The North American Third Edition

Cambridge Latin Course

Unit 3

Teacher's Manual

Revision Editor

Ed Phinney

Chair, Department of Classics & Director, University Foreign Language Resource Center
University of Massachusetts at Amherst, U.S.A.

Consulting Editor

Patricia E. Bell

Teacher of Latin & Assistant Head of Languages
Centennial Collegiate and Vocational Institute, Guelph, Ontario, Canada

Editorial Assistant

Barbara Romaine

Amherst, Massachusetts, U.S.A.

CAMBRIDGE
UNIVERSITY PRESS

Published by the Press Syndicate of the University of Cambridge
40 West 20th Street, New York, NY 10011, U.S.A.

The Cambridge Latin Course was funded and developed by the University of Cambridge School Classics Project and SCDC Publications, London, and is published with the sponsorship of the School Curriculum Development Committee in London and the North American Cambridge Classics Project. The work of the School Curriculum Development Committee has now been taken over by the National Curriculum Council.

This edition first published 1989
Reprinted 1997, 1998

Printed in the United States of America

ISBN 0 521 34857 9

CREDITS

The North American editors gratefully acknowledge the work of the Cambridge School Classics Project in England, particularly the editorial skill of Robin Griffin, Revision Editor of the British Second Edition of the *CLC*. The Narrative Points and the plot summaries of the stories in the Stage Commentaries were written expressly for this Manual by William D. Gleason, Latin Teacher at South Hadley (Massachusetts) High School, and Director of the Resource Center, North American Cambridge Classics Project, Box 932, Amherst, MA 01004–0932; the Grammatical Points and Sentence Patterns, with Examples, were collected by Patricia E. Bell, Latin Teacher at Centennial Collegiate and Vocational Institute, Guelph, Ontario, and Consulting Editor for the North American Third Edition of the *CLC*.

Contents

Introduction

Cultural Content

Stages 21–28

Unit 3 of the Cambridge Latin Course was organized according to the objectives and guidelines described in the Unit 1 Teacher's Manual, pp.5–6. For direction in overall planning and in selecting methods of presentation, consult the relevant sections in the Unit 1 Teacher's Manual, pp.8–19. The stage commentaries that follow this introduction will provide further suggestions.

Stages 21–28 conclude the Roman Britain episode, which began in Stages 13–16 but was interrupted in Stages 17–20 by Quintus' long narrative "flashback" to his stay in Alexandria. Two themes alternate in Stages 21–28: a "high life" story of the political intrigue involving Salvius, Cogidubnus, and eventually the provincial governor, Agricola, and a "low life" story modeled after Roman comedy, in which appear Modestus and Strythio, two soldiers of the Second Legion. Stages 21–23, and part of 24, are set in the Romano-British town of Aquae Sulis (modern Bath, in the county of Avon). They introduce students to some aspects of Roman religious life. In Stages 25–27, the narrative moves to the Roman fortress at Deva (modern Chester, in Cheshire, near the Welsh border), where the Second Legion was stationed in A.D. 83, the time the events supposedly take place. Thus the theme of the Roman army is introduced. In Stage 28, the narrative returns to the palace at Fishbourne, which by then, after the death of Cogidubnus, has come into the possession of Salvius.

Stages 29–34

Stages 29–34 begin the final, Roman episode by describing the life in the capital and introducing students to intrigue within the imperial household and bureaucracy. (In Stages 35–40 of Unit 4, Agricola and Salvius, hero and villain respectively of the earlier Roman Britain episode, will find themselves caught in the tangle of the emperor's grim suspicions.) The events of Stages 29 and 30 are set in September, A.D. 81, and thus are earlier by two years than the events of A.D. 83 described in Stage 28. In the year A.D. 81, the first year of Domitian's reign, the emperor, though he had hardly loved his other brother Titus, attempted to capitalize on Titus' popularity by dedicating a commemorative arch in his honor. Stage 31 and 32, describing the visit of the Greek philosopher Euphrosyne in Rome, are set in A.D. 82. Stages 33 and 34 bring us back up to the year A.D. 83, when the Empress Domitia Augusta was divorced by Domitian for adultery with the pantomime actor Paris. Domitia's place in the imperial household was temporarily filled by a mistress named Flavia Julia, the daughter of Titus and therefore niece of Domitian. Julia was also the widow of T. Flavius Sabinus, who had been executed by Domitian in A.D. 84. This is the Sabinus who, when consul in A.D. 82, is imagined as a guest of honor at the "cēna Hateriī" in Stage 32.

A link between Stages 29–34 is the wealthy contractor Haterius and his house, family, and connections, who include his patron Gaius Salvius Liberalis. Salvius, the senator and successful lawyer of Stages 13–16 and Stages 21–28, who was sent by Domitian as public commissioner and private emissary to the province of Britain some time after A.D. 80, in Stages 29–34 returns to Rome, where he connives with the emperor's minister Epaphroditus to entrap the lovers Domitia and Paris. Services like these perhaps helped Salvius attain the consulship some time before A.D. 86.

The Romano-British Setting of Stages 21–28: Bath and Chester

Stages 21–24 are set in Roman Bath, or ancient *Aquae Sūlis* "The Waters of Sulis." Here King Cogidubnus might have come, like many Roman-Britons of his day, for hydrotherapy. He would have soaked a long time in the soothingly warm waters which flowed then (and flow now) into large reservoirs. Afterwards, for good measure, he would have drunk a cup of water drawn for him from the mineral hot-spring. Although the king probably would have assumed that the water restored his energy by grace of the goddess Sulis (whose temple stood nearby), he might well have gone away feeling better than when he came because of the relaxing thermal action of the water.

Sulis and her hot-spring had been honored by the native Celts before the Romans came. The Romans, however, identified Sulis with their own goddess Minerva and by A.D. 83, the time our events supposedly took place, had built up the holy place into a widely known resort. Visitors came from Britain and elsewhere, visitors like the fictitious legionary soldiers, Modestus and Strythio, who are said in the story to have traveled south, for rest and recreation, from their fortress at Chester, or as an inscription indicates, like the Roman diviner-priest, L. Marcius Memor, who is here imagined as the administrator appointed by the Romans to oversee the sacred spa. A stone altar, dedicated by Memor to Sulis, was discovered during excavations in 1965, on what had been the

Hadrian's Wall
Eboracum
York
Mona
Anglesey
Deva
Chester
(ORDOVICES)
Viroconium
Wroxeter
Camulodunum
Colchester
Londinium
London
Aquae Sulis
Bath
Fisbourne
Noviomagus
Chichester

paved floor of the temple precinct (see photograph in Unit 3, p. 9 and frame 25 of Filmstrip 2, "Roman Britain"; for more information about this filmstrip, see below, pp.16–17). Memor, though he in actuality may have been only a visitor to Aquae Sulis, is the only attested example of a *haruspex* in Roman Britain. Whether he was actually an administrator or not, the importance at Rome of the elite priestly assemblage to which he belonged argues for the reputation of the provincial hot-spring complex that was famous enough to bring him there.

The Romans, in the first century A.D., surrounded the spring with a wall and piped water from it to the large, lead-lined "Great Bath" and to two other reservoirs, or pools. Originally, these baths were protected by a roofed building, but by the fourth or fifth century A.D., the temple and the protecting structure around the baths and the spring had collapsed and the foundations sank into a marsh that had been slowly encroaching because of flooding from the hot-spring. The town of Bath survived through the Middle Ages; in the eighteenth century, new Georgian-style structures were built over the temple precinct and Bath once more became a fashionable resort.

In 1790 there was discovered the stone relief of an atypical Medusa, who like a native Celtic warrior sports a man's mustache and who once decorated the center of the pediment of Sulis Minerva's temple (filmstrip 2, frame 24). In 1880–81 there was uncovered the Great Bath, which, now roofless, is open to the sky and to modern tourists (see photograph in Unit 3, p.17 and filmstrip 2, frame 23). The hot-spring and its muddy sediment, though covered by a fairly modern hydropathic establishment called the King's Bath, have been excavated in this century, in the mid-1960s and most recently in 1979. Since the excavations, the hot-spring now stands open to the air in an approximation of its original contour (see photograph in Unit 3 p.32). See Cunliffe and Davenport for details of the temple precinct.

Judging from the finds, we know that worshipers threw into the hot-spring thousands of gifts for the goddess: many coins and some silver and pewter containers, now and then inscribed *DMS* or *deae magnae Sūlī*. For texts of incriptions and photographs of containers, see Cunliffe (ed.), *Temple*, pp.41–49 and 55–57.

Most fascinating among the finds were the *dēfixiōnēs*, small thin sheets of pewter, each a few inches square at most, on which angry visitors scratched "magic" words, frequently backwards, against their enemies. See Cunliffe (ed.), *Temple*, vol. 2, pp.107–277, for transliterations of *dēfixiōnēs*, and pp.270–77, for photographs of some of the tablets. One of these *dēfixiōnēs* (partly illustrated on the title page of Unit 3, Stage 22; fully, in filmstrip 2, frame 26, and translated and discussed in Cunliffe (ed.), *Temple*, vol. 2, pp.112–13) mentions Vilbia, who is imagined in the story as the fickle girlfriend first of a local boy, named Bulbus, or

"Onion-Head," and then the paunchy, middle-aged Roman soldier-on-leave, ironically named Modestus ("Humble" he is not!).

Stages 25–27 are set in Chester, where Modestus and his sidekick Strythio were stationed, according to our story, with the Second Legion. The name of the river Dee, which flows through Chester, partly preserves the word *Dēva*, the ancient name of the town. The name of the modern town, Chester, preserves the Latin *castra*, the word for the fortress which the Romans began building there in (A.D. 76 or 77) at the orders of Frontinus, who preceded Agricola as governor of Britain. Frontinus' purpose was to secure the northwestern part of the province from the Welsh tribespeople, and to provide a backup base for the further conquest of northern Britain (Strickland 5–7). The fortress was probably still incomplete when Agricola first came there in A.D. 79.

The modern walls of Chester, which have survived, with many repairs and additions, through the Middle Ages until today, are laid for the most part in the trenches of the Roman fortress walls. The north half of the Roman-period amphitheater, excavated only since 1960, is still visible just outside the Newgate. From here the base of the southeast angle tower of the Roman-period fortress can also be seen.

Stage 28 is set in Fishbourne. For information about the palace there, see the Unit 2 Teacher's Manual, pp.4–5, and Cunliffe, *Regni*, 79–82.

The Roman Setting of Stages 29–34

Stages 29–34 are set in the city of Rome. Among the topics presented or mentioned are the topography and physical appearance of the city, the contrast between the lives of rich and poor, social institutions like the patron-client system, different kinds of public and private entertainment, the driving ambition of many Romans for status and prestige, the different ways in which a philosophical sect or religion—Stoicism or Judaism or Christianity—offered alternatives to the official state religion, and the struggle for power and influence among the emperor's advisers and officials. The students' background material supplements the presentation of the stories.

The Emperor Domitian

The story of Stages 29–34 occurs in the hub of the empire, Rome, during the reign of the Emperor Domitian. Although students are likely to know much about the power and importance of the city of Rome, they may know little about Domitian, and even that little may be entirely negative. But Domitian's reputation for greed and cruelty should not cloud the general efficiency of his administration, especially in the provinces. Even if an autocrat, he was continuing the absolutist, but operative policies of his father Vespasian, who had been a successful general before he became emperor. If from the beginning of his rule he seemed at times, to the senatorial nobles, highhanded, he was perhaps reacting to the long years he had spent in the shadow of his brother Titus, who seems to have been favored over Domitian by their father. Vespasian, for example, had made Titus, but not Domitian, colleague of most of his consulates. How discrepant with Domitian's inner feelings must have been his officially cheerful face when he officiated, in A.D. 81, at the dedication of the arch consecrated to the memory of his highly successful, popular, and posthumously deified brother (see "arcus Titī" in Stage 29).

Domitian, however, was not content with building the arch of Titus. He completed the *Amphitheātrum Flāvium* (later called the Colosseum) which his father started and Titus continued. He expanded the area of the imperial forums with the Forum Transitorium, which his successor Nerva completed. He built a stadium, whose outline can still be traced around the Piazza Navona. But most important, he built the *domus Flāvia/ Augustāna*, a mansion so splendid that its location, the Palatine hill, has become the modern word for a magnificent house, or "palace."

The hostile tradition that Domitian persecuted the Christians is perhaps exaggerated. True, he ordered the executions in A.D. 95, on charges of atheism, of both a consular, M'. Acilius Glabrio (a character in Stages 35 and 37 of Unit 4), and of his relative, Flavius Clemens (father of the two sons whom Domitian adopted as heirs; cf. Stages 38 and 39 of Unit 4). Perhaps these men were less atheists than they were converts to the ancient religion of Judaism or possibly—as many early Christians could not be easily distinguished, by outsiders, from Jews— to the younger one of Christianity (see also hint in Stage 33, p.228, line 15). Clemens was married to Flavia Domitilla (a character in stage 38 of Unit 4), who traditionally owned the land on which an early Christian cemetery, still bearing her name, was built. In any case, atheism was a political charge easily leveled at Jews and Christians, because they did not worship the deities traditional to the Roman nation. Christianity is discussed further in Stage 33 (see pp. 141–43 below).

A Hierarchy of Clients: Epaphroditus, Salvius, and Haterius

The historically attested affair between Domitian's wife Domitia and the pantomime actor Paris led to the emperor sending her away (Suetonius, *Life of Domitian* 3.1). But he took her back later. In Stages 33 and 34, it is not Domitian himself who catches his wife in adultery, but his freedman-agent Epaphroditus who, along with Salvius, is imagined as inveigling the lovers into keeping an apparent assignation at the house of Salvius' client and perhaps dupe, Haterius.

Both Epaphroditus and Salvius were historical persons, but their plot against the empress and her lover in our story is fictitious. It is nonetheless typical of the behavior of Salvius in Stages 13–16 and 21–28 and of the Epaphroditus who is described by Tacitus as uncovering the plot of Gaius Calpurnius Piso against the Emperor Nero in A.D. 65 (*Annals* XV.55.1). (On Salvius, see Unit 2 Teacher's Manual, pp.5–6 and 23–4; on the conspiracy which Epaphroditus uncovered, see Tingay's translation of Tacitus, *Empire and Emperors*, pp.89–97.) Although a freedman, Epaphroditus, who had held the sword on which Nero committed suicide in A.D. 68, was himself executed at Domitian's command in A.D. 95, after a long, successful, and immensely lucrative career in the highest echelons of the imperial service. As for Haterius, the fictitious son of a freedman of the historical Haterii, who is imagined in Stages 29–30 as the contractor who built the arch of Titus, he too managed to acquire great wealth, but failed to attain social or political success, perhaps because he rather foolishly, for a man socially so new, set his sight on a priesthood traditionally reserved for members of old families.

Study of Social and Historical Topics

The theme of *urbs Rōma* in Stages 29–34 offers wide scope for the study of aspects of Roman civilization. Both the Latin stories and the English background material supply the student, directly or indirectly, with much factual information about features of Roman life. But there is more to historical studies than the acquisition of information; inquiry, analysis, inference, speculation, imagination, and evaluation all have their place. From time to time, therefore, you should treat the students' material as an opportunity for considering questions like the following:

1 Why were the facts as they were? E.g. "Why were the markets close to the river?" "Why did the public prefer *pantomīmī* to comedy and tragedy?"

2 What were the consequences of these facts? E.g. "What would the senators have felt about an emperor who relied heavily on ex-slaves to run the empire?" "How would Domitian's building program have affected (i) unemployment, (ii) those who lived on main roads?"

3 What judgments of value or taste are suggested by the facts? E.g. "Were the Jews at Masada right to prefer suicide to slavery?" "Was the patron–client system a sensible one?" "Would you have found a Roman banquet pleasant or disagreeable?"

Discussions of this kind are generally more productive if they include an attempt to see the situation through the eyes of both the first-century participant and the twentieth-century observer. For example, if the question "What do you think made the Jews prefer suicide to slavery?" is discussed first, a second question, "Were they right?" will receive an answer which is better-judged because it is better-informed.

4 How do we know? E.g. "How do we know the arch of Titus was at the southeastern end of the Forum?" "How do we know what Nero did to the Christians?"

Such questions raise the crucial matter of evidence, first discussed in Stage 28 of Unit 3. Students should continue in Stages 29–34 working back from a statement in their textbook to the relevant evidence for the statement, whether literary, archaeological, or epigraphic. Sometimes too they should examine the relation in reverse, by first looking at the evidence itself and then attempting to draw conclusions from it with your guidance. Accordingly, the students' textbook continues to include occasional quotations from the literary and epigraphic evidence. Literary evidence is usually presented in translated form; inscriptions are normally given in the original. Archaeological evidence is sometimes presented in relevant photographs, and you will be able to present more examples with slides (see "Slides and Filmstrip" below, pp. 16–17) or videocassette tapes, or in museums.

Presentation of Grammar

Stages 21–28

Stages 21–28 introduce as their chief grammatical items the following:

1 perfect participles, first the perfect passive, then the perfect active (deponent) in Stages 21–23;

2 a series of clauses using imperfect and pluperfect subjunctive verbs: *cum* ("when"), indirect question, purpose, result, and indirect command in Stages 24–27;

3 the ablative case. Students have met the ablative since Unit 2 in prepositional phrases, but in Stage 28 they meet it in other situations.

Stages 21–28 also review forms which students learned earlier: in Stages 21–23, indicative forms of the verb prior to the introduction of subjunctive forms in Stage 24; and in Stages 24–27, case endings of the noun prior to the extension of the uses of the ablative in Stage 28. The students' textbook provides review exercises for both verbs and nouns, and the stage commentaries below contain further suggestions for oral drill.

Stages 29–34

Stages 29–34 systematically introduce several passive forms of the verb into the sentence patterns of the linguistic scheme; they are the 3rd person singular and plural of the present and imperfect passive in Stage 29 and of the future passive in Stage 34, all persons of the perfect and pluperfect passive in Stage 30, as well as the present infinitive passive in Stage 34. Uses of the ablative are extended to include the ablative absolute phrase in Stage 31, and the ablative of description in Stage 33. Also new are many finite forms of deponent verbs in Stages 32 and 34 (participles of deponent verbs were met in Stage 22 of Unit 3), the present infinitive of deponent verbs in Stage 34, and the future and future perfect active tenses in Stage 33.

All of Unit 3, while introducing new grammatical points, simultaneously reviews and integrates items already met in Units 1 and 2. At the same time, Units 1, 2, and 3 themselves become the foundation of Unit 4 yet to come. You should, therefore, make sure that students have assimilated all the grammatical and cultural information presented in the earlier Units. For purposes of review, refer students often to the Language Information (hereafter LI) Sections in Units 1 through 3. Otherwise, students may not be able to give full attention to the major linguistic advances, e.g. indirect statement, that lie ahead in Unit 4. In particular, by the end of Unit 3 (Stage 34), students should know all case-forms of the five declensions; all finite active indicative verb-forms, the most common passive indicative verb-forms, present active and passive infinitives, and present, past, and future participles of the four conjugations; and all past-tense subjunctive forms and their most common uses in subordinate clauses.

Time Allocation for the Course in School and College

We suggested in the Unit 1 Teacher's Manual, p. 14, that in a four-year high-school level sequence, Unit 3 should normally constitute the second year's work. In a three-year sequence, students should finish Unit 3 by the middle of the second year so that they can also read Stages 35–40 of Unit 4 and thus have more time in the third year to finish Unit 4 and/or read selections from authors stressed in the American "College Board" Achievement Test in Latin. Poet-authors stressed in the Achievement Test are Vergil, in the *Aeneid*, and Ovid, in the *Metamorphoses*.

At the college or university level, Unit 3 should be begun in the middle of the second semester of a non-intensive elementary-year course, and completed in the third semester along with part of Unit 4. Most of Unit 4 should be completed in the fourth semester. In colleges or universities where only three semesters are allotted to the elementary and intermediate sequences, Unit 3 should be begun near the end of the second semester, thus allowing students time in the third semester both to finish Unit 3 and to read Stages 35–40 of Unit 4 and perhaps selections from Stages 41–48. Where only two intensive semesters are allotted to elementary and intermediate Latin, Unit 3 should be completed, and

Stages 35–40 of Unit 4, and perhaps selections from Stages 41–48, read in the second semester. In colleges or universities with quarter-terms instead of semesters, the fourth quarter-term of a six-term non-intensive sequence should comprise Stages 21–28 of Unit 3; the fifth quarter-term, Stages 29–34 and, if possible, the beginning stages of Unit 4; the sixth quarter-term, Stages 35–40 and most of the remainder of Unit 4.

If you discover that either the limitation of time or the learning disabilities of students will not allow completion of the work planned, omit a story here and there, rather than omit groups of consecutive stories or, worse, entire stages. If necessary, you might omit the stories listed below, providing a brief summary of the plot in English to insure continuity. If the story to be omitted contains difficult new grammar or basic vocabulary, you should not only summarize the story but also ask students to translate sentences which contain either the new grammatical points or examples of vocabulary that will appear in that particular stage's words-and-phrases checklist.

Stage 21	"Lūcius Marcius Memor" I, lines 12–32 *or* II; exercise 4
Stage 22	"Modestus"
Stage 23	"epistula Cephalī;" exercise 3
Stage 24	exercise 2, exercise 4
Stage 25	"Modestus custōs;" exercise 2, exercise 3
Stage 26	"contentiō;" exercise 4
Stage 27	"sub horreō;" exercise 3
Stage 28	"in aulā Salviī" II
Stage 29	"Masada" I and II; exercise 4
Stage 30	"dignitās," lines 29–46; exercise 2
Stage 31	exercise 3
Stage 32	"philosophia," lines 14–38; exercise 2
Stage 33	"Tychicus"
Stage 34	"exitium" I; exercise 3

You might also save time by dividing a story into sections and assigning different sections to different groups of students for exploration and translation. See Unit 1 Teacher's Manual, p. 11. Or you might guide students through any exercise (especially one with completions) orally, but not ask them to write it out, or, alternatively, guide them through part of an exercise orally and then assign the entire exercise as written homework.

Classroom Procedure

Many of the teaching methods set out in the Unit 1 Teacher's Manual, pp. 8–12, continue to apply. By this point, however, you may wish to modify previous routines slightly, especially if the students are mature and have developed their reading skill.

Your main concern will be to avoid monotony and to keep a good pace. It is *not* necessary for students to translate every word, since they are developing skill in comprehension as well as in translation. Accordingly, you may introduce variety by any of the following ways:

1 Allowing the class to begin their study of a passage by working in pairs or small groups and by exploring the first two or three paragraphs for answers to specific questions contained in the textbook (see Stage 28, pp. 128–31, "in aulā Salviī") or provided by you (for an example, see below, pp. 40–41, "in thermīs").

2 Inviting students, after they have read a story, to prepare and perform a dramatized reading (in class or, on a cassette recorder, at home) as an alternative to a final, polished translation (see below, pp. 23–24 "Memor rem suscipit").

3 Conducting regular oral reviews. They should not be longer than five minutes each, and they might fit conveniently at the beginning or the end of a lesson or, during a very long or a double period, in the middle. An oral review might be conducted on the basis of a question-per-line or be focused on relevant examples of a particular grammatical point.

You will also find variety in the materials themselves. New kinds of written exercises have been incorporated among the stories. Many stories, though on the average somewhat longer than in previous Units, have in some cases been subdivided where a narrative breaks naturally.

Comprehension questions have, as in previous Units, been attached to some of the stories. They range from the straightforwardly factual ("What is the time of day at the start of the story?") to, increasingly, the interpretation of situation, character, and motive ("What do you think makes Cephalus smile and why does he try to hide the smile?"). Some of these questions, such as those in Stage 32, p. 215 of Unit 3, are fairly demanding; others, like those in Stage 33, p. 231, are sufficiently straightforward for students, though unaided, to try to answer even during their first reading of the passage.

You should not, however, ask comprehension questions only where they are printed. The questions printed are only examples of what you will want to devise yourself, often extemporaneously, and use regularly. And to encourage teachers in this practice, we have added examples in the stage commentaries below. Comprehension questions are crucial for developing in students both a sensitive attention to what they are reading and a critical enjoyment of it.

The illustrations in the students' textbook also give opportunities for useful questions, sometimes on historical points ("What is the object on the left? What would be its purpose?"), sometimes in connection with the text ("Which sentence is illustrated by the picture?")

Some questions again, like those suggested in the commentary to Stage 29 below, p. 97, are designed to guide students to the meaning of complex sentences. Meaning, nevertheless, should not always be cued for students with comprehension questions. Sometimes students should work unaided, without immediate help from either you or a fellow student, so that they can develop fluency and self-confidence. Here you will have to judge precisely which students should be asked to work on their own, for how long, and at which task. You should avoid pushing students into working unaided on, say, a written translation of a long passage which contains much new grammar or many new vocabulary words; otherwise, students, by failing, will lose the sense of achievement which they need to maintain their motivation.

There are several ways you may keep a balance between helping and not helping students. You may guide the students in working out an exercise orally in class before sending them home to write the whole unaided. Or you may help students by guiding them in their first look at a Latin passage, e.g. you may read a portion aloud and then conduct a quick oral "word check" by asking students for the meanings of key words (especially old ones not glossed on facing pages) before assigning a translation of the passage as homework. Or, if the passage is not too difficult, you may read it aloud *twice* and then ask the class to write down answers to straightforward comprehension questions (see suggestions below, p. 40). As the months pass, you may lengthen the portions which students, after the first reading, are asked to translate aloud or to look over by themselves. Always encourage students to try remembering vocabulary or deciphering it from context before they look it up in the Complete Vocabulary part of the LI Section.

Finally, note that the language notes in the students' textbook are usually printed late in the stages so that students may meet examples of the grammatical point concerned before they analyze it. If the grammatical point is not difficult or if the students are quite able, they may read it earlier than where it is printed, but *never* as an introduction to the entire stage. Whenever the students are ready for the note you ought to guide them through it orally, not leave them to read it through by themselves, either in class or as homework. Because each language note usually contains a short exercise in addition to the generalizations and examples, you can adapt it to the needs of the class, answer individual queries, provide other examples extemporaneously, and keep control of the activity in general. Some students have difficulty understanding the notes, since these necessarily contain abstract (and sometimes abstruse) statements. It is your duty to make the note understandable for every student by rephrasing the abstract statement, analyzing the examples, or providing still more examples.

Lesson-plan Syllabi

As the stories become longer and the language and grammar increase in complexity, you should be more careful than ever in designing lesson plans. You will find a format suggested for plans in the Unit 1 Teacher's Manual, pp. 9–12. Such a format will insure pace and variety, though it should be modified during class if students' needs or interests demand. There follow four possible syllabi for high-school level lesson plans, centering on "Masada" II and "arcus Titī" of Stage 29:

First Lesson-Plan Syllabus

1 Write *rūpēs, mūnītiōnēs*, and *agger* on blackboard for class to translate. Let volunteer summarize story of Masada so far.
2 Read first two paragraphs of "Masada" II aloud. Let students in pairs explore meaning and grammar of each paragraph. Ask entire class comprehension questions, and let volunteers translate.
3 Let students read rest of story in pairs, and then let volunteers from class translate orally.
4 Ask one of the best readers in class to read Eleazar's speech aloud. Discuss the Jews' reason for committing suicide.
5 Pick out sentences with ablatives from "Masada" I and II, and write them on the blackboard for class to translate. Stress variety of translation. Refer students to LI Section, pp. 262–63, for examples of ablative forms in the paradigms.
6 Study with students the example at head of exercise 2 on p. 164.
7 Homework: have students review "Masada" II, noting especially participles and subjunctives, and do exercise 2 as written work.

The lesson-plan syllabus above may appear overfull, although many of the activities need occupy only a few minutes of class time. Naturally you should adapt it to your own circumstances, always keeping in mind the need for variety.

Second Lesson-Plan Syllabus

1 Ask students to pick out subjunctives in third paragraph of "Masada" II, identify tense, and say why subjunctive is being used. Pick out some participles from "Masada" II, and then ask students to identify type of participle, translate it, and say which noun it describes.
2 Discuss sources of our knowledge of events at Masada. Tell class about 1963–65 Masada excavation or read extract from translation of Josephus (see below, p. 100).
3 Write on blackboard some sentences from "nox" and "Masada" containing passive forms; write also some translations supplied by students. Compare with corresponding sentences involving active forms; e.g. compare *Templum ā mīlitibus dīripiēbātur* with *mīlitēs Templum dīripiēbant*, written on blackboard with its translation.
4 Homework: ask students to prepare "arcus Titī" I.

Third Lesson-Plan Syllabus

1 Give back exercise 2 and practice any points which have caused trouble.
2 Ask class to go through "arcus Titī" I, to answer your comprehension questions and to translate selected phrases and sentences. Ask volunteers to read part or all of "arcus Titī" I.
3 Discuss with students the description of the scene (see below p. 100 for suggestions).
4 Pick out sentences in "arcus Titī" I which contain passive forms; ask students to translate. Study with students the language note on passives.
5 Read aloud first two paragraphs of "arcus Titī" II. Follow reading with a mix of comprehension questions to be answered and sections to be translated by volunteers.

Fourth Lesson-Plan Syllabus

1 Study with students exercise 1 (p. 164 of Unit 3).
2 While reviewing content of first two paragraphs of "arcus Titī" II, ask supplementary questions like "What did a *corōna* look like? Where had the *candēlābrum* come from? What is the difference between *incēdere* and *ambulāre*?"
3 Study with students picture of procession on p. 163 of students' textbook (see below, p. 100, for suggestions). Ask students to read third and fourth paragraphs of "arcus Titī" II in pairs or groups, then let volunteers translate for the entire class.
4 Read remainder of "arcus Titī" II together with class: read aloud, let students explore, answer comprehension questions, and translate. Keep the class moving.
5 Homework: have students read Stage 29 background material.

Correlation of Unit 3 with American National Examinations

Some ambitious students who have completed Unit 3 may wish to take the Latin Achievement Test (AT) in Latin, offered every June by the Admissions Testing Program of the College Board, Princeton, NJ. But the Latin AT is not recommended for most students of the course until they have finished Unit 4 in their third year (= Latin, Level III), when they will have completed the entire gradient of grammar, including indirect discourse, and will have been introduced to original verse and slightly adapted original Latin prose. If an especially able student decides to take the Latin AT when s/he has only finished Unit 3 at the end of his/her second year (=Latin, Level II), s/he will have to do work in Unit 4 ahead of time, particularly in conditional sentences with the subjunctive, indirect discourse, and verse metrics—with an emphasis on Stages 42

(Phaedrus, Catullus, Martial, Ovid, and Vergil), 44 (Ovid), 45 (Catullus), and 47 (Vergil).

Many American and Canadian high school students take the Level II National Latin Exam (sponsored by the American Classical League and the National Junior Classical League, Oxford, OH) in early March of their Latin II school year. Since Latin II students using the course will normally have reached the middle of Unit 3 by March (*ca* Stage 30), they will be quite prepared to succeed on the Level II exam. If you wish, prepare the students ahead of time with some of the constructions taught in Stages 31–34, especially the forms of the deponent verb (Stages 32), the gerundive of obligation (Stage 32), and future and future-perfect tense forms (Stage 33).

Because the exam caters to students using many different kinds of textbook, however, some of the non-grammatical questions will deal with Classical mythology and history of the Roman Republic. If you wish, prepare the students for these kinds of questions by assigning them readings in widely available books like K. McLeish's *Myths and Legends of Ancient Rome* (Longman Inc. 1987) and Nichols and McLeish's *Through Roman Eyes* (Cambridge U.P. 1976) or any available handbook of mythology and survey of Roman history and civilization. For further information about the National Latin Exam, back copies, and syllabi, write to A.C.L./N.J.C.L. National Latin Exam, P.O. Box 95, Mt. Vernon, VA 22121.

Many American and Canadian high school students also take a Cambridge Latin Examination (sponsored by the North American Cambridge Classics Project) in the middle and at the end of their Latin II year. Examinations are based on a passage of facsimile Latin which incorporates the basic grammar, vocabulary, and socio-historical background of each Unit, with questions in two parts, one testing comprehension and grammar; the other, socio-historical background. There are four different examinations, one to follow the conclusion of each of Units 1, 2, 3, and 4. A new set of four examinations is available to the teacher every year in September, and they may be administered by the teacher at any time during the school year. Attractive certificates for high-scoring students are available free of charge. For more information about the Cambridge Latin Examination, back copies, or blank students' certificates, write to the Resource Center, North American Cambridge Classics Project (NACCP), Box 932, Amherst, MA 01004–0932, U.S.A.

Audiocassette Recording for Unit 3/Slides and Filmstrip

Recording

The second of the two C-60 audiocassettes accompanying the course contains dramatic readings, made by professional actors (sometimes with sound effects), of the following stories:

Stage 21 "Memor rem suscipit"
Stage 22 "amor omnia vincit" (three scenes)
Stage 23 "in thermīs" I and II
Stage 25 "Modestus perfuga"
Stage 26 "contentiō"
Stage 28 "Belimicus rēx"
Stage 30 "dignitās"
Stage 31 "salūtātiō" I and II
Stage 32 "philosophia"
Stage 33 "in aulā Domitiānī" II
Stage 34 "īnsidiae" and "exitium"

Play one (or part of one) of these dramatizations for the class after the students' second or third reading of the story. Younger students should follow the action and dialogue in their books. Older students might test their aural comprehension by listening only. Afterwards, ask the students to answer comprehension questions orally or on paper.

If students buy their own audiocassettes, they can listen to them at home on their Walkmen, or in class on a regular cassette player, while miming the action with suitable gestures or expressions. A good classroom activity is to have the class guess the story from the performer's miming action alone and to suggest some of the Latin words or phrases which accompany the action.

Slides and Filmstrip

Because Unit 3 of the North American Third Edition has been so richly illustrated, no slides or filmstrip have been produced expressly for use with it. In the Stage Commentaries (below, pp. 18–155, however, references have been made to visual material produced for use with the North American Second Edition and British First Edition for the convenience of teachers who own them. The reference "filmstrip" is to the *Cambridge Classical Filmstrip 2: Roman Britain* or the *Cambridge Classical Filmstrip 3: Rome*, and the number after it, to the frame within the strip. Information about the frames within the strip is contained in a booklet distributed with the filmstrip. (Note: these filmstrips are British and will not fit American filmstrip projectors; cut each frame and mount them all in plastic or cardboard mounts which can be obtained at any camera store.) The reference "slide" refers to a slide in the *Cambridge Latin Course Unit III Slides*, and the number after it, to a particular slide. Information about the slides is contained in the first Edition *Unit III Teacher's Handbook*, pp. 17–38.

Cambridge Classical Filmstrip 2: Roman Britain contains visual material suitable for use with Stages 13–16 of Unit 2 and with Stages 21–28 of Unit 3. It includes the following topics (asterisks indicate frames of particular relevance to Stages 21–28):

The conquest (Title frame – 1)
Romanization (frames 2–14)
Daily life (frames 15–22)
Religion (frames *23–29)
The army (frames *30–35)

Cambridge Classical Filmstrip 3: Rome contains visual material suitable for use with Stages 29–34 of Unit 3 and with Stages 35–40 of Unit 4. It includes the following topics:

Forum, arch of Titus, and other monuments (frames 1–12)
Entertainment (frames 13–17)
Trade and grain supply (frames 18–26)
Insulae ("apartment houses") (frames 27–28)
Water supply (frames 29–31)
Death and burial (frames 32–35)

An additional filmstrip, *Cambridge Classical Filmstrip 4*, contains new material, i.e. material not taken from the original slides. It includes several frames of special relevance to Unit 3.

Unless stated otherwise, references are to Filmstrip 3 and Unit III slides.

Stage Commentaries

STAGE 21: AQUAE SŪLIS

BRIEF OUTLINE

Reading passages	Romano-British town of Bath Memor: soothsayer (continued in Stage 23)
Background material	Romano-British town of Bath
Chief grammatical points	perfect passive participle partitive genitive

NARRATIVE POINTS

Date	*Setting*	*Characters Introduced*	*Story Line*
Early Spring, A.D. 83	Britain: Cogidubnus' palace, and Aquae Sulis (Bath)	Lucius Marcius Memor (haruspex, and director of shrine at Aquae Sulis), Cephalus (his freedman)	Cogidubnus wonders whether to go to Aquae Sulis. Salvius advises him to make his will. Salvius orders Memor to kill Cogidubnus; Cephalus suggests poison, but Memor orders *him* to administer it.

GRAMMATICAL POINTS

increased incidence of perfect passive participle
  e.g. *faber, ab architectō laudātus, laetissimus erat.*
participial phrase + preposition
  e.g. *saepe ad aulam Cogidubnī ībat, ā rēge invītātus.*
partitive genitive
  e.g. *rēx aliquid novī audīre semper volēbat.*
neuter plural
  e.g. *Quīntus eī multa dē vītā suā nārrābat.*
increased incidence of *dēbeō, iubēō, volō* + infinitive
  e.g. *ad fontem sacram īre dēbeō?*
increased incidence of descriptive genitive
  e.g. *tū es vir magnae prūdentiae.*

SENTENCE PATTERNS
participial phrase + preposition
e.g. *faber, ab architectō laudātus, laetissimus erat.*
V + ACC + NOM
e.g. *vexant mē architectī et fabrī.*
DAT + V + (NOM)
e.g. *nōnne aegrōtīs remedia praebēre vīs?*
increasing complexity of elements governed by infinitive
e.g. *volō tē mihi cōnsilium dare.*

Title Picture

This shows the interior of the Great Bath, as it was at the end of the first century A.D. It will be useful for establishing the change of scene from Alexandria in the second half of Unit 2. For a description of the Great Bath, see below, pp. 26–27. Note the conduit bringing the water from the sacred hot-spring in the far corner and the fountain half-way down the right-hand side. The doorway just visible through the pillars at the far end leads to the hall where the Stage 22 model sentences are set. Students may also like to see filmstrip 2 frame 23 (slide 1).

Model Sentences

These deal with the building of the baths. Some of the sentences contain new vocabulary items, but the pictures supply strong clues to the meanings. You should discuss cultural details in the pictures while students are construing the captions.

Three men are at work. The first, a sculptor, is making the head for a statue of Sulis Minerva. The second workman is putting the coping stones on the wall which the Romans built around the spring itself. The third workman is bringing water in buckets, perhaps to make cement or wash down newly laid paving slabs. The main water supply from the spring to the Great Bath was through the pipe shown in the pictures (see also slides 2 and 3). The architect's final gibe, "*linguam sordidam habēs. melius est tibi aquam sacram bibere,*" hints at the curative properties of the water.

The model sentences introduce the perfect passive participle. Occasional examples have already occurred, but been treated like adjectives. Now their verbal nature becomes prominent and the examples more numerous. Here and in the following two stories, the participle is limited to the forms ending in *-ātus* (*laudātus*) and *-ītus* (arcessītus). In the model sentences themselves, each participle is preceded by an example of the finite form of its verb; thus *laudātus* is anticipated by *laudāvit*, etc. The first three participles are masculine singular nominative; one plural example is introduced near the end. A further aid is provided by expressing the agent, e.g. *ab architectō laudātus*, which highlights the passive meaning of the participle.

Many students feel more secure at first if encouraged to use a standard form, e.g. *laudātus* = "having been praised" or, perhaps a less awkward one, "after being praised." But as soon as students can recognize the participle readily, encourage them to use normal English equivalents, e.g. "after he had been praised."

Flexibility in handling the participle is one of the most important skills the learner needs to acquire. Perhaps the first natural variation is to omit the "having been" and to say simply "praised." Examples where this translation is appropriate are found early in the stage: e.g., in "fōns sacer," *prope thermās stat templum . . . ā meīs fabrīs aedificātum* (line 14), where the version "a temple built by my workmen" is more idiomatic than "a temple having been built . . ."

Again, a student may translate *faber, ab architectō laudātus, laetissimus erat* by "The workman was praised by the architect and was very pleased." You would be misguided to reject this as wrong. Simply say, "Good. That gives the sense of the Latin, but can you, for the time being, word the English differently and do without the 'and'?" Many students often have an intuitive preference for the finite verb. This can lead to another common mistake, viz. "The workman was praised by the architect, he was very happy," where the "and" is wrongly omitted. Again, help the student rephrase.

One other new language feature appears in the model sentences (one example only): the neuter plural, *īnsolentia verba*. The context, however, is clear, and you should not make any special comment at this point. A language note in Stage 23 will discuss neuter plurals.

The following words are new: *oppidō, fabrī* (new meaning), *exstruēbant, sculpēbat, minimē* (new meaning), *īnsolenter, verba, linguam.*

fōns sacer

The scene switches back to Fishbourne, where Cogidubnus, now seriously ill, contemplates a visit to Bath where he hopes to be cured by the waters. When he asks Quintus his opinion as to the advisability of the journey, Quintus asks, "Where is that spring?" Cogidubnus explains about the town of Bath and its healing waters, and then turns to Salvius, to ask *his* advice. Salvius curtly recommends that Cogidubnus make his will.

The guardian deity of the hot-spring was the Celtic goddess Sulis. In the stories, we have imagined that Cogidubnus himself played a part in the development of the temple and baths. This is possible since the spring lay in territory which he may have controlled (see map above, p. 3);

moreover, the buildings date from the late first century A.D. Once the students have read the model sentences and the first story, discuss with them the background material.

Cogidubnus' attitude, expressed in the words *"ego deam saepe honōrāvī; nunc fortasse dea mē sānāre potest"* (line 15), may strike some students as naïve or irreligious by its implication of a bargain between worshiper and deity, but it is an authentic Roman attitude towards the gods. Motives for worship included the hope of favors in return, especially favors of health and safety. Although you should touch on the theme of religious attitudes here, a fuller discussion might wait until Stage 23.

The passive meaning of the participle continues for the moment to be reinforced by *ā* or *ab* with the agent (with one exception: *ad aulam arcessītī*, line 6). The reinforcement is reduced in subsequent stories by replacing the agent with an adverb or other prepositional phrase; finally, the participle appears on its own. If students translate *ā rēge invītātus* (line 2) as "by the king's invitation," accept this as conveying the sense, but ask for a more literal rephrasing to make sure that the actual structure has been recognized.

Two other grammatical items should be noted here: (1) *volō tē mihi cōnsilium dare* (lines 9–10) and similar sentences. They closely resemble their equivalent English structures and are unlikely to cause difficulty. (2) *vir magnae prūdentiae* (line 9). Students may want to take phrases like this literally at first, but you should encourage them, as early as possible, to vary their translations. A language note on the descriptive genitive appears in Stage 22.

Lūcius Marcius Memor

The scene shifts to Aquae Sulis (Bath), and the curator of the baths, Lucius Marcius Memor, is introduced. He is portrayed as a man of frustrated ambitions, who came to Britain to further his political career, only to be relegated to a backwater where he can make few contacts with powerful men. Consequently, rather than attend to his duties, he drinks heavily, sleeps late, and delegates his responsibilities to his freedman, Cephalus. In this passage, Cephalus tries, at first in vain, to rouse Memor from his drunken stupor; he succeeds only when he manages to convince Memor of Salvius' imminent arrival at the baths, for Salvius is one of the those powerful men whom Memor would like to impress.

Memor is a historical figure, though later than our period (his character as depicted in the story is entirely fictitious): his name and presence at Bath are attested by a statue-base still standing in the temple precinct (see p. 9, and filmstrip 2 frame 25; slide 5), discovered in 1965. The inscription reads:

DEAE SVLI
L MARCIVS MEMOR
HARVSP
D D

(HARVSP = *haruspex*, DD = *dōnō dedit*)

On this evidence, Memor was a member of the priestly college of haruspices and perhaps involved in the administration of the baths and temple. The narrative imagines him in charge of the religious community and a leading figure in the government of the town. Although less important than Salvius, he belongs to the equestrian order and is quite wealthy. It is interesting that the temple of Bath was sufficiently important to attract a man of this status.

However, in the hierarchy of Roman priests, a haruspex ranked lower than a pontifex or an augur, and Memor's hopes of *maiōrēs honōrēs* (I, line 28) suggest his lower position within the priestly system. No doubt he also regarded a move to Rome as likely to benefit his career prospects; the province of Britain must have been outside the consciousness of people in Rome most of the time. More details about haruspices will be found in Stage 23, pp. 48–49 and pp. 45–46 below.

The policy of Romanization which Cephalus ironically attributes to Memor was practiced systematically by the governor Agricola (if we accept Tacitus' account, *Agricola* 21). Memor was part of the process of bringing the two cultures together and of superimposing, to some extent, the Roman upon the Celtic. So the goddess Sulis became Sulis Minerva; tribal leaders began to live in Roman-style villas, do business in newly built forums and basilicas, wear the toga, and mix socially with the conquerors. The extent of the change is debatable. Much may have been superficial. Maybe twenty or thirty miles from the Romanized town few patterns of Celtic life were changed.

This story is divided into two parts. The questions following Part I are intended to be studied by students, preferably in pairs or small groups, after a fairly rapid first reading. Most of the questions are concerned with character and motive, but question 3 can prompt a discussion of the activities around the baths. After students have read Part II, discuss with them the questions below; these too require interpretive responses rather than straightforward comprehension.

What does Memor find boring about his work at Bath?
Where would he prefer to be? Why?
What impression do you get of the way he is doing his job?
When Cephalus announces the arrival of Salvius, what effect does the news have upon Memor?
Explain Memor's comment about Salvius: *quem colere maximē volō* (line 21).

You might now, especially if a summer has intervened between Unit 2 and this Unit, review verbs. For example:

in line 1 "What tense is *erat*? Translate it."

in line 2, "Find a verb in the imperfect tense. Translate it."

Do not ask students to affix labels to tenses without also translating them; otherwise, students may start dissociating grammar and meaning.

First Language Note (Perfect Passive Participle)

After taking the class through the note on pp. 10–11, ask students to pick out examples of perfect participles in "Lūcius Marcius Memor" and to say which noun each describes. The main objective at this point is to develop students' ability to:

1 identify perfect participles in the text (you should accept the adjectival *perterritus, vexātus*);
2 translate them appropriately;
3 distinguish between the perfect participle and the present participle (several examples of which also occur in "Lūcius Marcius Memor");
4 link the participle to its associated noun.

These skills are more important than mastery of the term "passive," which has been postponed to the end of the language note and is included there only to prepare the way for the term "active" in Stage 22.

Paragraph 5 concentrates on agreement of number. When students have become familiar with participles, have them turn back to this language note and consider agreement of gender. Examples here include the feminine *laudāta* (paragraph 4) and *parāta* (paragraph 6) and the neuter *ōrnātum* (paragraph 2). Other neuter examples can be drawn from the stories.

Memor rem suscipit

Salvius orders Memor to kill King Cogidubnus, informing him that the order comes directly from the Emperor Domitian. The astonished and frightened Memor turns for help and advice to Cephalus, who glibly suggests killing the king with a poisonous cup containing some of the healing water. The matter no longer seems so easy to Cephalus when Memor assigns *him* the task of giving the poisoned cup to the king.

The passage allows students to explore feelings, attitudes, and intentions of the characters. The dialogue portrays a battle of wills, which should be explored with students first by questions and then perhaps a dramatic reading. Possible questions might be:

Why does Salvius call Memor *vir summae prūdentiae* (line 2)?

Are Memor's first words true? What dilemma is he caught in?

What does Memor think Salvius is asking of him, when Salvius says

Cogidubnus, quī in morbum gravem incidit, aquam ē fonte sacrō bibere vult (lines 8–9)?

What arguments does Salvius employ to overcome Memor's scruples (or fear)?

Do you expect Memor to execute the plan? Why?

Why do you suppose Memor passes the task on to Cephalus?

Why is it difficult for Cephalus to refuse?

Why does Salvius proceed in a roundabout way rather than kill Cogidubnus outright with sword or dagger?

Students usually enjoy speculating about the technical details of the cup used for the poison. You might draw their attention to other mechanical devices like the eagle escaping from under the wax effigy of the Emperor Claudius in Stage 15, or the Emperor Nero's booby-trapped ship designed to kill his mother Agrippina (Tacitus, *Annals* XIV. 3–6).

Finally you might ask some of the better readers in the class to read the parts of Memor, Salvius, and Cephalus aloud. You might involve more students by dividing the parts of Memor and Salvius between two readers each. Before these students read aloud, all the students should discuss key moments in the dialogue and consider how they should be read. For example: Memor, in his first speech, replies hastily to Salvius' unspecified request, but pauses before *sed quid vīs mē facere?* (line 6) as the possible seriousness of it begins to dawn. In his long speech in the middle, Salvius tries to coax his man, *num praemium recūsāre vīs, tibi ab Imperātōre prōmissum?* (lines 25–26). After Salvius' departure, Memor's next two speeches are extremely anxious in tone; but in his last two speeches his mood changes fast, perhaps because he begins to believe that Cephalus' suggestion can be carried out and perhaps because he sees an opportunity to pass the buck. Hence his final sarcastic comment, *vīta, mī Cephale, est plēna rērum difficilium* which mirrors exactly the tone of Salvius saying these same words in line 31.

After students have read the story, you might ask them to:

1 pick out the perfect participles and the nouns they describe (seven examples);

2 review the use of the dative case with verbs like the Stage 21 checklist word *cōnfīdere*. You might write on the blackboard the sentence *nūllīs tamen servīs cōnfīdere ausim*, lines 48–49, retranslate it and then take the class through further examples like *Memor Cephalō cōnfīdit*. Lists, from previous stages, of verbs taking the dative will be found in the Unit 2 Teacher's Manual, pp. 71 and 88.

Second Language Note (Partitive Genitive)

If some of the students are studying French, ask them to compare this Latin usage with the French, e.g. *plus de vin, assez d'argent*. Extend the discussion by asking them to suggest why the genitive case is used in such phrases as Latin *plūs cibī, nimium vīnī.* (Answer: Each pronoun indicates a quantity or part *of* something.) Finally, contrast the Latin phrases with their natural English equivalents "more food" and "too much wine," in which the "of" does not occur.

If time allows, do further work with harder phrases in which the genitive depends on *nihil* or *aliquid*, e.g. *nihil perīculī, aliquid novī. aliquid* may lead to a genitive adjective, as above, which is translated by "something new" or "some news," or it may lead to a genitive noun, e.g. *aliquid vīnī*, translated by "some wine."

Drills and Suggestions for Further Practice

In this and other stages which contain numerous exercises, do not work through all five consecutively. Provide variety by doing, for example, Exercise 1 before students read the stories.

Exercise 1 Type: vocabulary
Grammatical point being practiced: recognition of adverbs in *-ē*

This is the first of a series of exercises designed to increase students' word power by encouraging them to notice cognate forms. Guide students through them orally; if students write them out, they should not look up items or the exercises become pointless. The examples, both old and new, make the point that words not previously met can be interpreted correctly if a cognate form is known. Encourage students to generalize for themselves about the way that adverbs are formed from adjectives ending in *-us*. Extend this exercise with similar examples from the list of 1st and 2nd declension adjectives drawn from the checklists of Stages 1–17 (in the Unit 2 Teacher's Manual, p. 69), and from subsequent checklists: *cārus* (19); *doctus* (20); *dūrus* (21); *lātus* (20); *occupātus* (21); *perītus* (21); *pessimus* (20); *plēnus* (21); *plūrimus* (19). (Warning: The adverbial form of *bonus* (16) is usually *bene*; of *magnus* (3), *magnopere*; of *parvus* (6), *parum*; and of *plūrimus* (19), *plūrimum*.) Choose a selection of adverbs formed from the adjectives in the lists above, put them into short sentences, and have them translated.

Exercise 2 Type: completion
Missing item: noun
Test of accuracy: correct case
Grammatical point being practiced: nominative, genitive, and accusative, singular and plural.

Exercise 3 Type: completion
Missing item: noun or verb

Test of accuracy: sense and syntax
Grammatical point being practiced: sentence structure

If this exercise is too difficult for students, ask them to translate some of the items in the pool orally before they write the exercise on their own.

Exercise 4 Type: translation from English, using restricted pool of Latin words
Grammatical points being practiced: nominative, genitive, dative, and accusative, singular and plural; perfect tense

Do one or two sentences orally for the students first, and write the correct version on the blackboard. Make sure that they understand what to do and know how to use the LI Section to help themselves. In this exercise the position of the dative is later than it normally is in the stories.

Exercise 5 Type: completion
Missing item: verb
Test of accuracy: correct personal ending
Grammatical points being praticed: 1st, 2nd, and 3rd persons singular of present, imperfect, perfect, and pluperfect (including one example of imperfect of *possum*)

Use this exercise as a diagnostic test to determine whether students have grasped the different endings.

The Background Material

The outstanding feature of the Roman town of Aquae Sulis was the group of buildings consisting of the temple of Sulis Minerva, the temple precinct, and the suite of baths. The plan on p. 18 shows the complex at its earliest stage. The visitor entered through the doorway at the bottom left and passed through the frigidarium to reach the hall overlooking the sacred spring in which the Stage 22 model sentences are set. The doorway to the Great Bath was then on his right (see title picture and photograph on p. 17). This bath, lined with lead sheets, was 72 ft long, 29 ft wide and 5 ft deep (22 × 9 × 1.5m) and was entered by steps along all four sides. Warm water flowed into it through a lead pipe that ran directly from the sacred hot-spring. Around the bath ran wide covered walkways, paved with hard limestone. On each of the long sides were three recesses (*exedrae*), which provided sitting areas well clear of splashing water. The roof was probably about 44 ft (13.5m) above the bath and the upper walls must have contained apertures to allow daylight to enter and steam to escape.

The photograph on p. 17 shows the Great Bath as it is today, looking in the opposite direction from that in the title picture. The columns and superstructure are Victorian.

The spring which supplied the baths with their constant hot water was enclosed within the southeast corner of the temple precinct. The Romans lined the spring with lead sheets and built a wall around it (see model sentences, p. 3). Many items were thrown into it as offerings to the goddess, like the pewter and silver bowls in the photograph on p. 20. These may have been part of the temple possessions. They were used for pouring libations and are inscribed with dedications to the goddess. They show signs of wear and may have been consigned to the goddess' spring when worn out.

In the center of the precinct stood the temple. Much of it lies beneath the present Bath Abbey church, but modern techniques have made excavation possible and allowed archaeologists to examine the site. It cannot be definitely dated, but was probably first built in the first century A.D. with modifications later. Work is still proceeding on reconstructing it. For detailed accounts, see Cunliffe's *Roman Bath Discovered* or his more elaborate *Roman Bath.*

One of the most interesting discoveries is the pediment of the temple (see drawing on p. 41), which has been pieced together from fragments. In the center is a Gorgon's head (see photograph on p. 40; filmstrip 2 frame 24; slide 4) with snaky hair and, unusually, a male face with mustaches in the Celtic style. Supporting it on either side are winged Victories carved in the classical manner. This blend of styles denotes more than a meeting of different artistic traditions; it is a powerful example of religious synthesis. The local Celtic goddess Sulis has become identified with the Roman Minerva, symbolically suggested by the Gorgon's head which she traditionally carried upon her shield.

The town was smaller than a typical Roman market town. Although excavations have shown several large private houses as well as taverns, boarding-houses, and the homes of ordinary people, the site as a whole was not densely built up during the first century A.D. But its mineral waters insured that Aquae Sulis was widely known and much visited. Regular repairs and modifications to the Great Bath and the evidence of wear on steps and paving-stones testify to the constant passage of visitors. So too do the surviving inscriptions, which are mainly of two types: altars erected to the goddess in thanksgiving for a safe journey or in hope of a cure, or tombstones. In addition to Memor, the name of one priest is known, Gaius Calpurnius Receptus (see slide 7).

Tourism may have been the chief basis of the town's economy, but the surrounding countryside was a prosperous agricultural, and to some extent, industrial area, where farmers built many villas, grazed sheep and cattle, and grew barley and wheat. Nearby, others quarried stone and manufactured utensils from pewter, a cheap alternative to silver, which was alloyed from tin mined to the southeast in Cornwall and lead mined to the south in the Mendip hills of Somerset.

Suggestions for Discussion

1 Show views of the interior of the Great Bath at Aquae Sulis and those of the baths at Herculaneum. What similarities and differences are there? Which baths most resemble a modern swimming pool? Why?

2 Discuss with the class the idea that a spring was a religious place. What activities and objects would impress upon visitors, when they came to the baths at Aquae Sulis, that they were in a religious setting?

3 Read in translation Tacitus, *Agricola* 21, and using the example of Sulis Minerva and the religious complex at Aquae Sulis, explore with students the cultural policy of Romanization. Consider modern parallels, e.g. the colonization of Africa in the nineteenth century by various European powers; the "melting pot" policy adopted by the United States toward immigrants from Europe in the latter part of the nineteenth century; the multi-cultural character of contemporary Canadian society; the impact of Western technology on oil-producing countries of the Middle East, Africa, and Central and South America.

Suggestions for Further Activities

1 Tell something of the story of the gradual discovery of Roman Bath. An excellent account, including excerpts from the Anglo-Saxon poem "The Ruin," which almost certainly describes the site as it appeared in the eighth century, will be found in Cunliffe, *Roman Bath Discovered.*

2 With data from this stage, from Cunliffe and other sources, ask students to write an imaginary diary of a Roman while visiting Aquae Sulis. They might illustrate the diary with small maps or illustrations.

3 Show students filmstrip 2 frame 27, the model of the temple of Claudius at Colchester, or another picture of a Roman temple. Discuss the similarities with and differences from the temple at Bath.

4 College students who have studied European history might enjoy writing a research paper on the history of spas, or resorts with mineral springs, in Europe. They might consider, besides e.g. Aachen in West Germany, Aix-les-Bains in southeastern France, and the original Spa in eastern Belgium—all of which were colonized by the Romans—the Shrine of Our Lady of Lourdes, in France, where the sick still come to drink glasses of healing water, or even ancient Thermopylae (modern Loutropolis), in Greece, where Herakles supposedly bathed.

STAGE 22: DĒFĪXIŌ

BRIEF OUTLINE

Reading passages Background material	magic and superstition
Chief grammatical points	perfect active (deponent) participle descriptive genitive

NARRATIVE POINTS

Date	*Setting*	*Characters Introduced*	*Story Line*
Spring, A.D. 83	Britain: Aquae Sulis (Bath)	Modestus and Strythio (Roman soldiers), Latro (local innkeeper), Vilbia and Rubria (Latro's daughters), Bulbus (Vilbia's lover), Gutta (Bulbus' friend)	Modestus buys Vilbia's affections and alienates her from Bulbus. Gutta, dressed as a woman, distracts Modestus, so that Bulbus can shove him into the Sacred Spring. Vilbia hears Modestus reject her, and is reunited with Bulbus.

GRAMMATICAL POINTS

perfect active (deponent) participle, nominative case
 e.g. *fūr, thermās ingressus, ad fontem sacrum festīnāvit.*
clauses with *cui*
 e.g. *quam celerrimē ēgressus, Guttam petit, cui cōnsilium callidum prōpōnit.*
increased incidence of descriptive genitive
 e.g. *Latrō, quī tabernam tenēbat, erat vir magnae prūdentiae.*
 velim, ausim
 e.g. *velim cum eō colloquium habēre.*

SENTENCE PATTERNS

accusative/prepositional phrase + participle
 e.g. *fūr, senem cōnspicātus, post columnam sē cēlāvit.*
 fūr, ad fontem regressus, amulētum in aquā quaesīvit.
increasingly varied position of dative
 e.g. *tibi perīculōsum est Bulbum contemnere.*
 tum fībulam, quam puella alia tibi dederat, Vilbiae trādidī.
 puellīs nōn tūtum est per viās huius oppidī īre.

Title Picture

For this defixio, see below, pp. 33 and 35–36.

Model Sentences

An offering to the goddess is retrieved by a thief from the sacred spring. It bears an appropriate curse. The idea of invoking divine help against enemies by means of a defixio or curse tablet will reappear in this stage. The episode takes place outside the Great Bath in the hall with the windows, one arched, flanked by two square, looking over the sacred spring.

All the perfect participles in Stage 21 were passive. Now the perfect active (deponent) participle is introduced. The term "perfect active," instead of "perfect deponent," has been adopted here in order not to complicate unduly students' perception of the contrast between the passive and active voices which should be the focal point of their attention. Deponent verbs, together with the term "deponent," are discussed in Stage 32, and use of the term should be postponed until then.

You will find that the best way to teach these model sentences is to make full use of the accompanying picture, the story line, and factual comprehension questions. These aids provide such powerful clues to the meaning that students, though unaware they are using different voices of the verb, normally have little difficulty in treating perfect participles as active and passive. Let students learn through discussion the difference between the perfect active participles of this Stage and the perfect passive participles of Stage 21, but not until they have read one or more stories in this Stage besides the model sentences. If a student incorrectly translates e.g. *fūr thermās ingressus* as "the thief having been entered . . ." do not lecture on grammar, but simply ask, "Who entered the baths?"

A student is more likely to mistranslate perfect participles as present ones, as, for example, in the sentence "Entering the baths, the thief . . ." However, while students are learning the important distinctions of voice and tense in the participle, encourage them to express clearly in their translations the correct tense of a particular participle. Again, you should use concrete, not abstract guidance. So you should ask, "Did the thief enter the baths and look around at the same time? If he entered *before* he looked around, how could we say that in English precisely?" Allow students to answer within a reasonable range of alternative translations, e.g. "When he had entered . . .," "Having entered . . .," or "After entering . . ." If a student offers the idiomatic "On entering . . ." or simply "Entering . . .," accept it, but request also an additional, more literal translation for the time being.

The following words are new: *ingressus, cōnspicātus, columnam, precātus, regressus, adeptus.*

Vilbia

In Bath, Vilbia and Rubria, the daughters of Latro, are in the kitchen of Latro's inn, where they are supposed to be washing dirty cups, but instead are gossiping. Vilbia is showing off to Rubria the brooch she has received from Modestus, a Roman soldier on leave. She has become infatuated with him, losing interest in Bulbus, her erstwhile boyfriend.

The stories of this stage provide a view of the life and character of ordinary people in Aquae Sulis. They are seen as lighthearted types. Vilbia and Rubria are the daughters of the local innkeeper. Vilbia has fallen for the fast-talking Modestus, a Roman soldier on leave from Deva. The prototype of Modestus is the braggart warrior Pyrgopolynices in Plautus' *Miles Gloriosus*, while his friend, Strythio, is modeled on the parasite, Artotrogus, in the same play. Bulbus is the local boy whom Vilbia has jilted for the bedazzling soldier.

Dialogue fills the passages. It serves not only to reveal character and define relationships, but also to express humor; each speaker builds on, caps, and rebukes what the other has just said, scoring points in the process. Sensitize students to the tone by asking, for example, whether Rubria really sympathizes with her sister's feelings or is she out to make mischief? Be sure to ask, "Why has Vilbia jilted Bulbus for Modestus?" Sutdents should see that it is Modestus' bluster which has won her heart. She has also fallen for Modestus' physical attractions (*quantī erant lacertī eius*) and apparent integrity (*Modestus probus*). Students, however, after looking at the picture of him, may conclude that Vilbia's judgement has been influenced by the gift of a beautiful brooch! But remind students that because a Roman legionary usually served twenty years before he was discharged, many a Roman soldier, like Modestus, was approaching middle age.

In the college-age class, students might want to discuss seriously the relationships of Roman soldiers with British women. They should remember that relations varied with place and time. In the early days of Roman conquest and occupation, some women would deliberately avoid contact with the invaders, while others would willingly or unwillingly become prostitutes. In time, however, civilian *vīcī*, or settlements, would grow up outside the forts and long-term relationships develop between soldiers and their women-friends (who could thus live nearby). A soldier, however, could not claim a serious relationship as legal marriage until after his discharge.

Examples of descriptive genitive phrases begin from line 3, *vir magnae dīligentiae sed minimae prūdentiae*. Do not comment on the construction until the language note on p. 34, but encourage varied translations, e.g. "a man of great diligence," "a hard-working man," "a man who worked hard."

If the position of *autem* (line 20) puzzles students, write the sentence on the blackboard, ask for a translation, write that too on the board, and invite comment on the respective positions in the sentences of *autem* and "but." When the students have observed the position of *autem*, ask them to recall other connectors they have met in this same position (Answer: *enim*, *igitur*, and *tamen*).

If the students feel that "heart-throb" (in the glossary) is too old-fashioned as a translation of *suspīrium*, invite alternative suggestions. Mention the literal meaning "a sigh."

Modestus

This short piece of dialogue introduces the principal male characters, Modestus and Strythio, both on leave from the Second Legion at Chester. Of the two, Modestus is an unmitigated windbag, though evidently possessed of some charm. Strythio is somewhat more complex, since he makes fun of his buddy. You might suggest to students, at the beginning, that they look out for differences between these two so that they can produce brief character sketches.

Modestus and Strythio discuss Modestus, who brags about his military prowess and his way with women, while Strythio feeds the braggart's vanity. As they approach Latro's inn, Strythio mentions that he has given a brooch, which Modestus had previously received from another girl of his acquaintance, to Vilbia, and that Vilbia is now head-over-heels in love with Modestus.

Ask students to observe the links between this and the previous story. For example, Strythio's remark, *Vilbia . . . statim amāvit* (line 9), confirms Vilbia's claim that she fell in love at first sight. Strythio, lines 13–15, also confirms that Modestus gave her the brooch as a present, but adds more detail.

First Language Note (Perfect Active Participle)

The note introduces the term "perfect active participle" and by illustrating it with several examples, contrasts it with the perfect passive. The note accounts for the difference between them simply with the contrasting translations, "having . . ." and "having been . . ." The fact that these participles belong to different categories of verbs is not discussed until Stage 32.

While students are translating the examples, draw their attention to the context surrounding a given participle: e.g. "Look at the whole sentence. It isn't just *parātus*, but *ā servīs parātus*. Which makes better sense, 'having prepared by the slaves' or 'having been prepared by the slaves'?" Or "Look at the sentence *Modestus, thermās ingressus, avidē circumspectat*. Would it make sense to describe Modestus as 'having been entered'? Look at *thermās* next to *ingressus*. How will that fit in?" If you treat the participle in this way, the students are likely to take it in their stride. Some students will make mistakes, but resolve them for now by taking the students back to familiar examples, not embarking on an analysis of passive/deponent distinctions.

amor omnia vincit

Bulbus and his friend Gutta play at dice, while Bulbus laments his ill fortune, not in gambling (although he is, in fact, losing), but in love. He tells Gutta that he has put a *dēfīxiō* on Modestus, and intends thus to ruin his rival. Unfortunately, Modestus overhears Bulbus, and, with Strythio's help, knocks Bulbus to the floor. Vilbia condescends to intervene on Bulbus' behalf, then agrees to a midnight assignation with Modestus near the sacred spring. Bulbus, having overheard this exchange, goes to the spring at the appointed hour. Gutta comes with him, and, disguised as Vilbia, distracts Modestus, so that Bulbus can throw him into the water. The cowardly Modestus begs for mercy and disowns Vilbia, who arrives just in time to hear him. She returns to Bulbus, and the lovers depart happy. Gutta is also pleased, having been paid by Bulbus for his help. Modestus, soaking wet and humiliated, slinks away.

scaena prīma

In Latro's inn, Bulbus is drinking and playing dice with Gutta, until interrupted by the entry of Modestus and Strythio. Roman dice had six faces with the same markings as modern dice. A "Venus" was a double six, a "dog" was a double ace. Some pupils may find Bulbus' run of bad luck suspicious; this would be a suitable moment to mention the loaded bone die discovered at Vindolanda, which produces sixes 8 times out of 10!

The *tabula* Bulbus talks about in lines 20–22 is the one illustrated on the title page and filmstrip 2 frame 26 (slide 8), which was found in Bath. It is discussed below on pp. 35–36.

During this and the next scene, review forms of the verb. Begin by asking students to change *āmīsistī* (line 4) to the form meaning "I lost," then to "he or she lost." After several drills of this type, ask students to change e.g. *āmīsistī* to "you (sg.) lose," then to "you (sg.) were losing." If students cannot do this drill, make the Latin transformations yourself, but ask students for the meaning, e.g. "What did *āmīsistī* in line 4 mean? What would *āmīsī* mean?" In either case, remember to vary only person or tense at first, then proceed to vary both simultaneously.

scaena secunda

Bulbus has to face alone the anger of the two soldiers, but Vilbia's intervention saves him from further punishment. Modestus urges Vilbia to meet him later. For a moment she hesitates, but quickly agrees to her lover's proposition. Ask students to comment on Vilbia's reasons for (1) trying to save Bulbus from further maltreatment, (2) her abrupt change of mind, lines 19–20. Ask them to suggest the best way to express this change when reading aloud *pater mē sōlam exīre nōn vult. ubi est hic locus?*

The sentence pattern *possum* or *volō* + infinitive, e.g. *tibi resistere nōn possum* (lines 23–24), is well represented here. Drill students in this construction, sometimes changing the finite verb, e.g. *possumus* or *potest*, sometimes substituting an infinitive of another verb taking the dative (see lists above, p. 24), then write the new sentence(s) on the blackboard and ask students to translate.

scaena tertia

The villain gets his comeuppance.

Notice that now, in accordance with normal Latin usage, the position of the dative case in a sentence is more varied than previously.

Review the construction of negative commands by contrasting them with corresponding positive ones: e.g. *nōlī lacrimāre* (line 38) with *lacrimā*, and *stā prope fontem* (line 10) with *nōlī stāre prope fontem*. Then write both the negative and positive plural forms (e.g. *nōlīte stāre* and *stāte*) on the blackboard and ask students to translate them.

You might encourage discussion by asking students the following questions:

How does Bulbus overcome Gutta's reluctance to put on a woman's dress?

Modestus describes himself as *fortissimus mīlitum* (line 15). Does he behave like this when attacked by Bulbus? Yes or no, and why?

Bulbus claims, line 28, that he could now easily kill Modestus; and Modestus does not seem to doubt it. Why?

When Vilbia hears Modestus readily give her up, *nōn amō Vilbiam* (line 29), how does she react?

What does Bulbus say to calm her fury?

High school students might practice this play until they can represent it as a full production, which could be recorded on an audio- or videocassette. Four speaking (and two non-speaking) parts are required. Sound effects would include the rattle of dice, grunts and groans of men fighting, and the splash when Modestus hits the water. Finally, each group might compare for expressiveness its own recording with the professional recording on the audiocassette.

College students might prefer to read the play from their seats, with a few volunteers providing sound effects.

Second Language Note (Genitive of Description)

Allow students, at first, to use the familiar "of" translation. Encourage them, however, to be more flexible and adventurous as soon as they have become accustomed to these phrases.

Drills

Exercise 1 Type: vocabulary
Grammatical point being practiced: adverbs in *-ter*

Exercise 2 Type: completion
Test of accuracy: correct case
Grammatical points being practiced: genitive and dative, singular and plural

Exercise 3 Type: sentence composition from pool of Latin words
Grammatical points being practiced: nominative, dative, and accusative, singular and plural; 3rd person singular and plural of perfect

Students might work in pairs, taking it in turns to produce a sentence which the other translates. Encourage natural Latin word order and the use of as many different words as possible, but chiefly insist on the choice of correct inflections from the word-pool. Also encourage the production of sentences whose meaning is plausible rather than implausible, though grammatically correct.

The Background Material

Defixio Tablets

Many defixiones, or formal curse-tablets which consecrate one's enemy to the gods of the Underworld, have been found in Roman Britain. The tablet on which the stories of this Stage are based was found at Bath and reads as follows:

> [I] VQ IHIM MAIBLIV TIVALO / [V]NI CIS TAVQIL (OD)[O]MOC AVQA / [A]LLE ATVM IVQ MAE TIVA / [RO]V IS ANNIVLEV SVEREPV / SXE SVNAIREV SVNIREV / ES SILATSVG(V)A SVNAITI / MOC SVNAINIMSVTAC / [A]LLINAMREG ANIVOI (*R.I.B.* 154)

The backward writing is quite a common feature of defixio tablets; when the order of the letters is reversed this inscription emerges as:

> QVI MIHI VILBIAM INVOLAVIT SIC LIQUAT[1] COMO(DO)[2] AQVA ELLA[3] MVTA QUI EAM VORAVIT SI VELVINNA EXSVPEREVS VERIANVS SEVERINVS A(V)GVSTALIS COMITIANVS CATVSMINIANVS GERMANILLA IOVINA

([1] = *liquēscat,* [2] = *quōmodō,* [3] = *illa*)

The text and its interpretation are uncertain in parts. A translation of the version given above reads:

> May he who has stolen Vilbia from me dissolve like water. May she who has devoured her be struck dumb, whether it be Velvinna or Exsupereus or Verianus, etc.

The number of possible candidates to be cursed implies more about Vilbia than about those who caused her lover's angry jealousy. You might write on the blackboard the part of the curse printed at the beginning of the stage (i.e. as far as AVQA), ask a student to rewrite the letters, and work out a translation.

A large collection of defixiones in the form of lead scrolls was discovered in 1890 at Uley, in Gloucestershire, some miles north of Bath, on the site of a small temple of Mercury which probably also served as a local market. It seems likely that the curses were drawn up by the temple clerk at the request of local people, mainly farmers, who were perhaps hedging their bets in a legal case against a neighbor. If so, it was a fairly public way of damning one's enemy and suggests the importance of insuring that he got to know about it. Clearly such curses were more than a conventional ritual. Many a Roman or Celt must have believed in the efficacy of the divine agent and feared this god's power; even if he did not, he would have been disturbed, even frightened, by the knowledge that someone hated him enough to damn him publicly.

Further discussion of superstition will be found in Paoli pp. 279–91; Balsdon, pp. 65–67.

Source of picture on p. 37

On a defixio tablet, a demon is shown in a boat. He may be a representation of Charon, the ferryman who carried the souls of the dead over the Styx. The figure holds an urn and a torch, symbols of death. The text on the left reads CVIGEV, CENSEV, CINBEV, PERFLEV, DIARVNCO, DIASTA, BESCV, BEREBESCV, ARVRARA, BAGAGRA; on the demon's breast, ARITMO, ARAITTO; on the boat, NOCTIVAGVS, TIBERIS, OCEANVS. See Paoli, pp. 285–86.

The reverse of the tablet reads:

> ADIVRO TE DEMON QVICVMQVE ES ET DEMANDO TIBI EX ANC DIE EX AC ORA EX OC MOMENTO VT EQVOS PRASINI ET ALBI CRVCIES ET AGITATORES CLARVM ET FELICEM ET PRIMVLVM ET ROMANVM OCIDAS COLLIDAS NEQVE SPIRITVM ILLIS LERINQVAS[1]: ADIVRO TE PER EVM QVI TE RESOLVIT TEMPORIBVS DEVM PELAGI CVM AERIVM IAW LASDAW . . .

([1] = *relinquās*)

> I adjure you, demon, whoever you are, and I demand of you, from this day from this hour from this moment, that you torture the horses of the Greens and The Whites and destroy and smash their drivers Clarus and Felix and Primulus and Romanus and leave no breath in them. I adjure you by that god of the sea who has released you in due season and by the god of the air, Iaw etc. (quoted in Dudley, p. 215)

Some have suggested that the names on the boat are those of the horses being cursed. The tablet was written in the third century A.D. at Hadrumetum, or modern Sousse (Tunisia), and was found in a tomb.

Other defixiones

Here are some other defixiones which have been discovered in Britain:

(a) TRETIA(M) MARIA(M) DEFICO ET / ILLEVS VITA(M) ET ME(N)TEM / ET MEMORIAM [E]T IOCINE / RA PULMONES INTERMIX / TA . . . SCI[1] NO(N) POSSITT LOQVI / (QVAE) SICRETA SI(N)T . . . (*R.I.B.*7)

([1] = *sic*)

I curse Tretia Maria, her life, mind, memory, liver, and lungs mixed up together. Thus may she be unable to speak what is hidden . . .

(b) DONATVR DEO IOVI / OPTIMO MAXIMO VT / EXIGAT PER MENTEM PER / MEMORIAM PER INTVS / PER INTESTINVM PER COR / [P]ER MEDVLLAS PER VENAS / . . . SI MASCEL SI / FEMINA QVI (SQ)VIS / INVOLAVIT DENARIOS CANI / DIGNI VT IN CORPORE / SVO IN BREVI TEMP[OR]E / PARIAT DONATVR / DEO DECIMA PARS (*Journal of Roman Studies*, vol. 53 (1963), pp. 122–24)

This tablet is given to Jupiter Optimus Maximus with the prayer that he may smite through the mind, memory, inward parts, guts, heart, marrow, veins whatever person, man or woman, has stolen the money of Canus Dignus. Let him quickly restore the money in person. A tenth of the money is offered to the god.

(c) Among the 130 defixiones found in the hot-spring at Bath was an engagingly comprehensive "insurance policy" directed against an unknown enemy: *utrum vir, utrum mulier, utrum puer, utrum puella, utrum servus, utrum liber.* Moreover, to insure that the magic had the best chance of working, someone wrote the whole backwards (for this and other defixiones from Bath, see Hassall, in *Omnibus* (see Bibliography), and Cunliffe (ed.), *Temple*, vol. 2, pp. 107–246.

(d) At Lydney, also in Gloucestershire (see above, p. 36), there was an important temple of the god Nodens, a Celtic god of hunting, who was worshiped too for his healing powers. Defixiones were found there too, including one by a certain Sylvianus who had had a ring stolen from him. Sylvianus promised to pay the god half its value if it were recovered, and cursed the suspected thief: "Among those who are called Senecianus, do not allow health until he bring the ring to the temple of Nodens."

Suggested Activities

1 Write on the blackboard or the transparency of an overhead projector one or both of the defixiones (a) and (b) above (these were not originally written backwards), work out the meaning with contributions from the class and invite students to suggest either the incident which may have led to the curse or the possible outcome of it. After the discussion, ask students to write, each individually, a fictitious short story about the curse, perpetrator, and victim.

2 Invite students to design an imaginary defixio of their own, including in it a mysterious drawing and abracadabra-type formula like those given on pp. 36–37.

3 Ask junior high or high school students to write out rhymes and formulae which they themselves, when younger, used to avert danger or express dislike of somebody. Ask college students to compare Roman (and Greek) superstitious practices with universal ones. For universal practices, they may begin with a reference book, containing a bibliography, like Frazer; for Roman and Greek practices, J. Ferguson, *Greek and Roman Religion*, pp. 118–39.

4 What does the use of defixiones suggest about the popular conception of the gods? Older students may discuss the related but not necessarily overlapping ideas of a "god as powerful being" and of a "god as having a moral will."

5 Explore with the class possible reasons for the widespread belief in defixiones and similar magico-religious practices. Possible reasons may include personal cowardice or helplessness; lack of confidence in the public system of justice; lack of scientific understanding of the natural world which results in the tendency to believe in irrational forces.

STAGE 23: HARUSPEX

BRIEF OUTLINE

Reading passages	Memor the soothsayer (continued from Stage 21)
Background material	divination and religion
Chief grammatical point	neuter plural

NARRATIVE POINTS

Date	*Setting*	*Characters Introduced*	*Story Line*
Spring, A.D. 83	Britain: Aquae Sulis (Bath)		Cephalus offers Cogidubnus poisoned drink; Quintus recognizes the Egyptian poison cup; Dumnorix forces Cephalus to drink it; he dies. Letter warns king of Emperor Domitian's poison plot; Cogidubnus dismisses Memor, and is placed by Salvius under house arrest.

GRAMMATICAL POINTS

Increased incidence of neuter plural

e.g. *iubeō tē ōmina īnspicere.*

genū

e.g. *Cephalus pōculum haurīre nōluit, et ad genua rēgis prōcubuit.*

īdem

e.g. *servus enim, multa tormenta passus, in eādem sententiā mānsit.*

SENTENCE PATTERN

V + NOM + ACC

e.g. *scrīpsit Cephalus epistulam.*

No major new grammatical points appear in this stage and so there are no model sentences. Use this stage to help students review and integrate the perfect participle, particularly to

1 associate the participle with the correct noun;
2 translate the participle appropriately, using a variety of English equivalents;
3 distinguish perfect active from perfect passive participles and both of these from present participles. Assess students' initial grasp by the correctness of their translation. Gradually follow this with the request to say whether the participle is perfect active or perfect passive.

Title Picture

This shows Memor examining the entrails of a lamb on the altar in the temple precinct at Bath. The altar platform, which is 14 × 18 ft (4.3 × 5.5 m), has survived as have also three corners of the altar. They are carved with gods and goddesses on adjacent sides. For a full description, see Cunliffe, *Roman Bath Discovered*, pp. 22–23. The picture of Memor is based on one of the figures from a second-century relief of *haruspicēs* now in the Louvre (see slide 54).

in thermīs

The plot against Cogidubnus is resumed. The king visits the baths for the first time. At the sacrifice the omens are bad, but Memor, in his role of haruspex, interprets them falsely. They promise, he says, a recovery for the king. Cogidubnus proceeds to the bath, and is helped in and out with a great deal of fuss and shouting. (Quintus, meanwhile, is marveling at the grandeur of the baths.) After the king finishes his bath, he approaches the sacred fountain, where Cephalus nervously presents him with a poisoned goblet of water. At the last moment, Quintus, who has seen such a cup in Alexandria, prevents the king from drinking. The king is unconvinced that anyone would want to kill him, until Cephalus, forced by Dumnorix to drink the cup, dies on the spot.

Begin by reading the first two paragraphs aloud and then ask students to work in pairs or small groups to look for answers to comprehension questions like these (write them on the blackboard and let students refer to the plan in Stage 21, p. 18):

Where does this ceremony take place? Who are present?
What kind of ceremony is it?
What happens in the second paragraph?
What state of mind does Memor seem to be in? Can you suggest why?

Then bring the class together, check that the storyline has been clearly understood, and ask selected students to read quickly the dialogue which follows. Afterwards, discuss with the class the two following topics:
(1) the practice of divination. Refer students first to the background material, pp. 48–49, for information, then invite them to say why Cogidubnus sacrificed a lamb to Sulis Minerva before taking his water-treatment: firstly, to inquire whether he would recover and secondly, by making a present of the lamb, to try to secure a favorable outcome. What reply did Sulis Minerva appear to be making? If Memor had announced what the priest had actually found in the liver, how might Cogidubnus have acted? (2) the behavior of Memor. Why is he trembling and sweating? Why does he show alarm at the priest's statement that the liver is *līvidum* (line 12)? "A guilty conscience" or "He thought the goddess was trying to warn Cogidubnus" may be sufficient comment. But note also he begins to panic. Memor lacks the cool judgment of Salvius.

The picture on p. 41 shows the exterior of the temple. Note the pediment, described above in Stage 21, p. 27.

Keep the pace rapid during the first reading of Part II. If necessary, read it aloud in Latin, pausing only to ask brief comprehension questions after each sentence.

Some teachers break off at the words *rēx pōculum ad labra sustulit* (line 15), resuming in the next class-period, by which time most students will have read at least the next three lines on their own!

Cogidubnus' remark, *aqua est amāra sed remedium potentissimum* (lines 11–12), refers to the naturally strong taste of water with a high mineral content; on this occasion he does not actually taste it since Quintus intervenes.

You might encourage further discussion by asking the following questions:

Why did the slaves find it difficult to lower the king into the bath (lines 5–7)? What do you think were the commands (*mandāta*, line 6) given by Cogidubnus at this moment? Why do you think the chiefs were mean to their līberti?

Why, after the king had come out of the Great Bath, did he approach the *fōns sacer*?

Why are the words *anxius tremēbat* used of Cephalus in line 14?

What caused Quintus to suspect the cup was poisoned (lines 17–18)? Was his guess about the origin of the cup correct (see Stage 21, p. 13, line 41)?

How did Dumnorix propose finding out whether the contents were drugged (lines 27–29)?

epistula Cephalī

After Cephalus dies, one of his slaves delivers a letter to the king, in which Cephalus blames Memor for forcing him to attempt to poison the king. The letter also mentions that the emperor, according to Memor, has ordered the king's death.

While students are reading this letter, they will often begin to notice certain discrepancies between what Cephalus claims and what actually happened. Encourage their discernment by re-reading the relevant part of Stage 21, "Memor rem suscipit," and discuss with them the purpose of the letter. Cephalus had in fact attempted to poison Cogidubnus. Therefore, could the letter have been a warning in advance? Perhaps it was to provide an alibi if the plan miscarried and Cephalus bore the blame. Invite students to speculate about Cogidubnus' response. Will he be skeptical? Credulous? Or will he guess that both Cephalus and Memor were jointly responsible? Let the next story, "Britannia perdomita," itself attest to Cogidubnus' actual response.

Review with students the 1st and 2nd persons singular of the perfect tense. Ask students to pick out, e.g. in lines 6–9, the verbs in the perfect and then to identify which of these is 1st person. After establishing the endings, review the perfect stems by asking students to translate 1st or 2nd person singular forms of *irregular* perfect-tense verbs from previous checklists, e.g. "What does *ascendī* mean?" "What does *ascendistī* mean?"

Consult Unit 2 Teacher's Manual, p. 70, for perfects of verbs from the checklists of Stages 1–17; to that list, add the following perfects from the checklists of Stages 18–23:

Perfects with *-ĭ-*: *adiī* (20); *saeviī* (18).
Perfects with *-u-*: *monuī* (22); *pāruī* (23); *prōcubuī* (18).
Perfects with *-v-*: *administrāvī* (23); *amāvī* (19); *arcessīvī* (20); *castīgāvī* (19); *cēlāvī* (21); *cōgitāvī* (19); *cognōvī* (18); *collocāvī* (20); *commemorāvī* (23); *comparāvī* (19); *cūrāvī* (19); *dēmōnstrāvī* (18); *equitāvī* (20); *errāvī* (23); *iactāvī* (22); *līberāvī* (20); *nōvī* = "I know" (19); *ōrnāvī* (23); *petīvī* "I begged for" (18); *recūsāvī* (18); *scīvī* (or *sciī*) (23); *temptāvī* (20); *vexāvī* (19); *vītāvī* (22).
Perfects with *-s-* or *-x-*: *cessī* (23); *discessī* (18); *dissēnsī* (22); *extrāxī* (21); *flūxī* (19); *gessī* (23); *iussī* (21); *persuāsī* (20); *vīxī* (19).
Strong perfects: *adiūvī* (21); *coepī* (18); *cōnfēcī* (19); *dēcēpī* (22); *dēiēcī* (21); *effēcī* (21); *ēlēgī* (22); *frēgī* (18); *fūdī* (22); *grātiās ēgī* (19); *iēcī* (23); *incēpī* (22); *iniēcī* (22); *irrūpī* (20); *relīquī* (20); *suscēpī* (21).
Perfects with stem unchanged: *ascendī* (21); *dēfendī* (19); *induī* (23).
Perfects with reduplicated consonants: *cecīdī* (19); *cōnstitī* (18); *obstitī* (18); *pepercī* (22); *poposcī* (19); *restitī* (18).
Perfect with stem different from the present stem: *intulī* (20).

Help students determine the meanings of the harder verbs by setting them within the context of an English sentence (e.g. "I *adiūvī* her to finish the lesson") or providing English derivatives drawn from the inventories in the North American Second Edition Unit I Teacher's Manual, pp. 119–41, Units IIA/IIB Teacher's Manual, pp. 95–114, and Units IIIA/IIIB Teacher's Manual, pp. 167–200. Or assign to students some of these perfects to be studied at home for a quiz the next day: have them learn the meanings of verbs selected from the list above by finding the present stem and the lexical meaning in the Complete Vocabulary part of the Units 2 and 3 LI Sections.

The passage is on the list of those which you may omit (see above, p.10) when time is short. If you prefer to spend the period reviewing verbs as suggested above, you may yourself translate the story for the students, while they follow in their books, and invite them to suggest idiomatic English equivalents for the various phrases with *rem* that occur in the story.

Language Note (Neuter Plural)

Neuter plural nouns have been met quite frequently since Stage 21, but comment has been postponed until now. Paragraph 2 of the note invites the students to volunteer the generalization that all neuter plural nouns end in *-a* in both the nominative and the accusative cases. You should bring out this point, not hand it over. Then students may turn to the paradigm of the adjective in the LI Section, p. 265, and confirm their previous generalization about the identical endings. If students worry about not being able to distinguish a nominative from an accusative neuter plural form, advise them to look at the whole sentence before translating it.

Britannia perdomita

Salvius and Memor are confronted by Cogidubnus, who arrives in full official regalia and accompanied by an escort, to announce that he is dismissing Memor from his position as manager of the baths. Salvius cuts off Memor's indignant response with an open declaration of hostilities against Cogidubnus, declaring that the emperor has ordered Salvius to seize Cogidubnus' kingdom, and commanding the king to return to his palace at once. The shocked old man realizes that his years of cooperation with the Roman conquerors of Britain are of no avail to him now, because Roman policy has shifted.

In the hands of operators like Salvius and Memor, the old king is helpless. Students should discuss motives. What reasons are suggested to explain why Salvius conspired to bring down Cogidubnus? Why should Cogidubnus feel wronged by Salvius' remark, *numquam contentus fuistī. nōs diū vexāvistī* (line 31)? In answer, students should cite the king's hospitable treatment of Salvius and his honoring of the Emperor Claudius (Unit 2, Stages 15 and 16). You might add historical evidence: Cogidubnus' possible role in the invasion of A.D. 43 is considered in the Unit 2 Teacher's Manual, pp. 4 and 44, and Tacitus describes him as being *ad nostram usque memoriam fidissimus* (*Agricola* 14).

So far as Cogidubnus' past record was concerned, he might reasonably have expected *fidēs Rōmāna* to continue towards him. If the *arrogantia* imputed to Cogidubnus was not the real reason for Domitian's action against him, what might it have been? Although students may want to speculate, they will find a plausible answer in Stage 26, p. 97.

The questions following the passage are designed to establish the protagonists' relative positions of power and to show how their actions were the outcome of assumptions and prior calculations. You should begin the discussion by reminding students of the current situation. What do they suppose will be the king's feelings towards Memor at this moment? And what may be the mood of Salvius and Memor after the failure of their plot?

When students are discussing question 1, ask them to consider the way Cogidubnus has dressed for this visit, *togam praetextam ōrnāmentaque gerit* (lines 3–4). In question 4, make sure that students understand that Cogidubnus brought soldiers to put Memor out of his job. Was this a miscalculation? Or was it his best chance of dealing with the threat to his life? Students should observe carefully Salvius' reactions to Cogidubnus' display of force. Was he surprised? Memor reacts to the confrontation by protesting innocence, *tū mē dēmōvistī? innocēns sum* (line 27), and is about to continue when Salvius cuts him off. What was Memor about to say? In question 5, the answer is *Rōmānum* (line 29). The last question is looking for some consideration of Cogidubnus' state of mind at the end. What does he regret? What else could he have done at the time of the invasion?

There is no historical evidence for the letter which Salvius claims to have received from Domitian instructing him to expropriate the estates of Cogidubnus (lines 33–35), but an instruction of this kind would be consistent with what we know of Salvius' mission to Britain as *iūridicus* (see Unit 2 Teacher's Manual, p. 5) at a time when Domitian needed to replenish the imperial treasury. The emperor was financing an elaborate program of public works which he hoped would win him popularity (see above, pp. 5–6). Cogidubnus seems to have died at this time; whether from natural causes or foul play is not known.

Students will probably see the sense of *id quod* in *id quod dīcis, absurdum est* (line 15). Confirm that the single word "what" is sufficient as a translation. A short note and further practice appears in the Unit 3 LI Section, p. 274, paragraph 11.

The coin pictured on p. 45 is a didrachma from Caesarea, about A.D. 46. It shows the Emperor Claudius in a chariot, holding an eagle-topped scepter. The use of *dē* in this context ("a triumph *over* the Britons") is new to students.

Drills and Suggestions for Further Practice

Exercise 1 Type: vocabulary
Grammatical point being practiced: nouns ending in *-or*

Perfect participles are given where the cognate noun may seem to students remote from the infinitive, e.g. *pingere* (*pictus*)—*pictor*. Add the participles for the other verbs and so demonstrate that for all verbs the noun derives from the perfect participle, e.g. *amāre* (*amātus*)—*amātor*. Extend the exercise with examples from verbs in Appendix A, "Cumulated List of Checklist Words," below pp. 181–88.

Exercise 2 Type: completion

Missing item: verb
Test of accuracy: correct personal ending
Grammatical point being practiced: 1st, 2nd, 3rd persons plural of the present, imperfect, perfect, and pluperfect

Like Stage 21, Exercise 5, this is designed to help students review basic endings of indicative verbs before they proceed to the forms of the imperfect and pluperfect subjunctive active in the next two stages.

Exercise 3 Type: transformation
Grammatical point being practiced: infinitive with present tense of *volō, possum*, and *dēbeō*

This exercise reviews auxiliary verbs with the prolate infinitive; the examples have been selected to avoid the complication of a vowel change, e.g. *dormītis—dormīre*. If students have difficulty, point out that the infinitive is given in the Complete Vocabulary part of the LI Section. Extend this exercise by changing the verbs in the left-hand column (avoiding vowel changes) or by switching the auxiliary verbs around.

Exercise 4 Type: completion
Missing item: participle
Test of accuracy: sense and syntax
Grammatical point being practiced: perfect participles, passive and active

As in the stories, let students be guided principally by the context. The noun governing the participle is in every case nominative singular masculine.

If the students need further drill in the indicative before they begin the subjunctive, use some of the following transformation exercises:

1 Suppose the first paragraph of "in thermīs" were a stage direction, with all its verbs in the present tense. What would be the form and meaning of *erat* (line 1), *solēbant* (line 2), etc.?
2 Turn to the last paragraph of "epistula Cephalī" and using your knowledge of verb endings, work out the Latin equivalent of "he wrote," "we handed over," etc. You should not use English-to-Latin drills like these unless the students can do them in a reasonably confident way.
3 Turn to the LI Section, e.g. pp. 275–76. Look at the imperfect tense of *portō* and pick out the form which means "we were carrying." Look at the perfect tense of *doceō* and give the meaning of *docuistī*. You might follow up with paragraph 3, p. 275, and similar further examples.

Background Material

The *haruspicēs* belonged to a priestly *collēgium*, "college" or "association," which dated from the Etruscan dominance at Rome. Their name means literally "those who look at entrails" and, like the augurs, they practiced a discipline which purported to reveal the future. Their collegium at Rome consisted of sixty members. We also know that they were active at religious centers in the provinces, e.g. at Nemausus (Nîmes) in southern France and at Bath in Britain.

The respect popularly accorded to diviners and soothsayers reflects how the Romans viewed the future. They believed that the future cast a shadow in front of itself which could be recognized through correctly applied techniques; in this way, they could take precautions to avoid misfortune or at least mitigate its consequences. This belief in magical forseeability was widespread and by no means confined to the illiterate. Closely linked with it was a sense of the fickleness of fortune. A person could be a ruler one day and a slave the next. Hence the importance of recognizing the shadow of tomorrow's danger and avoiding it as far as possible. Some of the educated, however, were skeptical and tended to make fun of soothsayers; nevertheless, in varying degrees, the Romans found comfort or guidance in the words of those who read the stars, watched the flight of birds, or scrutinized the markings on the entrails of slaughtered animals.

The different areas of the liver (p. 48) were under the influence of different gods. This bronze model was possibly used as a teaching aid.

The life-size gilded bronze head of Sulis Minerva (p. 52) was found in 1727. The unfinished top of the head suggests that the goddess probably was wearing a detachable helmet. The statue to which it belonged may well have been the cult statue of the temple.

When discussing with students the official religion of Rome, stress its ritualistic character and public purposes.

A more personal experience was available from other sources: firstly, the continuation in rural communities of the old rituals which bound the individual to his family, his land, and its guardian spirits; and secondly, mystery religions and new cults from Greece and the Middle East which expressly addressed the individual. These offered purification, communion with the deity, personal significance, and existence after death. The worship of Mithras, a Persian fertility cult widespread in the Roman army, was one of these faiths; another which enjoyed much popularity during the first three centuries A.D. was Isis worship. From Greece came the orgiastic rites of Dionysus and the mysteries of Demeter. Evidence of these faiths, existing in parallel with the state religion, is to be seen at many places, for example, the temple of Isis at Pompeii and the temples of Mithras at Temple Court in London and at Carrawburgh on Hadrian's Wall.

By the first century, the Roman world had developed many different religious practices, and the official attitude was one of tolerance, except where, as in the case of Christianity, the religion was felt to be politically subversive. This diversity is comparable to the variety of religions in modern multi-ethnic societies. For further material on Roman religion, see Bibliography below, pp. 198–200

Suggestions for Discussion and Further Activities

1 Compare ancient mystery cults, like Isiacism or Mithraism, with modern religious sects, like Hare Krishna or the Unification Church, both of which offer personal enlightenment and salvation to their followers; the importance of ritual in both ancient and modern religious practices, e.g. in Judaism or the Orthodox, Roman Catholic, Episcopalian, and Anglican churches; and the links between religion and state both then and now, e.g. the American controversy about prayer in public schools.

2 Consider why the Romans placed so much trust in divination. Ask students to make a list of the different means of Roman divination which they have so far heard about. Ask them to collect and list examples of omens from, e.g. translations of Livy's history.

3 Remind students of the *larārium* in Caecilius' house depicted in filmstrip 1 frame 6, and discuss reasons why he had the scenes of the A.D. 62 earthquake carved on it. Then expand the point to include votive offerings which took many different forms, e.g. altars erected in fulfillment of a vow—usually with the words or initial letters of *vōtum solvit libēns meritō* "rightly and willingly he kept his promise" as the last line of the inscription; or objects like an oar, clothing, or jewelry hung up on a temple wall by the survivors of shipwrecks.

4 If you have visited churches in Italy or Greece, show slides of the small votive tablets—made usually of hammered silver—jewelry and watches which frequently hang beside sacred images or icons. The silver tablets usually depict the person or part of the body which Christ, the Virgin, or one of the Saints healed in response to the prayers of the dedicator.

5 Some students may enjoy the lighthearted view of divination in *Asterix and the Soothsayer*, a widely available comic book, in English or Latin.

STAGE 24: FUGA

BRIEF OUTLINE

Reading passages Background material	travel and communication
Chief grammatical points	*cum* with subjunctive 3rd person singular and plural of imperfect and pluperfect subjunctive

NARRATIVE POINTS

Date	*Setting*	*Characters Introduced*	*Story Line*
Spring, A.D.83	Britain: various locales	Gnaeus Iulius Agricola (governor of Britain)	Comic interlude when bridge collapses under chubby Modestus. Salvius orders all chieftains of Regnenses arrested. Dumnorix asks Quintus for help; they take horses and head northward to Agricola, who outranks Salvius. Salvius sends Belimicus with 200 horsemen to arrest Quintus and Dumnorix: also sends incriminating letter to Agricola. Dumnorix is killed in fight with horsemen. Quintus is wounded, but escapes.

GRAMMATICAL POINTS

cum-clauses

e.g. *cum ad pontem vēnissent, equus trānsīre nōluit.*

3rd person singular and plural pluperfect subjunctive

e.g. *cum dēscendisset, equus statim trānsiit.*

3rd person singular and plural imperfect subjunctive (including *sum, possum, volō*)

e.g. *cum Salvius rem sēcum cōgitāret, Belimicus subitō rediit exsultāns.*

neuter gerundive of obligation

e.g. *nōbīs festīnandum est ad ultimās partēs Britanniae.*

SENTENCE PATTERNS

ADJ + PREPOSITION + N

e.g. *Belimicus, multīs cum mīlitibus ēgressus, per oppidum dīligenter quaerēbat.*

extended prepositional phrase + participle

e.g. *Dumnorix tamen, ē manibus mīlitum ēlāpsus, per viās oppidī prōcessit.*

in itinere

The action in both the "high life" and the "low life" stories now leaves Bath and moves north. A short story, instead of the usual model sentences, brings back Modestus and Strythio. They are on their way to Chester (where the comically incompetent performance of their duties will provide the theme of Stage 25). A rickety bridge collapses beneath the overweight Modestus, after Strythio and a horse have successfully crossed it.

The new grammatical point is the use of *cum* with the pluperfect subjunctive, meaning "when" or "after."

Students should begin their reading with a brief discussion of the picture. They rarely fail to decide correctly which rider is which, though some may be surprised by the unglamorous figure of Modestus in the drawing. The two soldiers are not traveling in uniform, but the *pugiō* and the *gladius* are visible as are the bedding-rolls and cooking-pot by the horse's tail.

You might choose the following sequence for reading: (1) lines 1–3, you read aloud, ask comprehension questions, call for translation; (2) lines 4–9, you read aloud, students look over in pairs, call for translation; (3) lines 10–13, you read aloud, students look over individually, call for translation. During this reading, you should not comment on the new form of the verb; instead, you should use comprehension questions to bring out "when" as the meaning of *cum* and "had come" as the meaning of *vēnissent*.

Discuss the subjunctive after students have read the story, or leave it until after the next story, when students will have met more examples. Begin by asking students to pick out all the verbs in lines 1–3. Confirm that *vēnissent* is a verb and a part of *venīre*, and this new form may be spotted by the *-iss-* which is its regular feature. Invite students to find other examples. With further questions elicit that it may be translated by "had . . ." (confirm that it is a pluperfect tense), that *cum* means "when" in this situation, and that the endings *-isset* and *issent* are respectively the 3rd singular and 3rd plural. If students offer "they came" for *vēnissent*, accept this at first, but by the end of the stage, press for the pluperfect "they had come." At a convenient moment, you should introduce the label "subjunctive," treating it simply as a means of distinguishing this from other parts of the verb.

The next step is to associate in students' minds the conjunction *cum* with the subjunctive verb. The may be done by asking questions, e.g. "All the sentences that have a verb in the subjunctive also have another feature. What is it?" Confirm that it is the presence of *cum* that "causes" the subjunctive to be used.

Some students may be worried about the two uses of *cum* ("when" and "with"). If so, point out that the easiest way to decide which is which in a particular sentence is to look at the sentence as a whole. Demonstrate with examples, e.g. *rēx cum Quīntō ambulābat* and *cum Modestus dēcidisset, Strȳthiō rīsit*.

Some students may also ask at this point "Why does Latin have the subjunctive? What does it mean?" For suggested responses, see under the language note below, pp. 51–52.

Quīntus cōnsilium capit

On Cogidubnus' departure from Memor's villa, Salvius sends out soldiers to arrest all the chiefs of the Regnenses. Dumnorix, however, manages to elude them. He seeks out Quintus, who has always stood by the king and who has twice saved his life, and asks him to come to Cogidubnus' aid once again. Quintus proposes that he and Dumnorix should escape from Aquae Sulis, go to the north of Britain, and lay the king's case before the only man in the province who outranks Salvius: the governor, Agricola. A slave prepares food for them for six days' journey, they steal two horses from Salvius, and they flee the town under cover of night.

In this and the next story, the characters take sides in a way which cuts across ethnic and national boundaries: a Briton and a Roman (Dumnorix and Quintus) try to outwit a second Briton and a second Roman (Belimicus and Salvius). Encourage students to reflect on the motives for the behavior of all four men by asking questions like the following:

What reasons would Dumnorix have for trusting Quintus?
Why should Salvius wish to bring a charge of treason against Cogidubnus?
Do you think that Quintus' motives for wanting to protect the king are based on personal friendship or is a principle at stake?
Why should Quintus believe that an appeal to Agricola might be effective?
Is Quintus aware of the emperor's involvement?

When discussing the questions in Unit 3, p. 57, note that in question 4 Dumnorix has in mind not only Quintus' seizing the poisoned cup (Stage 21), but also his killing the bear (Unit 2, Stage 16).

When students read the sentence, *rēx . . . dē vītā suā dēspērat* (lines 13–14), discuss the meaning of *suus* and its contrast with *eius* and *eōrum*. Begin by writing the sentence on the blackboard, then write contrasting sentences, e.g. *Cogidubnus aegrōtat. medicus dē vītā eius dēspērat.* Ask a student to translate it, put the translation on the blackboard, then ask, "Both sentences translate as 'despairs of his life,' yet the Latin uses a different word for 'his' in each case. Can you suggest why?" Make sure that students recognize the referent of *suus* and *eius: suus* being used to denote something that belongs to the grammatical subject of the sentence and *eius*, something that belongs to any other person or thing in the sentence.

Review noun-forms and participles. Here and in the next three stages, drill most particularly the genitive and dative cases of the noun so that students will be ready for the introduction of the ablative without supporting preposition in Stage 28. Choose nouns from the current and previous checklists: from Stages 1–17, listed in the Unit 2 Teacher's Manual, p. 68, and from Stages 18–24:

First declension, feminine: *cūra* (23); *dea* (18); *fīlia* (19); *fortūna* (18); *hōra* (21); *lacrima* (22); *lūna* (20); *pompa* (19); *prūdentia* (22); *rīpa* (24); *stola* (19); *venia* (23).

Second declension, masculine: *annus* (21); *barbarus* (21); *locus* (19); *medicus* (20); *modus* (23); *morbus* (21); *numerus* (23); *oculus* (20); *umerus* (19).

Second declension, neuter: *caelum* (22); *colloquium* (24); *exitium* (22); *ingenium* (23); *mandātum* (23); *oppidum* (21); *perīculum* (19); *praesidium* (18); *pretium* (21); *remedium* (20); *venēnum* (23); *verbum* (22); *vērum* (24).

Third declension, m. or f.: *amor*, m.(22); *ars*, f.(20); *auctōritās*, f.(24); *auris*, f.(20); *carcer*, m.(24); *eques*, m.(24); *fōns*, m.(21); *haruspex*, m.(21); *hiems*, f.(20); *honor*, m.(23); *hostis*, m. or f.(22); *mīles*, m.(18); *mors*, f.(20); *nox*, f.(18); *parēns*, m. or f.(20); *pars*, f.(18); *pōns*, m.(24); *precēs* (pl.), f.(20); *sermō*, m.(20); *virtūs*, f.(22); *vōx*, f.(19). Of these, the following have *-i-* in the genitive plural: *artium, aurium, fontium, hostium, mortium, noctium, partium,* and *pontium.*

Third declension, neuter: *caput* (18); *flūmen* (24); *iter* (19); *vulnus* (20).

Fourth declension, m. or f.: *domus*, f.(20); *manus* "hand," f.(18); *sonitus*, m.(19).

Drill various forms of the nouns above and ask students to identify the meaning of each, and its number and case. If students have difficulty, place each noun in the context of an English sentence, e.g. "He gave the king a cup *venēnī*" *or* "They threw the coin into the *fontem*." Or have students open to the LI Section, pp. 262–64, "Nouns" and ask them which of the paradigm nouns resembles the form being drilled.

Also review, here and in the following stories, the participle. Using a story which students have just read, have them pick out the participles, link each with the correct noun or pronoun, and translate the whole phrase, and then say whether they are present, perfect active, or perfect passive.

First Language Note (*cum* with the Pluperfect Subjunctive)

When going through the final paragraph, encourage students to comment on the morphology of the pluperfect subjunctive in contrast to that of the "ordinary" (indicative) form. The paragraph has been so constructed that students usually perceive the difference for themselves. Confirm their comments and emphasize the importance of them.

At some point in this stage, students may ask, "Why have a subjunctive?" or "What does the subjunctive mean, if we can translate *trāxisset* exactly like *trāxerat*?" In the answer, make clear the priorities among things they should learn: (1) to translate a clause like *cum . . . advēnisset* into English and to identify *advēnisset* as a verb in the 3rd person singular; (2) to use the term "subjunctive" as a label which distinguishes this from the indicative form; (3) to realize that the subjunctive was used originally for things like wishes, prayers, and possible rather than actual events, as in the English expressions "Let's go out," and "It may rain tomorrow." The Latin subjunctive continued to have this meaning, but it also came to be used in other situations; one was in clauses with *cum*.

Salvius cōnsilium cognōscit

Salvius is furious that Dumnorix, of all the chiefs, has escaped his men, and, on hearing that Quintus is also missing, suspects collusion. He enlists the aid of Belimicus, the Cantiacan chief, whom he instructs to discover the whereabouts of Dumnorix and Quintus, or, failing that, to bring back one of their slaves who might provide information under torture. Belimicus captures a slave belonging to Quintus, who reveals, under duress, that he prepared food for the fugitives and that they have headed for the farthest parts of Britain. This leads Salvius to the correct conclusion, and he acts quickly. He sends a letter by special courier to Agricola and orders Belimicus to take two hundred horsemen in pursuit of Dumnorix and Quintus. This detachment catches up with the fugitives after several days, and in the ensuing confrontation Dumnorix is killed, but Quintus, although badly wounded, manages to escape.

By torturing Quintus' slave, Salvius discovers what Quintus and Dumnorix are up to and sends Belimicus in pursuit. Brutality towards slaves was portrayed in Stage 13. Here, when arrested for questioning about his master's disappearance, Quintus' slave is first tortured. Torture as a method of getting information out of slaves was practiced freely in the Roman world; in fact, evidence given by slaves in court was admissible only if it had been obtained in this way.

Invite students to comment on the following two topics: (1) the practical reasons for torturing a slave during an inquiry, (2) the morality of such treatment. The first will probably bring out comments like "A good slave would be loyal to a good master like Quintus and keep quiet unless forced to reveal what he knew" or "If a slave is tortured he is more likely to say what he thinks the torturer wants to hear." The Romans tended to believe that statements made voluntarily, especially by a slave, were inherently unreliable. Ask students to comment. How much more reliable would evidence given under force be than voluntary statements from non-slaves? Was such evidence any less dictated by self-interest?

By this time, comments on the morality of torture are likely to have cropped up, expressed variously but probably agreeing on the value of persons and the moral obligation not to do them violence or injustice. You might probe with questions, e.g. "Does it make any difference that slaves were not regarded by Roman law as persons, but as property owned by their masters?" You should keep the subject open to different views, clarify a point, help students listen to each other, and encourage the habit of reflecting on reasons.

The notion of *auctōritās* appears in line 33 and is worth considering. Ask first "Who is *ego*?" and "Who is *ille*?"; then "Do you think Salvius' claim is true? Why would he expect to have more influence with Agricola than Quintus? Because he is older? Holds a more important position? Is a friend of the emperor?" This could lead to an analysis of Belimicus' behavior. He could not have acted as he did without the *auctōritās* of a powerful Roman behind him.

Salvius himself is anxious only about the possible failure of his plan. About the morality of his actions, he has no visible qualms. He views others principally in terms of their usefulness or obstructiveness.

Second Language Note (Imperfect Subjunctive)

When taking students through paragraph 4, encourage them to compare the form of the imperfect subjunctive with that of the infinitive. Review with students the distinction between pluperfect and imperfect subjunctives by asking them to pick out the *cum*-clauses from the preceding story, translate them, and identify the tense of the subjunctive.

Drills and Suggestions for Further Practice

Exercise 1 Type: vocabulary
Grammatical point being practiced: negatives

In addition to observing the Latin negative prefixes in these examples (*n(e)-*, *in-*, *dis-*), draw attention to the English forms, both those which are the same ("n-," "in-," "dis-") and those which differ ("-less," "un-"). The exercise could also be used to introduce the notion of assimilation (without using the term). Ask the class, "If *īnsānus* and *dissentīre*, why not *inpatiēns* and *disfacilis*?" If students cannot answer, invite them to say the Latin aloud and contrast that with the ease of pronouncing *impatiēns* and *difficilis*. It would be inappropriate to go further into the rules of assimilation.

Exercise 2 Type: substitution
Grammatical point being practiced: oblique cases of *is*

This exercise emphasizes that "them" or "it" in English may represent any gender of the pronoun in Latin. Students might also use sentences 7 and 8 to practice orally the relative pronoun. The most difficult part of the manipulation of the relative, viz. the case of the pronoun itself, should be easier since students will have just performed the same manipulation with *is*. Students should probably do this exercise orally. For a further exercise, see LI Section, p. 274.

Exercise 3 Type: completion
Missing item: adjective
Test of acuracy: correct case endings
Grammatical point being practiced: agreement of noun and adjective

Examples are restricted to nominative and accusative cases, singular and plural. Some examples contain a noun and adjective of different declensions and different endings.

Extend this exercise by orally interpolating other adjectives of Stages 1–17 from the list in the Unit 2 Teacher's Manual, p. 69, and of Stages 18–24:

Adjectives of the 1st and 2nd declensions: *aureus* (22); *cārus* (19); *clārus* (23); *dīrus* (22); *doctus* (20); *dūrus* (21); *immōtus* (23); *īnfestus* (24); *invītus* (18); *lātus* (20); *longus* (18); *minimus* (22); *molestus* (22); *occupātus* (21); *perfidus* (24); *perīculōsus* (18); *perītus* (21); *pessimus* (20); *plēnus* (21); *plūrimus* (19); *prāvus* (23); *sacer* (18); *tardus* (22); *tūtus* (22).

Adjectives of the 3rd declension: *audāx* (neuter: *audāx*) (24); *crūdēlis* (20); *dulcis* (19); *gravis* (21); *īnfēlīx* (n.: *īnfēlīx*) (21); *neglegēns* (n.: *neglegēns*) (19); *potēns* (n.: *potēns*) (23); *sapiēns* (n.: *sapiēns*) (21); *trīstis* (24).

Also drill students in the meaning of these adjectives by applying them to the checklist nouns listed above, p. 51, and setting each adjective–noun pair in the context of an English sentence, e.g. "After a short summer, there came a *hiems longa*." Or give students practice in matching adjective to noun by gender and ask them to translate adjectives from the list immediately above with nouns from the list above, p. 51, in simple linking sentences, e.g. "The *hiems* was 'long'." (Answer: *longa*) If students cannot remember the gender of, e.g. *hiems*, tell it to them, since this drill focuses on the gender-specific forms of the adjective.

Exercise 4 Type: sentence composition from a pool of Latin words
Grammatical points being practiced: the noun in nominative, dative, and accusative, singular and plural; present tense

The Background Material

Consult Balsdon, *Life* pp. 224–43, for a very full account of travel in the Roman world illustrated by numerous anecdotes, Paoli, pp. 228–31, for descriptions of vehicles used in traveling, and Casson, *Travel*. The Roman road system took its official starting-point from the *mīliārium aureum*, or "golden milestone," probably in the form of a polygonal column set up by Augustus in the Forum and inscribed with place names and distances. The main roads (*viae pūblicae, viae mīlitārēs*) were constructed, owned and maintained by the state. Commissioners (*cūrātōrēs viārum*) appointed by the emperor were responsible for the network of main roads; smaller roads were provided and controlled by local magistrates, with local landowners contributing to the cost of maintenance. There were also some private roads.

Our knowledge of this road system comes from various sources:

1 The archaeological remains of the roads themselves including milestones and other monuments inscribed with distances and directions. This evidence provides a fairly complete picture of the methods of construction used (see, for example, filmstrip 2 frame 3). For an account of road building, see Chevallier, pp. 82–93.

2 Aerial photography, which has much increased our knowledge of the network where there are no physical remains on the surface.

There are also three documentary sources for roads:

3 *The Antonine Itinerary*, compiled at the end of the second century A.D., which gives details of the towns and stopping-places and the distances between them along most of the main roads and some minor ones all over the empire.

4 *The Peutinger Table*, a medieval copy of an ancient road map drawn in diagram form and covering the whole empire. The parts relating to Britain and Spain are unfortunately lost.

5 *The Jerusalem Itinerary* of the fourth century A.D. which shows the route from Bordeaux to Jerusalem via Arles, Milan, Istanbul, and Antioch. As far as Britain is concerned, the network has been well documented by Margary. See also the very useful Ordnance Survey map of Roman Britain.

Sea travel was often quicker and easier, especially in the Mediterranean, than the lengthy overland routes, and for that reason was frequently preferred, the seasons and weather permitting. Merchant shipping was controlled by corporations of ship-owners (*nāviculāriī marīnī*) who were responsible to superintendents appointed by the emperor. Much of their business was concerned with keeping Rome supplied with grain: they were well paid by the state for their services.

Inland waterways were also important parts of the system. Again we find corporations of merchants and barge-owners in control, making extensive connections across the empire from one waterway to another, like the rivers Rhine, Moselle, and Danube. For more information, see Casson, *Ships*.

Suggestions for Discussion and Further Activities

1 Consider with the class the various ways in which a relatively efficient road and maritime system could affect life in the provinces, using concrete examples wherever possible: for example, economic influence (luxury pottery made in southern Gaul was transported and sold across western Europe; glass vessels, made in Alexandria, Antioch, and the Rhine region, were sold in Gaul and Britain; wine, oil, and garum were exported from Campania in large quantities; the palace at Fishbourne clearly used imported materials and craftsmen); political and military influence (governors, other administrators, and troops could reach their provinces quickly, keep the emperor informed by the *cūrsus pūblicus*, and put his policies into action without delay, cf. Pliny, *Letters* X.18 and 96–97); religious influence (see *Acts of the Apostles*, e.g. 14, 17, 18.1–11, 19.21–27; and 27–28 for St. Paul's journey from Caesarea to Rome); private communication and travel (there was no public postal service for private mail. The usual procedure was to send a slave or to wait until a friend or friend's slave was going in the right direction, cf. St. Paul's Letters, e.g. *2 Timothy* 4.9–13. Urgent letters could be sent at some expense by special courier, cf. Pliny, *Letters* III.17; VII.12).

2 Why did people travel in the ancient world? How do the reasons compare with reasons for traveling today? Many wealthy inhabitants of Rome (then as now) moved out during the summer to country villas or the coast. Travel could also be undertaken in search of health. Thus Pliny sent his ex-slave Zosimus first to Egypt, then to Forum Iulii, or modern Fréjus on the French Riviera (*Letters* V.19). Consider also the religious pilgrimages made, in modern times, to Lourdes.

3 Obtain copies of the *Peutinger Table* (reproduced in Cunliffe, *Rome*, and in part on the cover of the Penguin *Atlas of Ancient History*) and ask the class to trace their way around the empire with it. Let them consult a conventional wall map while working with the *Table*.

4 Ask the class to calculate approximate distances and journey times over various routes, using different means of transport. Begin by looking at examples in Lewis and Reinhold II, pp. 148 and 198–207. For example, with the *cūrsus pūblicus*, an average of about 50 miles (80 km) a day could be maintained. How long might it have taken for a message from Agricola at Chester to have reached the Emperor Domitian in Rome?

STAGE 25: MĪLITĒS

BRIEF OUTLINE

Reading passages Background material	the Roman army
Chief grammatical points	indirect question imperfect and pluperfect subjunctive, 1st and 2nd persons, singular and plural

NARRATIVE POINTS

Date	*Setting*	*Characters Introduced*	*Story Line*
Spring, A.D.83	Britain: legionary fortress at Deva (Chester)	Valerius (centurion), Vercobrix (son of Deceanglian chieftain)	Vercobrix is put into military prison for spying. Modestus and Strythio are sent to guard him, but because of their inattention and inefficiency, he escapes. Modestus and Strythio flee in order to avoid punishment.

GRAMMATICAL POINTS

indirect question
e.g. *mīlitēs iuvenem iterum rogāvit quis esset.*

1st and 2nd persons singular and plural, imperfect and pluperfect subjunctive
e.g. *cum in Āfricā mīlitārēmus, sōlī tōtam prōvinciam custōdiēbāmus.*

perfect participle (active deponent), accusative case
e.g. *Strȳthiōnem, iam ad castra regressum, cōnspicit.*

clauses with *cuius*
e.g. *nam inter captīvōs est Vercobrīx, iuvenis magnae dignitātis, cuius pater est prīnceps Deceanglōrum.*

dative participle
e.g. *Modestus Vercobrigī dormientī exsultāns appropinquāvit.*

3rd person singular and plural, imperfect and pluperfect passive
e.g. *habēbat Strȳthiō libellum in quō nōmina captīvōrum scrīpta erant.*

SENTENCE PATTERNS

Variation of word order in sentences containing infinitive
e.g. *iuvenis dīcere nōlēbat quid prope horreum faceret.*
centuriō mīlitem iussit eum ad carcerem dūcere.
vōs ambōs carcerem custōdīre iussit.
coēgērunt mē portās omnium cellārum aperīre.

Title Picture

This shows three members of the Roman army in their uniforms. On the left is a centurion, holding his vine-staff of office. In the middle is an ordinary legionary soldier in armor, with his shield, sword, and javelin ready for battle. On the right is an *aquilifer*, wearing a bearskin and holding the eagle, or standard, of the legion.

Model Sentences

The pictures establish the scene, which is the legionary fortress at Chester during its occupation by the Second Legion (*ca.* A.D. 76 to 87). Notice in passing the turf-and-timber rampart and wooden granary typical of this period. Vercobrix, son of the chief of a Celtic tribe, the Deceangli, is found inside the fortress, hiding behind the granary. He is arrested.

The Deceangli inhabited the northern parts of what are now the counties Clwyd and Gwynedd, in northeastern Wales, westwards from the English county of Cheshire (where Chester is located). In A.D. 49 their territory was plundered by Ostorius Scapula, then governor of Britain, possibly partly in hope of gaining control over the mining of lead and silver. In *ca.* A.D. 76–77, the fortress at Deva/Chester was built to hold the boundary of Britain against the Deceangli and Ordovices tribespeople (see above, p. 5) and to provide a base for further conquests in northern Britain.

After students have read the model sentences and perhaps the story "Modestus custōs," draw their attention to the new grammatical feature: indirect question. Contrast it with the equivalent direct question by writing examples on the blackboard as follows:

"quis es?"	*mīles rogāvit quis esset.*
"quid prope horreum facis?"	*iuvenis dīcere nōlēbat quid prope horreum faceret.*

Have them translated and invite comments. Students are likely to pick out concrete points like the absence of a question mark or of quotation marks or the presence of a verb like *rogāvit*. Encourage them (1) to take the matter further by asking, e.g. "What do the examples in the right-hand column have in common compared with those on the left?," (2) to make comments like "The sentences on the right talk about or describe the questions on the left" or "The questions on the left look as they would in a dialogue, while sentences on the right look as they would in a narrative." After writing more examples on the blackboard, ask students to turn to the language note on pp. 74–75 and go through it with them. The only new word is *castra* (*ignōtum* occurred in exercise 1 of Stage 24, p. 62).

Strȳthiō

The Romans have now arrested Vercobrix and his companions from among the Deceangli and put them in the fortress-jail. The Romans are possibly less concerned with punishing the misdemeanor than with holding them, especially Vercobrix, as hostages.

Valerius, the centurion, sends his assistant (*optiō*) to order Modestus and Strythio to guard the prison. Strythio, who exasperates the optio by repeatedly interrupting him, at first misunderstands why he and Modestus are being sent to the prison, and assumes that he and his companion are in trouble, but once the optio manages to get the real message across, Strythio self-importantly assures him that he could not have chosen two better men for the job.

In line 1, the phrase *Strȳthiōnem . . . regressum* is a good example of participial agreement. After students have read the story, write the phrase on the blackboard and ask: "Who has returned, the optio or Strythio? How does the Latin show this?" Then consider suitable translations, including one with a relative clause, i.e. "He sees Strythio who has now returned to the fortress."

In line 8, if students offer "I am sent" for *missus sum*, guide them towards "I have been sent" by asking for an alternative which better fits the context. The perfect passive indicative will appear in full in Stage 30.

Some Suggested Questions

From the evidence of this story, was a soldier who had the rank of optio above or below a centurion?

What tone of voice do you detect in the optio's words, *mī Strȳthiō, . . . mē audīre* (lines 6–7)? Ask for the sentence to be read aloud, with a suitably sarcastic effect in *quamquam occupātissimus es.*

Why do you think the Romans keep Vercobrix and his companions in the fortress-jail? Can you think of similar tactics which are sometimes used in the modern world? (E.g. Shiites kept Americans hostage.)

When Strythio says *ad statiōnem prōcēdimus* (line 32), what does he mean? From what you know about Modestus and Strythio, how well do you expect them to carry out their duties?

The legionary helmet on p. 73 is bronze and the standard type of the first century A.D. A brow-ridge protected the nose and eyes and a flap on the left protected the neck. The sides of the face were protected by cheek-pieces (see drawings on pp. 69–71).

Filmstrip 2 frame 32 (slide II.54) shows a model of a legionary complete with armor and weapons.

Modestus custōs

At the jail, Modestus and Strythio take up their duties: they are inspecting the prisoners' cells. Modestus wants to see Vercobrix, and is indignant when Strythio interprets his hesitation to enter the cell as fear. As soon as Strythio brings him a lamp, he goes into the cell and gleefully waves his sword at the sleeping Vercobrix, but when a spider falls onto the cowardly Modestus' face, it sends him scurrying from the cell in terror. When Strythio comments on Modestus' pallor, Modestus hastily declares that he is pale from hunger. Strythio offers to go to the kitchen and fetch him some dinner, which Modestus thinks is a fine idea, but he thinks it would be even better if he went himself; so he does, leaving Strythio alone to guard the prisoners.

Modestus is portrayed here at his least attractive, by turns a liar, a bully, a coward. He threatens an unarmed, sleeping prisoner, but runs in panic from a spider which tickles his nose. But this is farce, and it may be made more acceptable for some students if they are reminded of the age-old tradition of comic duos. Ask the class to provide examples, e.g. Laurel and Hardy, Abbott and Costello, the Smothers Brothers, or John Belushi and Dan Aykroyd. In classical literature, the models are Pyrgopolynices and Artotrogus in Plautus' *Miles Gloriosus*, the braggart soldier accompanied by the sharp-witted fool who colludes, mocks, and debunks. Without revealing the sequel in "Modestus prōmōtus" hint that Lady Luck will control the outcome.

Several further examples of *cum* and the pluperfect subjunctive are present. Notice also the newly introduced indirect question in, e.g., *cognōvit ubi Vercobrix iacēret* (lines 4–5), *nesciēbat enim cūr Modestus clāmāret* (lines 23–24), *rogāvit quid accidisset* (lines 30–31).

Exploit the presence of several participles for further oral review. Ask students to pick out each participle, link it with its corresponding noun and translate the whole phrase. Continue, in subsequent lessons, with this kind of drill until students become thoroughly used to participles.

Continue also to review with students forms of the noun (see above, p. 51). This time, for variety, ask them to consider the different possibilities of, e.g., the *-ae* endings. The present story contains examples of *-ae* (nominative plural) *etiam arāneae eum adiuvant* (lines 28–29) and of *-ae* (genitive singular) *in angulō cellae iacēbat Vercobrix* (line 17). Make up other examples as needed, always using complete sentences. One benefit is to confirm to students that endings are more easily distinguishable if they study the whole sentence first.

The sword in its scabbard on p. 74 is the standard legionary sword. Students might like to look back at the picture in Unit 1, Stage 10, p. 154, of soldiers in battle. The Romans were trained to use their swords to stab or thrust at their enemies rather than slash at them. This was not only a more efficient way of inflicting fatal wounds, but also did not leave the soldiers' right sides exposed to the enemy.

First Language Note (Indirect Question)

Paragraph 2 helps students grasp the distinction between direct and indirect questions, but encourage students to express it in their own words. In the final paragraph, ask which are direct questions and which indirect. Ask students sometimes, after they have correctly translated an indirect question, to reconstruct in English the original direct question. Use examples 7 and 8 in this paragraph to show that in this construction the tense of the subjunctive is also the correct tense for translation.

Modestus perfuga

The incompetence of Modestus and Strythio has predictable results. Returning from the kitchen, Modestus is wondering how to explain to Strythio that he has eaten not only his own dinner, but *both* their dinners, when he notices that the prison door is open. Inside the prison, he finds the cells apparently all empty, but as he begins to consider his predicament, he hears a voice coming from Vercobrix's cell, and imagines, in his confusion, that at least the most important prisoner is still safely confined. He is still mystified, however, by Strythio's absence, until he finds a bloody dagger on the ground, and immediately concludes that Vercobrix has killed Strythio. Melodramatically, he laments his friend's death. Swearing revenge, he enters the cell and begins to beat the "prisoner," who turns out to be Strythio himself, much to Modestus' consternation. At this point, the two have no choice but to flee, or else face the consequences of their incompetence. Naturally, they flee.

Because the passage is quite easy, selected students should read it aloud in Latin quickly. Test their comprehension by questions appropriately placed throughout the story. At the end, invite the class, with their books closed, to listen to the audiocassette recording or to your own expressive reading. Alternatively, volunteers might read the passage aloud after discussing tone and points of emphasis.

If students have difficulty with *mihi fugiendum est* (I, line 19), remind them of *nōbīs festīnandum est* or *nōbīs effugiendum est* which were encountered in Stage 24. A language note on the gerundive appears in Stage 26; the term "gerundive" is introduced in a language note in Stage 32.

Second Language Note (1st and 2nd Persons, Singular and Plural, Imperfect and Pluperfect Subjunctive)

1 Make sure that students distinguish accurately between the two

tenses. If they cannot, ask them to identify tenses after reading a story.

2 Devise worksheets on which students sort out short lists of jumbled indicative and subjunctive verbs in both tenses or of jumbled persons, e.g. "Circle the pluperfect subjunctive in the following list: *prōcubuerat, prōcubuisset, prōcumberet, prōcumbēbat*" or "Circle the 'you (sg.)' subjunctive: *trānsīret, trānsīrētis, trānsīrem, trānsīrēs*."

Drills and Suggestions for Further Practice

Exercise 1 Type: vocabulary
Grammatical point being practiced: nouns with masculine/feminine contrast

Extend this exercise into oral practice of English derivatives, e.g. *captīvus/captīva* producing "captive," "captivate," *fīlius/fīlia* producing "filial," "affiliate." For additional derivatives, see inventories in the North American Second Edition Unit I Teacher's Manual, pp. 119–41; IIA/IIB Teacher's Manual, pp. 95–114; and IIIA/IIIB Teacher's Manual, pp. 167–200.

The final group of feminine nouns includes *patrōna*. If the notion of "patroness" in a Roman context sounds improbable to students, cite Eumachia, the *patrōna* of fullers and dyers at Pompeii (see Unit 1 Teacher's Manual, p. 45). Ask students to produce the masculine equivalents of the feminine nouns in the last group, in both Latin and English, but leave *rēgīna* to last.

Exercise 2 Type: completion
Missing item: verb
Test of accuracy: sense
Grammatical point being practiced: forms of perfect tense

The phrases *coquum occupātum* (*invēnit*) and *Modestum īrātum vīdit* are likely to produce "found the busy cook" and "saw angry Modestus." Encourage the predicative versions "found the cook busy" and "saw Modestus was angry."

Exercise 3 Type: transformation
Grammatical point being practiced: nominative and dative, singular and plural

Before assigning this exercise to be done by students on their own (with the help of the LI Section), work some examples on the blackboard so that students will understand the steps of the transformation. The last sentence may cause difficulty.

Exercise 4 Type: completion
Missing item: *cum*-clause
Test of accuracy: sense, based on "Modestus custōs"

Exercise 5 Type: completion
Missing item: adjective
Test of accuracy: correct ending
Grammatical point being practiced: agreement of noun and adjective
Incidentally practiced: *crēdō, pāreō,* + dative

The examples are restricted to dative and accusative, singular and plural.

If students ask about the word order in sentence 7, point out that the first position in a sentence is emphatic. English as well as Latin uses emphatic position to stress a point. Thus this sentence could be translated as "new dresses—that's what the woman was buying."

The Background Material

The life and work of the Roman soldier provide a new topic for study and one which often stimulates considerable interest. Its postponement until now is an advantage, because you may treat it with the sort of details needed to bring it to life.

If students ask about the modern equivalent of a soldier's pay (300 denarii in Domitian's time), work out equivalents from the information below, p. 131. E.g. since a denarius = 4 sestertii, one denarius is equivalent to a laborer's daily wage.

When studying the diagram on p. 81, students sometimes ask why there were not 100 men in a "century," since the term is obviously connected with *centum*. Originally there were, but with natural fluctuation, the term lost its strict numerical significance and just denoted one of the 60 divisions of the legion, each commanded by a centurion. In the beginning of the empire, this had been standardized to *ca*. 80 men. The change in the first cohort from six centuries of 80 men (=480) to five centuries of 160 (=800) took place in the eighties A.D.

The duty roster shown on p. 86 should be interpreted and discussed. There is considerable doubt about many of the readings and disgreement among scholars about what the abbreviations stand for and mean. The entries given in the students' textbook mainly follow the interpretations given by Watson. According to these:

C. Julius Valens was to spend October 1st training in the arena, October 2nd on guard duty in the fortress tower, October 3rd digging (?) drains, October 4th working on (i.e. mending?) boots, October 5th and 6th on duty in the armory (either guarding it or maybe servicing the weapons), October 7th cleaning the baths, October 8th working as orderly to one of the officers, October 9th in his own century (on guard duty?) and October 10th cleaning the baths again.

L. Sextilius Germanus was to spend October 1st on guard at the gate,

October 2nd guarding the standards, October 3rd cleaning the baths, October 4th on guard in the tower, and October 5th–10th on duty with D. Decrius' century.

M. Antonius Crispus was to spend October 1st cleaning the baths, October 2nd on stretcher duty, October 3rd in his own century, October 4th in plain clothes (perhaps civil police duties), October 5th in his own century again, and October 7th and 8th acting as a tribune's escort.

T. Flavius was to spend October 4th, 5th, and 6th cleaning the baths and October 7th on guard at the gate.

M. Domitius was to be away from October 3rd at the granaries in Neapolis (a suburb of Alexandria).

The quotation about recruitment on p. 82 is taken from Vegetius I.7. The terms at the bottom of the diagram of a legion are defined on p. 85 of the students' textbook.

Suggested Activities

This subject area is suitable for small group research (i.e. four or five students work together on a topic; each group reports its findings to the class and/or produces a display). This approach also economizes on time. Ask groups to investigate a selection of the following:

(a) the main items of protective equipment worn by a Roman legionary soldier;
(b) the legion on the march and what it did at the end of the day's march;
(c) the arrangement of a legion on the battlefield;
(d) rewards, decorations, and punishments in the Roman army (Watson is helpful here);
(e) the deployment of the Roman army, either over the whole empire or in Britain, could be studied with maps showing the location of fortresses, smaller forts, and frontier defenses;
(f) Hadrian's Wall: its construction, purposes, manning, and something of the events which affected it. Include the civilian population which lived close to the forts (remember, however, that Hadrian's frontier was not constructed until the second century);
(g) the *auxilia*: how they differed from the legions (different citizen status, more emphasis on cavalry, different style forts, different tasks, links with the legions). See note on *tribūnus mīlitum* below, p. 71, and filmstrip 2 frame 33 (slides II.59 and 60).

To supplement the information contained in this and the next two stages, the following material will be useful (for details of filmstrips and books see Bibliography on pp. 197–98).

1 Slides of military installations, e.g. Hadrian's Wall (see filmstrip 2

frame 35), Chester (see filmstrip 2 frame 30; slide II.56); York, military roads (see filmstrip 2 frame 3).

2 Drawings of Roman soldiers or photographs of military tombstones showing details of uniform and equipment (see filmstrip 2 frames 32–33; slides II.54, 59 and 60). These may also be found in Watson; Webster, *The Roman Army;* Cambridge School Classics Project, *The Romans discover Britain;* photographs of Trajan's Column in, e.g. Richmond.

3 Ground plans of forts of various types and sizes; also some aerial photographs. Sources include Van der Heyden and Scullard; Webster, *The Roman Imperial Army;* Birley, *Life.*

4 A selection of military inscriptions. *R.I.B.* is the definitive collection for Roman Britain, but a valuable and much less expensive alternative is LACTOR No. 4: *Some inscriptions from Roman Britain* (see Bibliography below, p. 198). Both contain translations of the inscriptions quoted.

Suggestions for Discussion

1 The self-sufficiency of the Roman legion and the very high proportion of fighting troops to support troops, compared with the corresponding proportion (1:8) in British and American armies in World War II. Invite students to comment on this difference (e.g. the greater need for specialized support skills as military technology becomes more complicated).

2 The mixture of professional soldiers and "amateur" commanders. Point to the value of having an army led by a man whose experience was not restricted to the military, but might also have included legal and political experience. Also mention that a *lēgātus legiōnis* would not be totally inexperienced since he would have served previously as a *tribūnus* (and men like Agricola took their military tribuneship very seriously); that the senior centurions played a crucial role in assisting and advising the commander; that the lēgātus would already have demonstrated ability to lead and organize in the civilian offices he had held.

3 The part played by the legions and auxiliary units in preserving the frontiers of the empire (most of them were stationed in the frontier provinces) and in maintaining or changing the central power in Rome, i.e. the emperor. At the death of one emperor, the next claimant, especially if the successor had not been identified in advance, relied upon the support of the military to press his claims. For example, in A.D. 68–69, the Roman senate helplessly recognized four emperors supported by legions in little more than twelve months. For colorful details you might read aloud selections from Books 1–3 in the Penguin translation of Tacitus, *Histories,* translated by K. Wellesley; and for background, consult P.V. Jones, *Handbook*, pp. 2–13.

STAGE 26: AGRICOLA

BRIEF OUTLINE

Reading passages Background material	Gnaeus Iulius Agricola
Chief grammatical points	purpose clauses gerundive of obligation (impersonal use)

NARRATIVE POINTS

Date	*Setting*	*Characters Introduced*	*Story Line*
Spring, A.D.83	Britain: legionary fortress at Deva (Chester)	Gaius Iulius Silanus (commander of Second Legion)	Agricola visits camp, is welcomed by soldiers. Salvius and Belimicus arrive to paint lurid picture of Cogidubnus' supposed rebellion. Quintus, in rags, but verifiably a Roman citizen, interrupts, proclaims Cogidubnus' innocence, and collapses. Agricola sends his military tribune, Rufus to question Quintus. Rufus turns out to be Barbillus' missing son for whom Quintus has been searching. Quintus gives Rufus Barbillus' letter, which establishes Quintus' good faith. Agricola orders Salvius to apologize to Cogidubnus, but Salvius informs him that the emperor wants tribute from the provinces, not victories over tribes in the north. Messenger brings news of Cogidubnus' death.

GRAMMATICAL POINTS

purpose clauses

e.g. *Agricola ad tribūnal prōcessit ut pauca dīceret.*

increased incidence of neuter gerundive of obligation.

e.g. *tibi statim cum duābus cohortibus proficīscendum est.*

impersonal verbs

e.g. *numquam nōs oportet barbarīs crēdere.*

expressions of time

e.g. *trēs continuōs diēs labōrāvērunt; quārtō diē Sīlānus adventum Agricolae nūntiāvit.*

num + indirect question

e.g. *cognōscere voluit quot essent armātī, num Britannī cīvēs Rōmānōs interfēcissent, quās urbēs dēlēvissent.*

id quod, ea quae

e.g. *renovāvit ea quae in epistulā scrīpserat.*

dative + participle

e.g. *Agricola tamen hīs verbīs diffīsus, Salvium dīligentius rogāvit quae indicia sēditiōnis vīdisset.*

future participle

e.g. *in animō volvēbat num Agricola sibi crēditūrus esset.*

SENTENCE PATTERNS

postponement of subordinating conjunction

e.g. *haec cum audīvisset, Agricola respondit.*

more complex examples of "stringing" and "nesting"

e.g. *mīlitēs, cum hoc audīvissent, maximē gaudēbant quod Agricolam dīligēbant.*
sollicitus erat quod in epistulā, quam ad Agricolam mīserat, multa falsa scrīpserat.

dative + participle

e.g. *Agricola tamen hīs verbīs diffīsus, Salvium dīligentius rogāvit quae indicia sēditiōnis vīdisset.*

Title Picture

This shows Agricola addressing the troops drawn up outside the principia at Chester, as described in the first story. Behind him stands Silanus. Students might like to pick out the various office-holders standing at the front.

adventus Agricolae

Instead of model sentences, the Stage opens with a short story introducing the new grammatical point: purpose clauses with *ut*. The scene is the fortress at Chester, where Silanus, legate of the Second Legion Adiutrix, is expecting Agricola, the governor of Britain and commander-in-chief of all the legions there. The soldiers have been working day and night, cleaning their quarters and polishing their weapons, in preparation for Agricola's visit, although they are not told the reason for their efforts until just before the governor's arrival. When Agricola arrives, he is greeted by the troops with a spontaneous show of enthusiasm. He delivers a speech praising the soldiers, inspects their ranks, and enters the headquarters. Agricola gives the impression of a successful and popular general. Thus the way is prepared for the contrast between him and Salvius.

Because the story is straightforward, expect a good level of understanding while you read it aloud to the class. After the reading, ask students comprehension questions. At the end, ask whether they believe Agricola's praise of his troops is sincere or consists of standard remarks which he might make to all his legions.

Initiate a discussion about purpose clauses by writing two sentences on the blackboard:

Agricola ad tribūnal prōcessit ut pauca dīceret (line 15).
omnēs . . . tacuērunt ut contiōnem Agricolae audīrent (lines 15–16).

Invite comment about any feature they share. Students will probably notice the subjunctive in each. Confirm this and ask them to identify the subjunctives. Underline these on the blackboard. Then ask whether either of the previously met reasons for the presence of a subjunctive (i.e. a *cum*-clause or an indirect question) applies here. After a little thought, students are likely to say "No." Confirm this and invite further comment. At this point, if not sooner, they will mention *ut*. Confirm that *ut* is a reason for the subjunctive, but encourage the class to continue looking for a common "idea" in the clauses *ut . . . dīceret* and *ut . . . audīrent*. The object is not to elicit the label "purpose" but to secure any appropriate observation. If students say that the words with the subjunctive verb give the "reason," orient this reply in a more appropriate direction by saying, "That's close. Do you mean that we could put the word 'because' into the translation? If we asked 'Why did Agricola march to the platform?' would the answer be 'because he was saying a few words'?"

in prīncipiīs

Inside the headquarters, Salvius has been waiting for Agricola, and he wastes no time getting down to matters at hand. He repeats the contents of his letter, and Agricola's response to the news of Cogidubnus' alleged treachery is grim. Without further ado, he dispatches Silanus with two cohorts to crush the rebellion. Only then does he question Salvius in detail. Salvius presents, as a witness, Belimicus, who gives a somewhat less than credible account of the situation, arousing Agricola's suspicions as to the veracity of the report. Here Quintus makes a dramatic reappearance: he bursts into headquarters, battered and on the point of collapse; he identifies himself as a Roman citizen, gives his name, declares that Cogidubnus is innocent, and falls unconscious.

As he waits for the confrontation, Salvius is uneasy, but conscious that he now has to deal with a superior. Agricola, for example, has already held the consulship; Salvius has not yet reached that office. Agricola is of senatorial rank by birth; Salvius has had to work for it. Such nuances of social difference would not escape the notice of either of these two powerful men.

At first, Agricola accepts without question Salvius' report of treachery by Cogidubnus. Such acceptance may surprise students, but as an administrator Agricola would not take for granted the loyalty of a client-king. He would recall his own experience of Boudica's revolt, A.D. 60–61, when as a young *tribūnus mīlitum* he witnessed the grim realities of insurrection.

Up to this point, Salvius' plan has worked. Now he decisively overplays his hand, by inviting Belimicus to confirm his story. The British chief exaggerates so much, however, that Agricola at last becomes suspicious and begins to ask the questions he should have asked before. But almost immediately, he is interrupted by Quintus' entrance. Read this story aloud, section by section, asking questions as you proceed, but postpone translation until after the students have discussed the questions on p. 93. Assign all or part of the story to be translated as a written exercise.

While taking the class through the questions, notice that:

Question 1: Salvius has changed his mind since we last saw him. Then he proposed to deal with Agricola by means of a letter alone; now he has decided to come in person.
Question 3: After reflection, Agricola breaks into a passionate denunciation of Cogidubnus: *quanta perfidia . . . prō amīcō habeō* (lines 11–16). Ask a student to summarize this speech in one sentence or, better, one word.
Question 6: Agricola is deceived by Salvius' story because he is predisposed to trust him in a matter which concerns Roman security. He only becomes suspicious when Belimicus embroiders on the story. As far as possible, elicit from the class possible reasons for Agricola's behavior. Questions like the latter part of 6 which probe the behavior of a character are important both in themselves and as a preparation for the time when students read Latin literature.
Question 8: Quintus begins by establishing his credentials, to insure that his statement will receive the full attention of his listeners.

Some sentences are quite complex grammatically:

1 "stringing" together of subordinate clauses or participial phrases, e.g. *cognōscere voluit quot essent armātī, num Britannī cīvēs Rōmānōs interfēcissent,*

quās urbēs dēlēvissent (lines 32–34);

2 "nesting" of one clause or participial phrase inside another clause, e.g. *mīlitēs, cum Agricolam castra intrantem vīdissent, magnum clāmōrem sustulērunt* ("adventus Agricolae," lines 12–13); or *sollicitus erat quod in epistulā, quam ad Agricolam mīserat, multa falsa scrīpserat* (lines 3–4).

To help students handle these expansions and the greater sentence length created by them, you should sometimes use very emphatic phrasing when reading aloud, sometimes ask questions directed at various bits of the sentence before students translate it, and, in due course, use the "Longer Sentences" part of the LI Section pp. 295–96, to consolidate.

On *id quod* (three examples), see p. 44 above. If students are at home with the term "antecedent," introduced in Unit 2, get them to compare, e.g., *id quod Salvius dīxit* with *verba quae Salvius dīxit* and hence to see that just as *verba* is the antecedent of *quae* so *id* is the antecedent of *quod*.

First Language Note (Purpose Clauses)

What should be at the forefront of the learner's attention is the *whole subordinate clause*, within which the subjunctive verb suggests the sense of "purpose" and the introductory *ut* is a useful but secondary characteristic. *ut* by itself has little meaning. It is a copula which links any of a considerable variety of subordinate clauses to the main or controlling clause. Encourage students to regard *ut* as part of the machinery of such clauses, to be translated in any way that is suitable to the sense of the whole clause.

Paragraph 3 takes students from the standard translation "in order that" to the more important idiomatic variations. Encourage students to use these variants. Write on the blackboard purpose clauses taken from previous stories and consider alternative ways of putting them into natural English. Periodically, from this point onwards, ask students to pick out the subjunctives in a passage, to say what tense they are and why they are subjunctive.

tribūnus

Agricola orders Quintus to be taken away and given medical attention. Then he sends Rufus, his trusted military tribune, to question Quintus. When Rufus has gone out, Salvius hastily tries to discredit Quintus, fabricating more stories about his conduct and character. Rufus, however, shortly returns, much astonished at what he has learned: Quintus is a friend of Rufus' late father, Barbillus, and has fulfilled his promise to the father by delivering a letter to the son. At this point, Agricola sends for Quintus, and dismisses the others. Salvius goes out, in some discomfiture, and Agricola proceeds to have a three-hour consultation with Quintus.

When the class has reached line 5, invite students to speculate about the outcome. The *bona fidēs* of Quintus is soon established; for Rufus is the estranged son of Barbillus (see Unit 2, Stage 20).

It is not surprising that Salvius is anxious. He hurriedly tries to undermine the credibility of anything that Quintus may say by launching into a highly distorted account of Quintus' behavior while staying with him. Ask students to spot the bias and distortion and to suggest what these reveal about Salvius' frame of mind. Agricola, on the other hand, now displays a determination to get to the truth.

On the staff of a legion there would be six *tribūnī mīlitum*, one of whom, the senior, was usually a young man of senatorial rank, while the others were members of the equestrian order. None was a full-time, professional soldier. The senatorial tribune (*tribūnus lāticlāvius*) was performing the period of military service required at the outset of the regular *cursus honōrum*; the equestrian tribunes (*tribūnī angusticlāviī*) were probably aiming at higher posts in the imperial civil service. An equestrian tribune would already have commanded an auxiliary cohort and could expect to return to the *auxilia* to command an *āla* of cavalry. After ten years he could be promoted to one of the equestrian prefectures, like commander of the fleets, of the praetorian guard, or governor of provinces like Judaea or even Egypt.

How seriously the young senatorial tribunes took their military duties probably varied. Tacitus (*Agricola* 5) implies that some used inexperience as an excuse for taking long leaves and explicitly commends Agricola, when tribune, for serving a hardworking apprenticeship to military command.

Second Language Note (Gerundive of Obligation)

After taking students through the note, ask them to turn back to "in prīncipiīs" and "tribūnus" and find the example of the gerundive in each: *tibi statim cum duābus cohortibus proficīscendum est* ("in prīncipiīs," lines 19–20) and *sī tālia fēcit, eī moriendum est* ("tribūnus," line 17). Illustrate the comparison between the two ways of expressing obligation by rephrasing the examples in paragraph 3 with *necesse* and writing both on the blackboard. Avoid examples which would require a deponent infinitive.

The last example in paragraph 3 advances slightly beyond the examples in the stories because it uses the gerundive with a noun instead of a pronoun. Watch for any difficulty and be ready to offer *necesse est omnibus servīs labōrāre* for comparison.

contentiō

Agricola, much displeased with Salvius' machinations against

Cogidubnus, as reported by Quintus, orders Salvius to apologize to the king and, moreover, to account for himself before the emperor. Salvius, however, is not disarmed, but points out to Agricola that the emperor himself is dissatisfied with Agricola's administration of Britain, and that it is Agricola, not Salvius, who must render accounts: the emperor, it seems, is interested in tribute, and the spoils of war, not in Agricola's victorious campaigns in Caledonia. In the midst of this dispute, a messenger arrives to announce that Cogidubnus is dead.

Perhaps because he is angry with himself, Agricola rounds on Salvius with considerable ferocity. Some students, despite disapproval of Salvius, may feel grudging admiration for the way he launches a counterattack, claiming that the real issue is not about justice to an ally, but about the new emperor's need of money. The politician mocks the soldier.

The situation may be interpreted in more than one way. At its simplest, it may appear to be a conflict of right against wrong. But it is also a battle of wits between two powerful men, and a clash of policies towards the allies of Rome. However, the personal struggle is still unfinished. Although Salvius is effectively rebuffed for the moment, he has not necessarily forfeited his credit with Domitian.

With older students, you might explore the comparison further: Salvius and Agricola are not wholly dissimilar. The ruthlessness of Salvius finds an echo in Agricola. Salvius' contempt for provincials is reflected, if only briefly, in Agricola's *numquam nōs oportet barbarīs crēdere* ("in prīncipiīs," lines 13–14). There is, finally, the irony of the positions adopted by the two men. For it is the soldier who speaks for the integrity of law, while the *iūridicus* argues the claims of expediency.

quī in line 2 is the first instance of a connecting or demonstrative relative. Advise students that a relative pronoun as the first word of a sentence is often best translated by "this," "she," or "he"/"these," or "they."

Some Suggested Questions

What is Agricola's mood when he sends for Salvius? Which Latin words indicate his feelings?

What does Salvius do as soon as he enters the room?

What does Agricola now say about Cogidubnus? What allegations does he make against Salvius? Which Latin words convey these allegations? (List them on the blackboard as the class selects them.)

Does this criticism put Salvius on the defensive? What is the tone of his reply?

Can you summarize the speeches of the two men in one line each? Which wins the argument?

Drills and Suggestions for Further Practice

Exercise 1 Type: vocabulary
Grammatical point being practiced: nouns of the form *amor, timor* etc.

Exercise 2 Type: completion
Missing item: noun
Test of accuracy: correct ending
Grammatical points being practiced: genitive, dative, and accusative, singular and plural

Sentence 6 contains *crēdō* + dative. If students cannot handle it, refer them back to Stage 25, Exercise 5, sentence 6.

Exercise 3 Type: translation from English using a restricted pool of Latin words
Grammatical points being practiced (the number in parentheses is the stage where the relevant language note appears):
agreement of adjectives (14)
direct question (11)
neuter plural (23)
oblique cases of *is* and present participles (20)
pluperfect tense (16)
present tense of *possum* (13)
vocative and imperative (19)

This exercise might serve as an excellent test of grammar in review.

Exercise 4 Type: completion
Missing item: noun *or* verb *or* participle
Test of accuracy: sense and syntax
Grammatical point being practiced: sentence structure

Additional Suggestions for Further Practice

1 The following exercise using the LI Section may seem complicated at first, but becomes easier after one or two examples have been worked by you and class together. You write on the blackboard a pair of nouns with the same ending, but different in case and sometimes number, e.g. *puerum* and *canum*. To identify each item of the pair, students will have to refer first to the Complete Vocabulary part to check the nominative and genitive singular of each word and then to the Review Grammar to relate that information to the appropriate specimen-noun on pp. 262–63.

Ask students to work out the case (or possible cases) of each item in the pair, whether it is singular or plural and which specimen-noun it resembles. Include examples which contrast *-ĭs* with *-īs*, examples which contrast *-ī* (genitive singular and nominative plural of 2nd declension) with *-ī* (dative singular of 3rd declension), e.g. *medicī* and *mīlitī*. Present some examples as whole sentences, reinforcing the point that context provides strong clues to the correct classification. For example:

clāmor canum puerum magnopere terrēbat.
stolae mercātōris fēminīs nōn placent.
strepitus urbis fēminīs Graecīs semper placēbat.
servī canī cibum cotīdiē dabant.
servī dē vītā Barbillī dēspērābant.
mercātor vīnum caupōnum Pompēiānōrum vituperāvit.

Construct further examples of noun-pairs, with or without contextualizing sentences, using nouns taken from previous checklists: from Stages 1–17, listed in Unit 2 Teacher's Manual, p. 68; from Stages 18–24, above, p. 51; and from Stages 25–26;

First declension, feminine: *dīligentia* (25); *perfidia* (26); *poena* (25); *prōvincia* (26).
Second declension, masculine: *captīvus* (25); *dī* (pl. irreg.) (25); *lēgātus* (26); *tribūnus* (26).
Second declension, neuter: *bellum* (26); *castra* (pl.)(25); *prīncipia* (pl.)(26); *rēgnum* (26).
Third declension, m. or f.: *cohors*, f.(26); *dignitās*, f.(25); *legiō*, f.(25); *statiō*, f.(25); *testis*, m. or f.(25).
Third declension, neuter: *facinus* (26); *nōmen* (25); *ōs* "face" (25).
Fifth declension, feminine: *fidēs* (26).

2 At the end of a story, spend a few minutes on the familiar exercise of picking out items, but extend the repertory to include, e.g., relative clauses, adjectives and the nouns they agree with, genitive cases and the nouns they depend on. Thus students will gain self-confidence and reading speed.

The Background Material

The inscription on the water-pipe, p. 100 (top picture), can be translated: "In the ninth consulship of the Emperor Vespasian and the seventh of Titus (victorious general), when Gnaeus Iulius Agricola was governor of the province."

For the other inscription on the same page, we have followed the version published in *J.R.S.* 1956 by R.P. Wright which remains the most generally accepted. Students may be surprised that so much of an inscription can be reconstructed with a fair degree of certainty when so little has actually survived. In this case, the "GRIC" at the bottom establishes that the inscription is about Agricola, and his official titles and the standard formulae are known from other sources. Note however that the fourth fragment shows that the reconstruction is incomplete, and in fact the purpose of the inscription has never been established. The version here may be translated:

> The Emperor Titus Caesar, son of the deified Vespasian, Vespasian Augustus, Pontifex Maximus, holding tribunician power for the ninth time, saluted as *Imperator* fifteen times, Consul for the seventh time, (Consul) designate for the eighth time, Censor, Father of the Fatherland, and Caesar Domitian, son of the deified Vespasian, Consul for the sixth time, (Consul) designate for the seventh time, Patron of the Youth, Priest of all the priestly Colleges, Gnaeus Iulius Agricola being Governor of the Imperial Province . . .

The students' textbook covers Agricola's career as far as his appointment as governor of Britain. Some aspects of his governorship will have emerged from the Latin stories, but you may wish to add a selection of the following details.

During A.D. 77 Agricola was a *cōnsul suffectus*. Because, at this time, the duration of the consulship might have been as short as two months, we do not know when during the year A.D. 77 Agricola was consul. This has given rise to uncertainty about the date of his arrival in Britain as governor. There are reasons (see the edition of the *Agricola* by Ogilvie and Richmond, Appendix 1) for assuming that he traveled to the province in the summer of A.D 78. That this province should have been assigned to him was not surprising in view of his experience and knowledge of it. What was unusual was that he should have been permitted to govern it for seven years.

On arrival Agricola dealt with the Ordovices, who had ambushed a regiment of cavalry in northern Wales and annexed the island now called Anglesey, just off the northwestern coast. His readiness to act so late in the campaigning season and so soon after arrival (Tacitus, *Agricola* 18) may indicate his familiarity with the province. In A.D. 79, he began the campaigns which took Roman forces to the far north of Britain. The line of advance chosen by Agricola was probably along the western route, going north from Viroconium (modern Wroxeter, in Shropshire) and Deva/Chester on up through modern Lancashire. As each tribe was defeated, it was offered "pardon and peace," and its area was penetrated by roads and guarded by forts. A road was built between the Tyne and Solway estuaries (between, roughly, the modern cities of Newcastle-upon-Tyne and Carlisle), the shortest and most easily defensible line across the island. Within fifty years, this road marked the line of Hadrian's Wall and became the northern frontier of the empire. Each summer, Agricola campaigned further northwards until he reached the southern part of what is now Scotland. During the winter, when the marching and fighting were brought to a stop, he worked at his policy of Romanization (see above, p. 22).

Tacitus perhaps exaggerated Agricola's virtues. He was, after all, writing to praise and to vindicate a man who was also his father-in-law. But the evidence of archaeology appears to confirm Tacitus' claims. Tacitus also ascribed to Agricola many good personal qualities and superior administrative ability. He seems to have been a man of simple tastes, careful judgment, honest and well-disposed to the native peoples. The rapid expansion of urban life in Britain in the second century may have owed as much to his civil policies as to his military successes.

The battle of Mons Graupius (perhaps in the modern Grampian region of Scotland), in A.D. 84, broke the final resistance of the far-northern tribes led by Calgacus. It also brought Agricola's public life to a climax and end. Recalled by Domitian, awarded triumphal honors, a statue, and a citation, he nevertheless thought it wise to retire into the safety of private life. Domitian did not call on him again to lead Roman armies; and when the governorship of Asia fell vacant, Agricola excused himself. Shortly afterwards, in A.D. 93, he died of an illness which Tacitus hinted might have been the work of a poisoner.

You might read to the class from the Penguin translation by H. Mattingly and S.A. Handford of Tacitus' *Agricola*: Chapter 21 on Romanization, and Chapters 33–34 with Agricola's speech to his troops at Mons Graupius. For further background information, consult D.E. Soulsby, *Handbook* to *Selections from Tacitus: Agricola*, pp. 1–5.

Words and Phrases checklist

On the importance of drilling orally different forms of verbs like *auferre*, see above, p. 42. *auferre* itself may be worth discussion: show its origin as *abferō, abtulī* etc. and let students appreciate, by experiment, the greater ease of pronouncing *auferō, abstulī*. It is important that such variations be seen as having logical reasons.

STAGE 27: IN CASTRĪS

BRIEF OUTLINE

Reading passages Background material	Chester: the legionary fortress
Chief grammatical points	indirect command impersonal verbs result clauses

NARRATIVE POINTS

Date	*Setting*	*Characters Introduced*	*Story Line*
Spring, A.D.83	Britain: legionary fortress at Deva (Chester)	Aulus and Publicus (friends of Modestus and Strythio), Nigrina (dancing girl)	Modestus and Strythio have been hiding under a granary for 6 days. Boredom and hunger force Modestus to send Strythio out for food, wine, dice, friends, and girls. Vercobrix and small band of men come to burn Roman grain supply, are inadvertently surprised by Modestus, whose tunic catches fire in struggle and whose shouts arouse whole camp. Valerius rewards him by putting him in charge of jail!

GRAMMATICAL POINTS

indirect command

e.g. *centuriō mīlitibus imperābat ut Modestum Strȳthiōnemque invenīrent.*

result clause

e.g. *sextō diē Modestus tam miser erat ut rem diūtius ferre nōn posset.*

increased incidence of impersonal verbs

e.g. *mē taedet huius vītae.*

increased incidence of extended participial phrase + preposition

e.g. *tum ē manibus Britannōrum ēlāpsus fūgit praeceps.*

SENTENCE PATTERN

DAT + NOM + ACC + V

e.g. *hominibus miserrimīs cibus sōlācium semper affert.*

Title Picture

This shows the fortress at Chester. The main streets in Chester today still follow the lines of the Roman ones. Students might use the plan on p. 117 to help them pick out important buildings.

Model Sentences

Modestus and Strythio flee, and the centurion orders the other soldiers to search for them. Meanwhile, Vercobrix is exhorting his men to attack the Roman camp. The scene is now set for the conclusion of the Modestus subplot. Note in the first picture that Modestus is pointing towards the granary which is the setting for the following stories.

The indirect command is highlighted. The direct, "quoted" form of each indirect command appears within the corresponding picture as a command uttered by one of the figures. Students need not study the direct commands in the pictures before proceeding to the indirect ones in the captions beneath; rather, they should read the captions first in the normal way and use the direct commands as clues. When students have read the captions, ask them to translate the direct commands too, but postpone discussion of the formal relationship between the direct and indirect utterances until students have reached the language note on pp. 109–10.

Some vocabulary may cause difficulty, e.g. *contiōnem . . . habēbat*. Help students infer the meaning by studying the picture. The only new word is *imperābat*.

sub horreō

Modestus and Strythio have been hiding under a granary of the camp for six days. Modestus, bored and hungry, readily consents when Strythio volunteers to go and organize some dinner for the two of them, and suggests, moreover, that while he is at it Strythio should bring along their friends Aulus and Publicus for a game of dice, and Nigrina the dancing girl, for additional entertainment. Strythio succeeds in all but the matter of Nigrina, who is unwilling to join the party.

Use this and the following story to build up students' understanding of the fortress. Some of the questions following the passage require discussion of the setting; reading the background material will therefore be a necessary preliminary to working on them. The questions may be used in turn to introduce a wider study of the legionary fortress, including guided reading in other books (see Bibliography below, pp. 197–98). As the students proceed with the story, deal with the following topics:

1 The design of the *horreum*. It stood raised above ground level on rows of low pillars, which left space of two feet (60 cm) or more between the floor and the ground. In this space circulated fresh air, keeping the foodstuffs above it dry and mice out. In the first century A.D., granaries were generally built of wood; from the second century onwards, of stone.
2 *coquus*. Although each *contubernium* of eight men would draw daily rations and prepare its own food, probably over a charcoal fire on the

verandah in front of their living quarters, a legionary fortress would also be equipped with ovens and kitchens for baking bread and cooking food (e.g. large casseroles) which the small fires could not cope with.

3 If students ask questions about dice-playing, remind them of Stage 22.

4 *vīcus*. Soldiers, when off-duty, met their womenfriends in the *vīcus*, not inside the fortress (nor under a granary!). At Chester, as at many other places of military occupation, a civilian settlement grew up. There may already have been a settlement near the site, but the arrival of the army insured that the settlement, which lay between the fortress and the river, grew and expanded while supplying the needs of a large, permanent garrison—fresh food, hardware, inns and shops, companionship.

Notice the build-up of clauses of indirect command at the end of the passage. Make sure that students read them with confidence before assigning the language note.

The description of Strythio as *vir maximī silentiī, minimīque iocī* (lines 13–14) should stimulate idiomatic translations. After inviting the class to write, for a few minutes, their suggestions on paper, compare and list the liveliest on the blackboard.

If the students, when doing the first part of question 4, think that Strythio is to bring the dinner, draw attention to *eum . . . coquere et hūc portāre* (line 21).

First Language Note (Indirect Command)

While students are working through this note, you should confirm that clauses of indirect command in Latin depend not only on a verb like *imperō*, meaning "command" or "order," but also and frequently on verbs like *persuādeō, ōrō, moneō*, whose meanings only imply command. The negative conjunction *nē* is postponed until Stage 29.

The word "usually" at the end of paragraph 2, p. 109, may prompt a question. If so, tell students about *iubeō* and *vetō* which control an infinitive instead of an *ut*-clause with subjunctive. Refer them to, e.g., Stage 26 "tribūnus," *tē iubēo hunc hominem summā cum cūrā interrogāre* (line 5).

In paragraph 4, ask students to say which sentences are direct commands and which are indirect. As a further exercise: (1) after reading an indirect command, ask students to reconstruct in English the original direct command, (2) convert a direct command into its past-tense, indirect equivalent, e.g. "*abī, Cogidubne*," *inquit Salvius* into *Salvius Cogidubnō imperāvit ut abīret*. Build up the sentence on the blackboard with students' help, but attempt this only with a very able class.

Lead a discussion on *sē* and *eum*. Write the sentence, *senex nōs ōrābat ut sibi parcerēmus* (paragraph 4, number 6), on the blackboard, have it translated and write the translation beneath. Then change *sibi to eī* and say "This sentence too is translated 'The old man begged us to spare him,' but it doesn't mean quite the same as the previous sentence. Can anyone suggest a difference?"

Modestus prōmōtus

Led by Vercobrix, ten Britons head for the granary where Modestus is waiting for Strythio to return with some good food and company. Modestus, in the time-honored manner of comedy, becomes an improbable hero, as events develop. The Britons' intent is to set fire to the granaries. The impatient Modestus mistakes them for his friends and hails them. Vercobrix recognizes his voice, reassures the astonished Britons, and leads his companions into Modestus' hiding-place. In the ensuing confusion, Modestus' tunic is set on fire by one of the Britons' torches. As he tries to flee, he bumps into his friends, grabs an amphora of wine from one of them, and uses it first to put out the fire, and then to plug the opening leading into the space under the granary. At the same time, he rouses the camp with his shouts. The commander of the legion summons Modestus and rewards him – by putting him in command of the jail!

The story is suitable for reading aloud. Because the plot has been fully prepared and the outcome is largely predictable, you might initially read it aloud in short portions, asking straightforward comprehension questions after each portion.

Because the story is a farce, the possibilities for serious discussion of character are limited, but at the end you might check that students clearly grasp the technical terms used: *vallum* (line 4), the defensive wall around the fortress, at that time a dirt mound topped by a strong wooden fence. Later, it was converted to a stone wall, parts of which have survived; *horrea* (line 5), the granaries (for details, see p. 119 of the students' textbook, and p. 78 above); *praefectus castrōrum* (lines 43–44), the legionary officer responsible for running the camp, its administration and supplies; *lēgātus* (line 49), the commanding officer of a legion. Agricola was *lēgātus* of the Twentieth Legion in Britain, A.D. 70–73. Distinguish the *lēgātus legiōnis*, however, from the *lēgātus Augustī prō praetōre*, who was the military governor of the whole province, as was Agricola, A.D. 78–84; *prīncipia*, the headquarters building (for details, see pp. 117–18).

The commas at the beginnings and ends of participial phrases are now being phased out. When students are reading aloud, you should observe whether they identify these boundaries.

Near the end, two sentences appear, each containing a participial phrase: *Rōmānī Britannōs ex horreō extractōs ad carcerem redūxērunt* and *tum lēgātus legiōnis ipse Modestum arcessītum laudāvit* (lines 48–50). The literal version is such unnatural English that students will attempt to produce something more natural. Accept and encourage this, but also write the Latin sentence on the blackboard, accompanied by a literal version to show that grammatically *extractōs* is a passive participle in agreement with *Britannōs*. After the analysis, go back to idiomatic English equivalents.

Notice also that the participial phrase is itself being expanded in new ways. In Stage 26 "in prīncipiīs," we had a dative case depending on the participle, *hīs verbīs diffīsus* (line 31). Now there is *ē manibus Britannōrum ēlāpsus* (line 34). In Stage 28, an important further change will appear when an ablative noun is attached without preposition, e.g. *morbō afflīctus*.

The antefix on p. 112 is early second century and comes from the army depot at Holt near Chester. Antefixes were set at intervals along the eaves of buildings, to cover the ends of the semi-circular roof-tiles (see title page of Stage 24, p. 54).

Second Language Note (Impersonal Verbs)

Impersonal verbs are often more naturally expressed in English by a personal construction: for example, *mihi placet* becomes "I am pleased." This may give students the impression that impersonal verbs are oddities, found only in Latin. Correct this impression by drawing attention to familiar impersonal usages in English, e.g. "it worries me," "it's getting late," "it hurts me to see . . ." If students remark on the profusion of ways in Latin for expressing the notion of obligation, compare the equally profuse variety in English, e.g. "ought," "must," "should," "have to," "got to," "I need to," and even "I am bound to."

Drills

Exercise 1 Type: meaning
Grammatical point being practiced: nouns in *-tūdō*

The aim is to build up awareness of abstract nouns in which the common ending *-tūdō* nominalizes a qualitative adjective, e.g. *altus—altitūdō*. Compare the similar relationship in English, e.g. "high" and "height," "pretty" and "prettiness," though English lacks the uniform ending.

Exercise 2 Type: completion
Missing item: participle
Test of accuracy: sense, syntax, and morphology
Grammatical point being practiced: present, perfect passive, and perfect active participles

Exercise 3 Type: transformation
Grammatical point being practiced: nominative and accusative singular and plural, including neuters

Exercise 4 Type: completion

Missing item: noun ending
Test of accuracy: correct ending
Grammatical points being practiced: nominative, genitive, dative, and accusative, singular and plural

This exercise is intended to diagnose how much more the students need to review cases. They should know the forms well, but if not, review cases of nouns from previous checklists in the ways suggested above, pp. 50–51. In Stage 28, students will learn the ablative without preposition.

Third Language Note (Result Clauses)

Restrain comment on the conjunction *ut*, treating it simply as a device to link one part of the sentence to another. Encourage students to translate *ut* according to context and the demands of natural English.

Draw attention immediately to the anticipatory words associated with result clauses. Gather these from the students' textbook and list them on the blackboard: *tam, tot, tantus, adeō;* mention also *tālis, ita*.

The Background Material

Chester has provided the setting for the stories in Stages 25–27. Supplement the general information about legionary fortresses in the students' textbook with some of the following details:

1 The site of the fortress was well chosen. It was near a tidal river and so could be provisioned by sea to function as a storage depot for military units in the area. It also stood between the mountains of north Wales, the hills of Derbyshire, and the northern Pennine mountain-range. Perhaps most importantly, it controlled the western military route to the north.

2 The Second Legion was withdrawn from Britain for service in Domitian's campaigns in Dacia (roughly modern Rumania), about A.D. 87. Its place at Chester was taken by the Twentieth Legion, which had been pulled back from Scotland when Agricola's strategy of conquering the whole island was abandoned by Domitian.

3 To begin with, the fortress had a turf-and-timber rampart and buildings constructed mainly of wood, as the drawings show, but in the second century it was rebuilt in stone. The later medieval city of Chester grew up directly over the fortress and made it impossible for the site to be excavated as a whole. Therefore, though the general layout has been identified, many details remain obscure. However, as most legionary fortresses were built to the same pattern, our knowledge can be supplemented by evidence from other sites, e.g. Neuss in West Germany (see Webster, *The Roman Imperial Army*, pp. 183–87).

The plan of a legionary fortress in the students' textbook, p. 117, is based on Chester, with some details added from the "standard" pattern where they have not been definitely identified in Chester. The drawing on p. 121 shows a corner of the fortress. Notice the cooking ovens against the rampart.

Suggestions for Discussion and Further Activities

1 After students have read the description of the legionary fortress, discuss with them the activities connected with the major structures. Recreate life within the fortress. For example, the ground plan of a barrack block becomes more interesting when one thinks about the eight men who lived, ate, and slept in each pair of cells with its colonnaded porch outside where they would cook and talk and keep up their equipment. What did they wear when off-duty? What did they cook? Did they take turns cooking? Did they eat with their fingers? What might they have talked about while eating? Etc. (You will not be able to find definitive answers to all these questions!)

2 Students might undertake a project on military life in Britain. The class, divided into groups of three to five students, might spend two or three consecutive periods researching (for sources, see Bibliography below, pp. 197–98) and reporting on some of the following topics:

(a) the main phases of the occupation of Britain from A.D. 43 to the arrival of Agricola;
(b) Agricola as a military commander;
(c) the history and design of a legionary fortress, e.g. Lincoln, York, Chester, Caerleon;
(d) the network of military roads which were developed soon after occupation began. Why were certain routes chosen? Did they follow high or low ground? How were they surveyed and built? What traffic, apart from the military, used them? How were the roads protected?

Students might make their reports orally or write them out. If they write them, you should display their reports, properly illustrated with foldout diagrams and drawings, so that every student can read and inspect the work of the others.

3 The military material in this stage provides students with an opportunity to draw conclusions from the evidence, whether in the course of the activities outlined above or during discussion while the stories are being read. For example:

(a) Why could a soldier, perhaps just transferred from Novaesium (Neuss) in Germany, find his way around the fortress at Chester without difficulty?
(b) At the time of these stories, a century contained 80 men. What do you think its original number was (see above, p. 63)?

(c) Why did Romans put ovens at the *edge* of the fortress (see picture on p. 121) and not, for example, in the middle of the barrack blocks?
(d) Why did the Romans locate the principia towards the center of the fortress instead of just inside the main gate?
(e) Why did the Romans dig a ditch, or *fossa*, around the fortress wall?

STAGE 28: IMPERIUM

BRIEF OUTLINE

Reading passages	conclusion of the Roman Britain narrative
Background material	sources of our knowledge of Roman Britain
Chief grammatical points	ablative singular and plural expressions of time prepositions

NARRATIVE POINTS

Date	*Setting*	*Characters Introduced*	*Story Line*
Spring, A.D. 83	Palace of King Cogidubnus	No new characters	By his own forgery of Cogidubnus' will, Salvius becomes heir to the king, since Dumnorix is dead and the Romans have abolished the Regnensian kingship. Belimicus, jealous, tries to unite surviving chieftains in a conspiracy, but the plot is reported to Salvius, who then lures Belimicus to palace with promise of reward at great banquet, and poisons him. After Belimicus' murder, the chieftains decide to play it safe under the Romans.

GRAMMATICAL POINTS

participle + ablative without preposition

e.g. *agricola, gladiō centuriōnis vulnerātus, exanimātus dēcidit.*

prepositions

e.g. *Belimicus enim mē ab ursā ōlim servāvit, quae per aulam meam saeviēbat.*

connecting relative

e.g. *quī tamen, Belimicō diffīsī, rem Salviō rettulērunt.*

increased incidence of expressions of time

e.g. *ibi novem diēs manēbat ut rēs Cogidubnī administrāret. decimo diē, iterum profectus, pecūniās opēsque ā Britannīs extorquēre incēpit.*

SENTENCE PATTERNS

more complex *cui*-clauses and *quibus*-clauses

e.g. *servus, cui Salvius hoc imperāvit, statim exiit.*

more complex examples of "branching"

e.g. *tam laetus erat ille, ubi verba Salviī audīvit, ut garum cōnsūmeret, ignārus perīculī mortis.*

Model Sentences

Salvius' punitive action against a farmer who resisted the demand for money represents the harsher side of Roman occupation.

The ablative case, previously used only in prepositional phrases or (more recently) in expressions of time, is now introduced in another of its important contexts: with a perfect passive participle, e.g. *gladiō centuriōnis vulnerātus*. The forms themselves of the ablative are familiar already, but students should explore and practice the meanings of the new usage.

In the last sentence on p. 125, *complētam* may cause difficulty. If students say "complete with money," remind them of *viās complēbant*, "they filled the streets." With this and other instances of elusive vocabulary, encourage students to seek clues in the pictures and make full use of the context before allowing resort to the Complete Vocabulary part of the LI Section.

The following words are new: *extulērunt, catēnīs, abdūxērunt, timōre.*

testāmentum

This first passage takes the form of a Roman will and is important for understanding the stories which follow. Each bequest is prefaced by the formula, *dō, lēgō*, followed immediately by the name of the beneficiary and then the details of the gift (see also Barbillus' will in Stage 20, p. 152). Draw students' attention to the careful drafting and standard phraseology which typify a formal document, and invite comparison with similar pieces of writing in English, e.g. a mortgage contract.

Cogidubnus begins by nominating the emperor as his heir. A Roman takeover after his death is inevitable and he accepts it. If, however, the opening of this will was predictable, the substance of what follows is certainly not. For it not only makes a friendly mention of Salvius, it also leaves him two silver tripods and, in the event of Dumnorix also being dead, a thousand *aureī* and the palace itself. In addition, it bequeaths to Memor a villa near Aquae Sulis, and to Belimicus, five hundred *aureī* and a swift ship; the will also commits entirely to Salvius the responsibility for seeing to the king's funeral.

Encourage comment. Some students may suggest that after the will was given to Salvius for safe-keeping, Salvius tampered with it. Ask whether Cogidubnus was likely to have entrusted his will to Salvius at all. Postpone any definite answer until the end of the next story. The will concludes with the standard formula, *dolus malus ab hōc testāmentō abestō!* Students will appreciate the irony.

For the most part, the language is simple, and you may guide students to its content by appropriate comprehension questions, e.g. "What legacy does so-and-so receive?" but it does contain one example of "branching" in lines 15–16, *L. Marcius Memor, ubi aeger ad thermās vēnī, ut auxilium ā deā Sūle peterem, benignē mē excēpit*, where the clause *ut . . . peterem* branches out of the clause *ubi . . . vēnī*. Sentence patterns of this kind have occurred occasionally since Stage 18. Handle this example by reading it aloud carefully and asking questions before it is translated, e.g. "Why did the narrator (Cogidubnus) come to the baths?" and "when did Memor kindly receive the narrator?"

Examples of the new use of the ablative with a passive participle also occur: *morbō gravī afflictus* (line 2), *spē praedae adductī* (line 7), *īnsāniā affectī* (line 7), *manū meā scrīptum ānulōque meō signātum* (lines 26–27).

If students ask about the use of the abbreviations *C.* and *Cn.* for *Gāius* and *Gnaeus*, point out that this is a convention, surviving from the time when the sounds of "c" and "g" were represented by the same symbol.

Some Suggested Questions

Can you suggest reasons why Cogidubnus should name the emperor as his heir in spite of the humiliation he has suffered?

Would you expect him to have bequeathed more to Agricola?

What conclusions may be drawn from the amiable references to Salvius and the legacies allotted to him? Can you recall the history of these silver tripods? (Answer: They were originally a gift from Quintus to Cogidubnus, Unit 2, Stage 14, p. 34; Salvius accused Quintus of stealing them, Unit 3, Stage 26, p. 94).

The will provides for the transfer of legacies from Dumnorix to Salvius, if Dumnorix dies before Cogidubnus. Notice the "coincidence" that in the one clause where this provision is made, the first legatee (Dumnorix) has in fact died. What does this suggest?

Cogidubnus thanks Belimicus for saving his life in the incident with the bear, Unit 2, Stage 16, p. 67. Was this true?

Why should Cogidubnus ask that *gemmās meās, paterās aureās, omnia arma quae ad bellum vēnātiōnemque comparāvī* (lines 24–25) be buried with him? What beliefs about the afterlife does this suggest?

in aulā Salviī

Salvius takes possession of his inheritance. After setting affairs at the palace, he travels around the countryside, extorting money from the Britons; he is assisted in this by chieftains who cooperate, either because of fear or because of their own ambition and greed. In practice, the way is open for him to seize control of the whole tribal area. But Belimicus is dissatisfied and embarks upon conspiracy. His supposed allies soon betray him to Salvius, who decides to retaliate by killing him. Consulting with friends, Salvius works out a plan to poison him. Salvius invites

Belimicus to a banquet, and Belimicus, suspecting nothing, appears at the appointed hour.

You might handle the first part of the story by asking students, before they proceed, to work in pairs or small groups on the first six comprehension questions, p. 129. The questions are straightforward and will guide students in exploring the text till the end of the third paragraph. You might also ask, e.g. "What sort of things would Salvius do *ut rēs Cogidubnī administrāret* (line 3)? What was the hope of Belimicus, *spē praemiī adductus* (line 6)? How did he set about achieving his ambition?"

Students might translate the rest of Part I and, afterwards, turn to the last two questions. Finally, you should guide students in interpreting the behavior of Salvius, e.g. "Does Salvius, in this passage, seem sad or happy, anxious or confident? How have his feelings changed since he sat in the *prīncipia* at Deva? What were Salvius' feelings after learning of Belimicus' conspiracy? How does Salvius show his character in the steps he takes? Considering what Belimicus had already done to help Salvius, do you think his ambitions were reasonable?"

In Part II, Belimicus plunges towards disaster. When he mentions what is owed him, *praemium meritum* (line 10), Salvius responds with practiced irony, *praemium meritum iam tibi parāvī* (line 24); there follows a thinly veiled note of triumph in Salvius' *volō tē garum exquīsitissimum gustāre* (line 25). Belimicus fails to sense the menace in the words and persists in his dream-world. When Salvius admits to having forged the will, Belimicus begins to realize the awful truth.

As with Part I, ask the class to work through the first two paragraphs in small groups and find the answers to questions 1 and 2. Then take the students carefully through the rest, using comprehension questions designed to help them sense the rising tension. Postpone translation.

Now that it has been established that the will is a forgery, students might look at it again and consider why Salvius bothered to include a legacy to Agricola. Would the omission of any gift to Agricola have aroused suspicion? Was Salvius dumping an unwanted objet d'art on his rival?

First Language Note (the Ablative Case)

In paragraph 1, the ablative case has been put in a participial phrase and translated in four out of five examples with "by." This is the first among several ways of conveying the sense of the ablative in English. If students ask whether other ways are acceptable, e.g. *iniūriā incēnsī* "angered at the injustice," reply with approval and confirm that the ablative can be translated in many ways.

In paragraph 2, demonstrate clearly the pronunciation of the ablative singular of the first declension, *puellā*, and ask students to state the difference between that and the nominative singular. Write more examples on the blackboard and get the class to say them aloud together.

In paragraph 3, begin to encourage alternative translations, e.g. "astonished by the audacity of Belimicus" or "astonished at Belimicus' audacity" for *audāciā Belimicī attonitus*.

At some point students may ask about the difference between, e.g., *pugiōne vulnerātus* (instrumental use of the ablative) and *ā Belimicō vulnerātus* (ablative with *ā* or *ab* to express the agent). This is, however, another of those grammatical points which is considerably more complicated to explain than practice. Unless your class is particularly able or mature, let students familiarize themselves with the ablative in varied contexts over the next one or two stages before making them conscious of the distinction between "instrument" and "agent."

Belimicus rēx

The cat now plays with his mouse. Salvius emerges from the episode an easy winner. While Belimicus is recovering from his astonishment at the news that Cogidubnus' alleged will was a forgery by Salvius, Salvius calls for more *garum*; it is brought in, mixed with poison. Salvius begins to describe to Belimicus the vast "kingdom" he has designated for him, as Belimicus devours the poisoned sauce and seals his doom. His suspicions are aroused when Salvius tells him his "kingdom" is greater than the Roman Empire, and it is then that Salvius reveals himself: "*Belimice, tē rēgem creō mortuōrum.*" In vain Belimicus threatens revenge against Salvius: he is already feeling the effects of the poison, and the most he can manage before he dies is to wound Salvius slightly with a knife. Salvius, unperturbed, has a doctor summoned, and Belimicus' body disposed of. Thus does Salvius insure the other chiefs' acquiescence.

Result clauses and indirect command, recently introduced, continue to appear. Note how students are now handling the participial phrases, especially the perfect passive with an ablative noun, e.g. *hīs verbīs perturbātus* (line 16), and an extension of this pattern, *metū mortis pallidus* (line 22), where an adjective replaces the participle. A useful exercise consists of writing these and similar phrases on the blackboard and having them translated orally. Encourage alternatives, e.g. *spē ultiōnis adductus* (line 31) as "driven by the hope of revenge," "inspired by hopes of revenge," or simply "in hope of revenge" or "hoping to get revenge."

The skeleton on p. 133 is a mosaic from Pompeii. It carries two wine-jars and probably came from the center of a triclinium floor

Some Suggested Questions

Was there a point when Belimicus might have recognized his danger and turned back to safety?

How does Salvius exploit Belimicus' greed?

Do you think Belimicus deserved his fate? If so, does this excuse Salvius? What reasons may have prompted Salvius to kill Belimicus rather than deal less severely with him?

Why, in your opinion, does Salvius succeed and Belimicus fail?

Second Language Note (Expressions of Time)

Preface work on this note by writing examples of both types of time phrases on the blackboard and asking students to translate and comment. Use the note as confirmation of what students have already deduced. After students have studied the note, provide further practice by giving them other examples in English and asking whether each phrase would, in Latin, be accusative or ablative.

If during this stage or later the class studies some Roman inscriptions, especially those on soldiers' tombstones, students will come across the use of the ablative for duration of time. Note this as a common alternative, especially in non-literary Latin.

Drills

Exercise 1 Type: vocabulary
Grammatical point being practiced: feminine nouns ending in *-ia*

Exercise 2 Type: completion
Missing item: clause
Test of accuracy: sense
Grammatical points incidentally practiced: uses and tenses of the subjunctive

Exercise 3 Type: completion
Missing item: noun
Test of accuracy: sense
Grammatical point being practiced: ablative

Third Language Note (Prepositions)

In view of the very many prepositional phrases students have already encountered, they are unlikely to have trouble with this note. If necessary, however, you should provide further practice:

1 Write on the blackboard pairs of phrases and ask for their meaning, e.g. *in urbe—in urbibus, sub mēnsīs—sub mēnsā ē vīlla—ē vīllīs*, varying the order of the singular and plural in each pair (see above, pp. 51 and 74, for

lists of nouns from checklists).

2 Ask for the meanings of the *untranslated* prepositions at the ends of paragraphs 2 and 3.

3 Ask students to translate into Latin simple phrases, e.g. "with the friend," "into the house," or "across the bridge." Keep vocabulary simple. Do the exercise both orally and written on the blackboard. Extend this by asking students to convert Latin singular phrases into plural and vice-versa.

The Background Material

Because students are now coming to the end of the sequence on Roman Britain, they might, before moving on, review this theme. In their textbook, the background section reviews the sources of our knowledge and emphasizes the interrelationship of the different kinds of evidence—literary, archaeological, and epigraphical. You should adopt the same approach: "How do we know?"

The first step may consist simply of recalling material from the stories. If, for example, slavery in Roman Britain is being reviewed, begin by asking the class what they remember of the treatment of the slaves they have encountered: e.g. Salvius' harsh treatment of the workers on his farm (Unit 2, Stage 13); the somewhat easier life of domestics in his villa (Unit 2, Stage 14); the torture of the slave after the flight of Quintus and Dumnorix (Unit 3, Stage 24).

This prepares the way for the questions: "How do we know that slaves were treated like this? What evidence supports the stories?" Cite information from the background sections here. Some students will remember the photograph (Unit 2, Stage 13, p. 6) of a slave chain, found in Britain, designed to fasten several slaves together by their necks. They may also remember Columella's advice (Unit 2, Stage 13, p. 18) to accommodate chained slaves in an underground prison. Help build up the picture of the literary evidence by quoting from Varro's *De Re Rustica* and Columella. Translations of parts will be found in Cambridge School Classics Project *The Roman World*, Book 7 *The Villa*, pp. 15–16.

Help students review other topics like the following:

1 The Roman invasion of Britain (Unit 2, pp. 36–41) Evidence: Caesar, *Gallic War* IV. 20–36; V. 8–23 (read to the class the Penguin translation by Handford, pp. 119–40); Dio Cassius LX. 19–23; Tacitus, *Agricola* 13.

2 Cogidubnus and the palace at Fishbourne (Unit 2, Stages 15 and 16) Evidence: Tacitus, *Agricola* 14 (Penguin translation, pp. 64–65); archaeological excavation at Fishbourne and the Chichester inscription. The diagram on p. 141 is a stylized diagram of the stratification at Fishbourne, to show how layers can provide evidence

for the occupation of a site.

3 The Roman baths and temple at Aquae Sulis (Stage 21). Evidence: Solinus, a third century A.D. geographer who wrote descriptions of well-known places in the empire (*Collectanea rerum memorābilium* 22.10); archaeological evidence including inscriptions, Roman coins, and defixiones found in the spring; and the Roman architecture of baths and temple.

4 The military presence, for example, at Chester (Stages 25–27). Evidence: the remains of the fortress; military inscriptions, especially on tombstones (see the section reprinted from *R.I.B* by Collingwood and Wright; also Webster, *A Short Guide to the Roman Inscriptions*); items of military equipment.

Useful sources of evidence, in addition to those cited above, are given in the Bibliography below, pp. 194–200.

The map on p. 138 shows in more detail than in Unit 2, Stage 14, p. 38, the early development of Roman Britain. The peaceful consolidation in the southeast (see p. 142) is clearly illustrated by the preponderance of roads, towns, and villas, compared with the north and west, where legionary fortresses indicate continuing military activity. Key to Roman names:

Aquae Sulis = Bath
Calleva = Silchester
Camulodunum = Colchester
Corinium = Cirencester
Corstopitum = Corbridge
Deva = Chester
Eboracum = York
Glevum = Gloucester
Isca (Wales) = Caerleon
Isca (south-west) = Exeter
Lindum = Lincoln
Londinium = London
Luguvalium = Carlisle
Mona = Anglesey
Noviomagus = Chichester
Pinnata Castra = Inchtuthil
Verulamium = St. Albans
Viroconium = Wroxeter

Inscriptions

p. 145: the expanded version reads:

D(is) M(anibus) / Caecilius Avit / us Emer(ita) Aug(usta) /optio leg(ionis) XX / V(aleriae V(ictricis) st(i)p(endiorum) XV vix(it) / an(nos) XXXIIII / h(eres) f(aciendum) c(uravit) (*R.I.B.*492)

To the spirits of the departed. Caecilius Avitus of Emerita Augusta, optio of the Twentieth Legion Valeria Victrix, of 15 years' service, lived 34 years. His heir had this set up.

Emerita Augusta was a *colōnia* in Lusitania, now Mérida in Spain. The Twentieth Legion received the second "V" (Victrix) in its name in acknowledgment of its victories during Boudica's revolt, A.D. 61. Caecilius holds in his left hand a square tablet-case; in his right, a long staff (the optio's badge of office).

p. 146: the expanded version reads:

C(aius) Lovesius Papir(ia tribu) / Cadarus Emerita mil(es) / leg(ionis) XX V(aleriae) V(ictricis) an(norum) XXV stip(endiorum) IIX / Frontinius Aquilo h(eres) f(aciendum) c(uravit) (*R.I.B* 501)

Gaius Lovesius Cadarus of the Papirian voting-tribe, from Emerita, soldier of the Twentieth Legion Valeria Victrix, aged 25, of 8 years' service. Frontinius Aquilo, his heir, had this set up.

Lovesius is a Spanish name.
Emerita = Emerita Augusta, or Mérida.

Suggested Activities

1 Take the class through the background material in Unit 3, pp. 143–44, to make sure they understand the explanations given there about reading military tombstones, then guide students through the inscriptions on pp. 145–46. The expanded versions are above.

2 Find more examples of funerary inscriptions, civilian as well as military, in Filmstrip 2, frames 33 and 34 and in Filmstrip 3, frames 16, 18, and 33 (slides 15–17 and 61–68); also in LACTORs No. 4 and No. 8.

Students should normally work on this material in collaboration with you before proceeding to work in small groups or alone. If time allows, younger students might enjoy re-creating large facsimiles on posterboard, Latin on one side, English on the other, as is done, e.g. on flashcards in C.S.C.P. *The Roman World* Unit I. Or the class together might collaborate in making a booklet of selected inscriptions with expansions, translations, and explanations where necessary.

There is unfortunately no simple guide to Roman epigraphy for young students. But older students may consult Gordon; he provides a full introduction to sources and technical details of Latin inscriptions, excellent plates of selected inscriptions, and accompanying commentary. See especially Pl.32, No.50, "Dedication of Arch to the Deified Titus."

STAGE 29: RŌMA

BRIEF OUTLINE

Reading passages	Rome: the arch of Titus
Background material	the Roman forum
Chief grammatical points	3rd person singular and plural, present and imperfect passive purpose clauses with *quī* and *ubi*

NARRATIVE POINTS

Date	*Setting*	*Characters Introduced*	*Story Line*
Switchback: September, A.D. 81	Rome: Arch of Titus; Mamertine Prison	Emperor Domitian, Haterius (building contractor), Glitus (Haterius' foreman), Simon (a Jewish captive boy), mother of Simon; references to (previous emperor) Titus, Eleazar (Jewish rebel leader), Lucius Flavius Silva (commander of Tenth Legion at Masada)	Haterius, building contractor for the arch, and Salvius, his patron, urge on workmen finishing arch. Meanwhile, in prison, a Jewish mother tells her children how Silva conquered Masada, and how Eleazar persuaded Jews to commit suicide, but she and her mother survived, with the children, by going into hiding. Next day, at the dedication ceremony at the arch, Simon kills his family and himself, in emulation of his father, preferring death to servitude or execution at the hands of the Romans.

GRAMMATICAL POINTS

3rd person singular and plural, present and imperfect passive

e.g. *in mediā Rōmā est mōns nōtissimus, quī Capitōlium appellātur.*

purpose clauses with *quī* and *ubi*

e.g. *inter eōs Salvius, togam splendidam gerēns, locum quaerēbat ubi cōnspicuus esset.*

purpose clause and indirect command with *nē*

e.g. *dē morte patris vestrī prius nārrāre nōlēbam nē vōs quoque perīrētis, exemplum eius imitātī.*

ablative + verb

e.g. *hīs verbīs Eleazārus Iūdaeīs persuāsit ut mortem sibi cōnscīscerent.*

adjectival *is*

e.g. *eō nocte ipse fabrōs furēns incitābat.*

dum + present indicative

e.g. *subitō, dum Rōmānī oculōs in sacrificium intentē dēfīgunt, Simōn occāsiōnem nactus prōsiluit.*

ablative absolute without a participle

e.g. *circiter mīlle superstitēs, duce Eleazārō, rūpem Masadam occupāvērunt.*

SENTENCE PATTERNS

ABL + V

e.g. *intereā dux hostium, Lūcius Flāvius Silva, rūpem castellīs multīs circumvēnit.*

increased complexity of subordinate clauses: "nesting" and combination of "nesting" and "stringing"

e.g. *tantum ardōrem in eīs excitāvit ut, simulac fīnem ōrātiōnī fēcit, ad exitium statim festīnārent.*

spectātōrum tanta erat multitūdō ut eī quī tardius advēnērunt nūllum locum prope arcum invenīre possent.

ille igitur fabrīs, quamquam omnīnō dēfessī erant, identidem imperāvit nē labōre dēsisterent.

Title Picture

This shows a model of the center of Rome from the air. Use it to establish the change of scene from Roman Britain in Stages 21–28. Also return to this when studying the map in Stage 31, p. 199.

Model Sentences

The students' introduction to Rome begins with the *forum Rōmānum*; the pictures and captions indicate its appearance and the part it played in the city's religious, political, and social life. The forum is the subject of this Stage's background material, and more information about the different buildings, with a plan (p. 168), is given there. The arch of Titus, which stood on the Sacred Way leading into the forum, provides a theme for two of the stories.

The passive, so far met only in the perfect participle, now appears in its finite form. Examples are restricted to the 3rd person singular and plural of the present tense.

Apart from the names, the following words are new: *appellātur, summō* (new meaning), *ignis, Virginibus, extrēmō.*

nox

At night, it is time for sleep in most of the empire, but not in Rome. Here, the wealthy are giving sumptuous dinner parties, while the wretched poor are devising schemes—legal and illegal—to alleviate their poverty. Adjacent to the forum itself, an extraordinary din surrounds a huge arch being erected in the Via Sacra. It is being rushed to completion, because the Emperor Domitian is planning to dedicate it to his deceased brother Titus on the next day. Haterius, the building contractor, and Salvius, his patron (by means of whose influence Haterius won from Domitian the contract for the arch), are at hand, anxiously pressing the workmen to get the job done. Finally, the work is finished, and the exhausted workers trudge home to bed. One workman's route takes him past the Mamertine Prison, where he hears the lament of some captive women.

The events of Stage 29 occur in A.D. 81, the year of the consulship of the Flavius Silva who had captured the Jewish stronghold of Masada in A.D. 73. It was also the year in which Domitian became emperor after his brother Titus' brief rule, A.D. 79–81. Among Domitian's first actions was building and dedicating an arch to Titus' memory. This, together with his other building schemes, was partly intended to attract to himself some of the popularity which both his brother Titus and father Vespasian had enjoyed. For details of the inscription and reliefs on the arch, see below, pp. 100 and 102–103. For the crane, see the background material of Stage 30, pp. 182–83.

The first story takes place on the night before Domitian's dedication of the arch. It touches briefly on the social stratification of Rome, the construction of the arch, the anxiety of the contractor Haterius and his patron Salvius that the arch be finished on time, and finally the misery of the Jewish women prisoners.

Although Haterius himself is a fictitious character, the Haterii, with whom we have associated him, were an ancient Roman family who had once possessed senatorial rank. They are thought to have built the magnificent tomb illustrated in the next stage.

The lament of the Jewish women is based on Psalm 22 (21).1. It is adapted from the Vulgate translation, which reads :*Deus, Deus meus, quare me dereliquisti?* (from *Nova Vulgata . . . Editio*) Should students be interested, you might also remind them that Jesus spoke similarly, in e.g. St. Matthew 27.46, when he was hanging on the cross.

Students' experience of the passive is now extended to include the 3rd person forms of the imperfect. The illustration on p. 155 of the students' textbook is intended to give help with lines 12–17 and 31–33 which contain a heavy vocabulary load and include examples of both the imperfect and present passive.

Lines 17–21 are difficult. After you have read them aloud to the class (or after the class have read them through to themselves), you might ask:

What was the Emperor Domitian intending to do to the arch?
What had been his feelings while Titus was alive?
What had he decided to do now that Titus was dead?
Whose favor did he want to win? What had their attitude been to Titus?

Using simple comprehension questions like these, guide students through new vocabulary or grammar (for instructions, see Unit 1 Teacher's Manual, pp. 10–11). Further examples of such questions are included in Unit 3 LI Section, p. 296, paragraph 4. But to help students develop a solid reading proficiency, follow up all comprehension questions with translation and discussion of grammar. Here, for example, the lines should in due course be translated and students asked to explain the case of *vīvum* and *mortuum* and the point of *sibi*.

If students translate *nunc īnscrībuntur* (line 31) as "are now inscribed," use *paene* in the previous sentence to establish that the arch is not yet finished, and thus encourage "are now being inscribed."

During this and the other stories in Stage 29, focus attention on the introduction of the passive forms and the consolidation of the ablative. A number of minor usages also appear, like the use of *nē* in the present story and of *dum* with the present indicative in "arcus Titī" II. Answer students' questions about these if they ask, but postpone full discussion of such minor points until they are described in the language note of a later Stage or in the LI Section. In practice, students often absorb these points with little difficulty, interpreting them from the context.

Masada

The story of Masada is told by one of the Jewish women prisoners to her son Simon, while they are waiting for their execution at dawn. Simon is determined to follow the example of his father who commited suicide at Masada. The boy elicits from his mother for the first time the story (based on the historical events described below) of what happened at Masada to his father and the other Jews who were besieged there by the Romans.

She has refrained, prior to this, from recounting the tale, because she feared that Simon would wish to follow his father's example, and indeed Simon, on hearing that his mother had spirited her children away to avoid the collective suicide of the Jews at Masada, calls her a coward, implying that she and her family should have died honorably with the rest.

The Jewish rebellion broke out in A.D. 66 and raged furiously until Titus captured Jerusalem in A.D. 70. The number of casualties on the Jewish side was enormous; Jerusalem was sacked, the Temple of Yahweh destroyed, and, to prevent any repetition of the revolt, many of the survivors driven out and scattered among the cities of the empire. Titus returned to Rome with prisoners and the treasures of the Temple.

But Jewish resistance had not completely ended. A group called Zealots, led by Eleazar ben Ya'ir, established themselves at Masada, a fortress on a high flat-topped hill overlooking the Dead Sea to its east. From this base they harassed the Roman occupation forces for two years until in A.D. 72 the above-mentioned (p. 96) Flavius Silva, commander of the Tenth Legion (who may have been related to Salvius), decided to get rid of them once and for all.

The story of what happened is told in the students' textbook. It is based on our only source, the history of Josephus, who gives a vivid account of the final resistance at Masada, ending in the mass suicide of the defenders (*The Jewish War* VII.389–40). He may have talked to eye-witnesses and questioned the survivors, who hid themselves in an underground aqueduct (*specus* in the students' textbook) and then surrendered to the Roman soldiers. Yigael Yadin, who led the excavation of the site in 1963–65, demonstrated the general accuracy of Josephus' account and brought to light much evidence of the last days of Eleazar and his companions.

An excellent translation by G.A. Williamson and M. Smallwood of Josephus' *The Jewish War* is available in the Penguin series; the account of the heroic defense of Masada is found there on pp. 395–405. There is also much helpful and interesting information about Masada in Yadin and Pearlman. Video-cassette tapes of the American PBS series *Masada* provide a colorful recreation of events there.

The illustration of the rock of Masada on p. 156 shows the palace and fortifications which had been built by Herod the Great about 100 years earlier. Silva and his force of about 7000 legionaries and auxiliaries besieged the rock for six months in A.D. 72–73. They built an encircling wall and eight camps. The ramp is clearly visible halfway along the right-hand side of the rock.

The story in the textbook shows the Romans from a hostile point of view. Contrast, for example, the abusive description of Titus as Beelzebub in I, line 21, with the reference to him in line 20 of "nox." The story also shows the results of uncharacteristically inept provincial management by the Romans. They failed to understand Jewish beliefs and feelings, and Roman governors displayed a mixture of antipathy and tactlessness which contributed to the Jews' final desperate bid for liberation. The Jews were deeply conscious of their own traditions and religion, and these contributed, as so often, to their passion for political independence.

For lesson-plan syllabi beginning at this point, see above, pp. 13–14.

The use of the ablative by itself to express means, method, or cause was introduced in Stage 28 in the context of participial phrases, e.g. *vīnō solūtus*. It is now also admitted to the main clause, where it is kept close to the main verb, e.g.:

aedificia flammīs cōnsūmēbantur. (line 23)
dux . . . rūpem castellīs multīs circumvēnit. (lines 31–32)

The examples demonstrate how the idiomatic English equivalent may vary (". . . by flames," ". . . with many forts").

First Language Note (3rd Person Singular and Plural, Present and Imperfect Passive)

Ask students to compare the passive examples in paragraph 2 with the active examples in paragraph 1, and to comment not only on the verbs but also on the sentences as wholes. The question "Is the meaning changed?" will often provoke valid comment, e.g. "It's a different point of view," "It's describing the same action in a different way."

Ask students where they recall meeting previously the terms "active" and "passive." (Answer: In Stages 21–22, of perfect participles.) But here finite passive forms are restricted, presenting only one spelling novelty: the addition of -ur to the active forms already learned. Nevertheless, do not be disconcerted if some students need more time and practice before they can consistently disentangle the various passive forms. If at first they seem uncertain about the correct translation of the tense of the passive, their difficulty may actually spring from unfamiliarity with the corresponding English translations, e.g. the difference between "was prepared" and "was being prepared."

arcus Titī

The procession, sacrifice, and dedication are carried out properly. All Rome enjoys a day off. Suddenly, at the end, Simon seizes a sacrificial knife from the astonished priest and finishes the mass suicide begun at Masada nine years before. (The story of the Jewish survivors in Rome, unlike the events at Masada, is fictitious.)

The ceremony is not, properly speaking, a triumph, but has features in common with one. Ask students to suggest modern parallels. Use their suggestions to illustrate the several different aspects of the occasion: national (e.g. Fourth of July or Canada Day); religious e.g. Christmas, Chanukah, Passover, or Easter); and victory celebration (e.g. the return of a World Series winning team or of Olympic winners to their home city).

Some Suggested Questions on Part I

In what way does Domitian intend to honor his dead brother today?

Where do the latecomers have to stand?

Which phrase suggests that many senators were insincere in their enthusiasm to see the ceremony?

In lines 9–12, how do the arrangements made for the senators differ from those made for the equites? Suggest a reason for this.

What arrangements are being made to discover whether the intended ceremony has the approval of the gods? (Students should recall from Stage 23 details of the procedure of haruspices and augurs.)

The first three paragraphs of Part II are linguistically straightforward. Students might read them without your help, listing on paper the persons and objects in the procession, perhaps with sketches, "stick people," and accompanying labels. Then they might look at pictures of the procession as it was represented in sculptured form on the arch of Titus, on the south side of the inner archway (left in the pictures on pp. 155 and 161 of the textbook: see filmstrip 4; slide 22), and the drawing (based on the arch relief) on page 163. Prominent in the pictures are the gold treasures from the Jewish Temple, referred to on page 162 of the story; students might pick out the Menorah, or seven-branched candelabrum, the trumpets, and the table for the showbread. The tilted rectangular objects (which resemble modern TV cameras!) are placards describing the treasures and giving details of the Romans' successful campaign. Discuss the mental outlook which the Romans displayed in such parades by asking students, "Why did the Romans want to show off their military prizes?" Cap this discussion by reading a translation of Josephus' description of Titus and Vespasian's triumphal parade after the fall of Jerusalem (*The Jewish war* VII.113–62: tr. Williamson and Smallwood, pp. 384–86).

In Part II, Domitian appears in person. Help students here by providing some historical context. Tell (or remind) them that there were three emperors of the Flavian family: Vespasian (reigned A.D. 69–79), and his two sons Titus (79–81) and Domitian (81–96). Vespasian, whose part in the Roman invasion of Britain was mentioned in Unit 2, Stage 15, p. 58 and Stage 16, p. 71, had originally, when a general under the Emperor Nero, been appointed to crush the Jewish revolt in 67; when Vespasian left Judaea in 69 to launch his bid for the principate, Titus remained behind to continue military operations as described above, p. 98.

Drill students in passive forms of the verb by substituting forms for those in the textbook, e.g. "What does *sacrificātur* in line 23 mean? What would *sacrificantur* mean? *sacrificābātur? sacrificābantur?*" Or ask students to pick out and translate some of the many numerals in the stories of this Stage.

Second Language Note (Purpose Clauses with quī and ubi)

After students have studied this note, ask them to compare pairs of sentences like:

augurēs aderant quī cursum avium notābant.
augurēs aderant quī cursum avium notārent.

Drills

Exercise 1 Type: vocabulary
Grammatical point being practiced: compound verbs with *dē*, *ex-*, and *re-*

Ask students, also, to translate additional forms of these verbs, e.g. *excurrō, reductus*, or *dēpōnēbātur*.

Exercise 2 Type: transformation
Grammatical point being practiced: imperfect subjunctive in purpose clause

Discuss the effect of replacing *ut* with *quibus* in sentence 4.

Exercise 3 Type: completion
Missing item: participle
Test of accuracy: sense and correct ending
Grammatical point being practiced: nominative and accusative, singular and plural, of present participle

Follow up this exercise by asking students to explain their choices or to identify the noun described by each participle.

Exercise 4 Type: translation from English, using restricted pool of Latin words
Grammatical points being practiced: present participle, perfect active and passive participles, ablative singular and plural, relative pronoun

For some students, this exercise might be more suitable as oral work in class than as written homework (see above, p. 12). Encourage students to refer to the Unit 3 LI Section, pp. 262–63 and 280, when they are in doubt about form-endings.

The Background Material

The students' textbook indicates the location and functions of some of the major buildings of the *forum Rōmānum*; it also suggests something of the forum's atmosphere and associations with Rome's history. Students should relate the reading material to the photograph and plan which accompany it, and refer where appropriate to the pictures and model sentences at the beginning of the stage. Filmstrip 1–9 (slides 19–22 and IV. 28–29) also contain relevant material. You can find further descriptions and illustrations in Dudley, Nash, and Platner and Ashby; or in Paoli, pp. 5–12, who is particularly lively and informative. Plautus, *Curculio* 470ff., contains a vigorous and mildly bawdy description of the forum and its occupants in the second century B.C., when it was also a marketplace.

Additional Notes on Some of the Features Shown on the Textbook Plan (p. 168)

Capitol: the spiritual and emotional center of Rome. By telling or asking the students to retell any of the associated legends, e.g. Tarpeia and the Tarpeian rock (Livy I.11) or the geese which warned of the Gallic invaders (Livy V.47), you might well illustrate the point that at the time of the stories in Stage 29, the Capitol was already a revered repository of religious and historical traditions stretching back over several centuries. On the summit was the temple of Jupiter Capitolinus, the focus of the state religion; compare its dominant position with that of the temple of Jupiter in the forum at Pompeii. The temple on the Capitol was burnt down during the civil war in A.D. 69; Tacitus, *Histories* III.72, conveys very forcibly the emotional shock caused by this event. Its replacement too was burnt down in A.D. 80 and was being replaced still again at the time of the Stage 29 stories. The effectiveness of the Capitol as a symbol of Roman power and permanence was readily exploited by poets like Vergil (*Aeneid* IX.448–49) and Horace (*Odes* III.30.7–9).

Basilica Iulia: the site of the Centumviral Court, specializing in inheritance cases, where the lawyer Pliny the Younger was frequently active.

Rostra: the place where, occasionally, the heads of proscription victims were displayed, e.g. the head and hands of Cicero: *ita relatum caput ad Antonium iussuque eius inter duas manus in rostris positum* (Seneca Rhetor, *Suasoriae* VI.17; see also Plutarch, *Cicero* 49).

Arch of Titus: covered with triumphal inscriptions and reliefs, including representation of the victory procession (see above, pp. 100–101). A relief on the underside of the vault (not shown in our pictures, but see filmstrip 5; slide 21) represents an eagle carrying Titus' soul to heaven. The inscription reads SENATVS / POPVLVSQVE ROMANVS / DIVO TITO DIVI VESPASIANI F(ILIO) / VESPASIANO AVGVSTO: "The Senate and People of Rome (dedicated this arch) to the deified Titus Vespasian Augustus, son of the deified Vespasian." The elaborate bronze statue on the top, which shows Vespasian and Titus in a four-horse chariot, no longer exists.

Mention other forum sites with historical or legendary associations. The shrine of Venus Cloacina (so called because it stood close to the point where the *cloāca maxima* passes beneath the forum) is located in front of the Basilica Aemilia, where according to tradition Verginius killed his daughter Verginia to save her virginity (Livy III.48). By the Basilica Aemilia stands the podium of the Temple of Julius Caesar, which was built to honor the deified Caesar on the spot where his body was cremated in 44 B.C. (Suetonius, *Caesar* 84.3–4). The three columns just to the south of the Temple of Julius Caesar are the remains of the Temple of Castor and Pollux, built to commemorate the victory which the Romans, with the help of the heavenly Gemini, Castor and Pollux, won over the Latin peoples at Lake Regillus (Livy II.19–20). There is an excellent map of the forum with accompanying gazetteer in Cunliffe, *Rome* pp. 124–25.

STAGE 30: HATERIUS

BRIEF OUTLINE

Reading passages	Haterius the builder
Background material	buildings and building methods
Chief grammatical points	perfect and pluperfect passive

NARRATIVE POINTS

Date	*Setting*	*Characters Introduced*	*Story Line*
Switchback (cont.): September, A.D. 81	Rome: Subura, Haterius' house on the Esquiline hill, Haterius' building site	Vitellia (Haterius' wife)	Haterius feels betrayed because Salvius promised him an influential priesthood; Vitellia suggests scheme: Haterius takes Salvius up in his crane to show him the city, and impress him; Salvius is terrified, but, instead of a priesthood, cunningly offers to Haterius, for a large sum, a parcel of land for a prestigious tomb. (The emperor had *given* Salvius the land.)

GRAMMATICAL POINTS

increased incidence of perfect and pluperfect passive (all persons)

e.g. *ego ā Salviō, quī mihi favēre solēbat, omnīnō dēceptus sum.*

genitive of present participle used substantivally

e.g. *apud Haterium tamen nūllae grātulantium vōcēs audītae sunt.*

further ablative usages

e.g. *quīntō diē uxor, Vitellia nōmine, quae nesciēbat quārē Haterius adeō īrātus esset, eum mollīre temptābat.*

SENTENCE PATTERN

continued use of complex sentence structure

e.g. *volō ad summōs honōrēs pervenīre sīcut illī Hateriī quī abhinc multōs annōs cōnsulēs factī sunt.*

tum fabrīs imperāvit ut fūnēs, quī ad tignum adligātī erant, summīs vīribus traherent.

Title Picture

This shows Haterius and his crane. The method of operating the crane is described on pp. 182–83 of students' textbook. Note also the thin stripe on Haterius' toga and tunic which marks him as an eques.

Model Sentences

These link the events of Stages 29 and 30. Haterius is at first euphoric at the praise heaped on his arch, then uneasy at the non-appearance of the promised reward. By the start of the first story in Stage 30, he begins to realize that Salvius has deceived him, and he becomes furiously bitter. Students are likely to make extremely appropriate comments about Haterius' last sentence.

The perfect passive is introduced. In these sentences it is chiefly restricted to the 3rd person singular, though a 1st-person example is included near the end. Temporal adverbs like *heri, hodiē, adhūc,* etc. have been freely used to guide students to an appropriate translation ("was dedicated," "was promised," "was praised," followed by "has been sent," "have been deceived").

Suggestions for handling the difficulties of the perfect passive are given under First Language Note below, pp. 107–108. When students are translating the model sentences, you confirm their "was dedicated" for "dēdicātus *est*," etc. If students demand an explanation or if they are very confused, you might use some of the explanations suggested under the language note. Normally, you should postpone linguistic comment until the students have met a few more examples of perfect passives in a connected context. There is no new vocabulary.

dignitās

This story opens with a brief narrative that sets the scene for the subsequent dialogue, presented in play-form, between Haterius and his wife, Vitellia. In the opening section, the city of Rome is celebrating a four-day holiday following the dedication of the arch, during which time many people go to admire the arch, and Salvius' clients offer him their congratulations. The emperor himself has expressed to Salvius his praise of Haterius' work. Haterius, however, broods in solitude, admitting no visitors, enraged because, in the midst of all the celebration, he, the creator of the arch, has been overlooked. Vitellia , concerned because her husband has not slept for several days, approaches him to offer some comfort and advice, which she does in the dialogue which follows. Vitellia's first suggestion is that Haterius should go to his country villa and try there to regain his peace of mind. Haterius insists that he is too overwrought because of the slight dealt him by Salvius, and explains to his wife that Salvius had promised him a great reward for his work on the arch, and that he was hoping Salvius would help him further his political ambitions by using his own influence with the emperor to obtain a priesthood for Haterius. The riches Haterius has amassed, of which Vitellia pointedly reminds him, mean nothing to him, he says, compared with this ambition. Vitellia, evidently shrewder than her husband, suggests that Haterius should invite Salvius to his building site and impress him by showing him his crane, then at some strategic moment, remind Salvius about the priesthood.

Quintus Haterius Latronianus is not in the highest level of society, but wishes he were. He enjoys undoubted advantges. He is related by marriage to the aristocratic Vitellii; because his wife is Vitellia, sister of Salvius' wife Rufilla, he is brother-in-law to the up-and-coming Salvius; he is also a very successful building contractor. Socially, however, he belongs to one of the less distinguished branches of the family of the Haterii and he is an eques. When, through Salvius' influence, he gets the contract to build the arch of Titus, he works nights to finish it on time and thereby win the favor of Domitian. But not satisfied with financial success, he is eager to become an honorary priest and win political and social prestige. For this reason he tries, through Salvius, to pull strings and get himself appointed priest by the emperor, who is also the *pontifex maximus*.

Some students may ask to what extent the Haterius story is based on fact. The reliefs on the tomb of the Haterii (illustrated on pp. 173, 177, and p. 183, and see notes below, p. 112) strengthen the inference that one member of the family worked as a builder, owned the giant lift-crane which is shown in one relief, and was involved in the construction of the arch of Titus, the Flavian Amphitheater (viz. Colosseum), and other public buildings. The Haterius of our story is imagined as the builder commemorated in the Haterii-tomb reliefs, but the details of the story, including his full name and his relation-by-marriage to Salvius, are entirely fictitious. There is historical evidence, however, that Salvius' wife Rufilla was connected with the family of the Vitellii. See Unit 2, Stage 13, p. 15, and Unit 2 Manual, p. 24. The most notorious member of the Vitellii was the grossly obese Emperor Vitellius, who reigned some ten months in A.D. 69. Latin passages describing Vitellius' final campaign and death are found in P. V. Jones, *Selections from Tacitus*, pp. 24–34, and explanatory information in the Teacher's Handbook.

Haterius' determined efforts at social climbing reflect the influence on Roman life of the ideal of *dignitās*. Many Romans believed that personal prestige was a major goal in life; the idea that virtue is its own reward would not have appealed to them.

The theme, though important, is necessarily abstract; students may find it difficult to develop a clear view of it. Take the class through the dialogue on pp. 174–75 as quickly as possible, while making sure they are following the thread of the argument; alternatively, let the class work through the passage in groups, writing down the answers to the printed comprehension questions as they go, but perhaps leaving until later the more complex questions 5 and 7. Then students may focus their discussion on question 5. They may suggest modern parallels, in either the adult or the adolescent world, for sources and symbols of status.

Supplement the questions in the students' textbook with others. After students have read the first two paragraphs, develop questions 1 and 2: "What were the feelings of Salvius? of Haterius? Why could Haterius not sleep?" or, testing the students' memory of the events of the previous Stage, "Why should Salvius (in lines 6–7) be so pleased at the emperor's praise of Haterius?" Probe for the implications of Vitellia's speech (lines 36–40): "Who is of higher social standing, Vitellia or Haterius? What impression do you have of Vitellia's personality? What is the effect of the word order in lines 49–50?" At the end of the story, raise a more speculative question: "Why is it that Salvius, but not Haterius, gets what he wants as a result of the arch being built?"

nōbilissimā gente depending on *nātam* (line 37) represents a further extension of ablative usages. Another small development is the use of the present participle in the genitive without an accompanying noun (*grātulantium*, line 8). *maius* and *mīrābilius* (lines 52–53) provide you with an opportunity to comment on the neuter of the comparative adjective, referring if necessary to p. 267 of the Unit 3 LI Section. Students have already met many examples of *melius* and *tūtius* with *est*; *suāvius* occurred in Stage 25 and *terribilius* in Stage 29.

First Language Note (Perfect Passive)

By the end of "dignitās," students have met several examples of the 3rd person singular and plural of the perfect passive, also two examples of the 1st person singular. The language note adds the remaining persons.

Although the forms of the perfect passive are easily grasped, many students will take some time to become proficient in translating them. *est* and *sunt* are by now so firmly associated with "is" and "are" that their occurrence with an apparently new meaning will be something of a stumbling block. Help students by encouraging them to pay close attention to the context.

After students have read the language note, pick examples of perfect passives from the model sentences and from "dignitās" and then, after reminding students of the context, ask them to recall the translation of these examples. Write the translation on the board, and invite comment. If students worry about *est* and *sunt*, ask what kind of word invariably appears next to them in these examples. Some students will identify it from the examples, others remember it from paragraph 3 of the language note. Confirm that it is the presence of the participle that is responsible for the "new" translation of *est* and *sunt*. Bring out from students the points that the participle is perfect, and as a finite verb it is compounded with a form of *sum*.

If students mistranslate this tense in their reading, e.g. "it is praised" for *laudātus est*, ask "Do you mean the arch is *being* praised at the moment Vitellia is speaking? Wouldn't that be *laudātur*, like the examples in Stage 29?" Later, when students have more experience of the perfect passive, advise, e.g., "Look again; what kind of participle is beside *est*?"

In a later lesson, help students with the other major difficulty in translating the perfect passive: the "double" translation of e.g. *portātus est* as "has been carried" and "was carried." Help as follows: "In Unit 1, you learned two ways of translating *parāvit*. Melissa, announcing that dinner is served, might say *Grumiō cēnam optimam parāvit*, meaning . . . (Students: 'Grumio has prepared . . .'). But somebody telling a story might say that Grumio was happy and so he . . . (Students: 'prepared . . . '). Similarly, there are two ways of translating the perfect passive. Melissa might announce the meal by saying 'an excellent dinner *has been* prepared,' but the storyteller would say 'an excellent dinner *was* prepared'." If necessary, provide more Latin examples, suppying contexts for the two types of translation.

polyspaston

Haterius adopts an unusual method of impressing Salvius and thus winning his support. He courteously invites Salvius to join him on a ride to the top of his crane, on a bench which has been attached for the purpose. Salvius, fearful but unwilling to appear so, reluctantly complies, and is presented thus with a splendid view of Rome, and in particular the arch, which reminds Salvius, somewhat belatedly, to convey to Haterius the emperor's praise and thanks. Haterius chooses this moment to mention his promised reward. Salvius, though suitably awed, remains evasive on the question of an honorary priesthood; however, he does satisfy Haterius' craving for *dignitās* by substituting, as a smaller favor, the "gift" of a plot in a patrician cemetery. This is a rather ingenious bit of subterfuge on Salvius' part, since what he is offering to Haterius—and he drives a hard bargain for it—he himself previously received *gratis* from the emperor: but Haterius is suggestible, blinded perhaps by his craving for prestige. He readily accepts and pays for this substitution for the priesthood.

Help students note that Salvius does not want to lose face in front of the *fabrī* by asking them, "Why did Salvius turn pale? Why did he nevertheless sit on the beam of the crane? What is the relevance of the fact that the workmen were watching him?"

Relate the panoramic view of Rome, on which Salvius comments in lines 22–24, either to pictures in the students' textbook (e.g. the title picture of Stage 29) or to the map on p. 199. Show some of the filmstrip frames or slides mentioned below, p. 120.

Salvius' customary astuteness seems to desert him momentarily when he gives Haterius (in lines 24–26) a convenient opportunity to raise the question of his priesthood. But Salvius easily diverts Haterius' attention from *sacerdōtium* to *agellus*.

The dialogue between Salvius and Haterius has both a comic and a serious side. Once the students visualize the physical circumstances, the comic side can be left to take care of itself. Approach the serious side by asking, "Which of the phrases *alter spē immortālitātis ēlātus, alter praesentī pecūniā contentus* (lines 47–48) refers to Haterius, and which to Salvius?" Which would students prefer, *spēs immortālitātis* or *praesēns pecūnia*, which leads easily to a further question: "Why does Haterius seize so eagerly upon Salvius' offer? Is it reasonable to want to be remembered long after one's death?" Some alert students may notice that the wish of Haterius (or, rather, his real-life counterpart commemorated on the Haterii-tomb relief) was in fact granted: his monument does survive, and does commemorate his achievements.

The pluperfect passive is introduced in this passage. A language note follows. Students may translate it as a perfect tense, e.g. "was prepared" for *parātum erat* (line 9). Do not dismiss this out of hand as wrong, since English usage here is more flexible than Latin. Encourage students to rephrase more literally. Postpone discussion until after students have met the final example of a pluperfect passive (*datus erat*, line 42, which demands more obviously than the other examples an English pluperfect translation). Then, when students have completed the story, ask them to reexamine examples like *parātum erat*. If a student translates this as "was prepared," ask "Do you mean 'was being prepared?' If not, how could we make that clear in English?"

strepitū . . . plēna (line 5) is a further extension of ablative usages. For *labōrantium* (line 5), cf. *grātulantium* in line 8 of "dignitās."

Drill perfect and pluperfect passives orally, but substitute personal endings different from that of a given example in the story. E.g.: "What did *admissī sunt* ('dignitās,' line 9) mean? What would *admissī sumus* have meant? *admissus sum*?" Do not substitute, unless you are teaching college-age students, one *tense* for another until after students have met more examples of the pluperfect passive.

Second Language Note (Pluperfect Passive)

Students usually find this easier than the perfect passive. (At least the forms of *eram* look past!) Drill the various forms, using different persons and conjugations by adding to the examples in paragraph 3, no. 5: e.g. *ductī erant, monitus erat, iussus erās*, and *vīsī erāmus*.

If there is time, take this occasion to review simultaneously perfect participles from recent words-and-phrases checklists: *ablātus* (26); *accūsātus*

(26); *affectus* (30); *apertus* (25); *cēlātus* (21); *circumventus* (29); *coāctus* (25); *collēctus* (26); *commemorātus* (23); *comprehēnsus* (24); *cōnstitūtus* (28); *cōnsultus* (30); *creātus* (30); *dēceptus* (22); *dēiectus* (21); *dēmissus* (30); *dēpositus* (25); *dēsertus* (24); *dīlēctus* (28); *doctus* (26); *effectus* (21); *ēlēctus* (22); *explicātus* (25); *exstrūctus* (30); *extractus* (21); *fūsus* (22); *gestus* (23); *iactātus* (22); *iactus* (23); *incēnsus* (27); *inceptus* (22); *indūtus* (23); *iniectus* (22); *īnstrūctus* (26); *iussus* (21); *laesus* (25); *mandātus* (28); *monitus* (22); *occīsus* (28); *occupātus* (26); *oppugnātus* (24); *ōrnātus* (23); *patefactus* (24); *perfectus* (29); *praebitus* (26); *praefectus* (28); *reductus* (29); *relātus* (26); *solūtus* (28); *sprētus* (29); *susceptus* (21); *vītātus* (22). Help students with an analysis as follows: "*servātus* means 'having been saved' and *erat* means 'he was,' so *servātus erat* means 'he was (in a state of) having been saved,' i.e. 'he had been saved.'"

If necessary, help students practice agreement between noun and participle in compound verbs. After students have read the stories and language notes, pick out examples of perfect and pluperfect passive forms from the stories, choosing at first only masculine forms. Ask students to distinguish between singular and plural forms. Then pick out examples of feminine and neuter singular forms (e.g. *parātum erat* and *fīxa erat* in "polyspaston," lines 9 and 10) and ask students to identify their gender and number; finally, cite the one example of a feminine plural (*audītae sunt* in "dignitās," line 8) and ask students to identify its gender and number. Later, they may study the note on agreement in the Unit 3 LI Section, p. 278, paragraph 7.

Drills and Suggestions for Further Practice

Exercise 1 Type: vocabulary
Grammatical point being practiced: nouns in *-itās*

Exercise 2 Type: transformation
Grammatical point being practiced: genitive, dative, accusative, and ablative, singular and plural

Supply extra help, if needed, by telling students which word in the table of nouns (Unit 3 LI Section, pp. 262–63) provides the closest parallel to the noun in boldface, e.g. *leō* for *legiō* (sentence 2), *cīvis* for *testis* (sentence 4) and *mercātor* for *flōs* (sentence 6). *māter* (sentence 8) has no exact parallel in the table, but if students are puzzled, tell them that it belongs to the third declension.

Practice further the ablative forms, in preparation for the introduction of the ablative absolute in Stage 31, by asking volunteers to translate simple prepositional phrases from English into Latin, e.g. "with a flower" into "flōre." Include easy adjectives with the nouns as well as pronouns.

Exercise 3 Type: completion

Missing item: participle
Test of accuracy: correct ending
Grammatical point being practiced: nominative, accusative, and ablative, singular and plural, masculine and feminine, of perfect passive participle

Exercise 4 Type: transformation
Grammatical point being practiced: pluperfect subjunctive with *cum*

Students will find the transformation of the singular form *-it* to *isset* easier than the transformation of the plural from *-ērunt* to *issent.* Preface the exercise with a short oral drill of 3rd person pluperfect subjunctives (both singular and plural) from a variety of perfect stems. Besides perfect stems listed above, p. 42, new perfect stems learned in the checklists of Stage 24 to 30 are:

Perfects with *-ĭ-*: *trānsiī* (24).
Perfects with *-u-* or *-v-*: *accūsāvī* (26); *aperuī* (25); *appāruī* (27); *cōnsuluī* (30); *creāvī* (30); *dēposuī* (25); *dēseruī* (24); *docuī* (26); *doluī* (28); *explicāvī* (25); *haesitāvī* (25); *imperāvī* (27); *latuī* (25); *māluī* (29); *mandāvī* (28); *nescīvī* (25); *nocuī* (27); *occupāvī* (26); *oppugnāvī* (24); *palluī* (30); *praebuī* (26); *servīvī* (29); *sprēvī* (29).
Perfects with *-s-* or *-x-*: *arsī* (27); *dēmīsī* (30); *dīlēxī* (28); *exstrūxī* (30); *incessī* (29); *īnstrūxī* (26); *laesī* (25); *redūxī* (29).
Strong perfects: *affēcī* (30); *circumvēnī* (29); *coēgī* (25); *collēgī* (26); *patefēcī* (24); *perfēcī* (29); *praefēcī* (28).
Perfects with stem unchanged: *accidī* (25); *comprehendī* (24); *cōnscendī* (24); *cōnstituī* (28); *dēscendī* (24); *incendī* (27); *occīdī* (28); *occurrī* (27); *solvī* (28).
Perfects with reduplicated consonants: *adstitī* (24); *praestitī* (30).
Perfects with stem different from present stem: *abstulī* (26); *rettulī* (26).

Students should translate each pair of sentences in Exercise 4 before combining them, but they need not write down these translations.

The Background Material

There is a wealth of reference material available on Roman buildings and building methods (e.g. Green, Hamey, Hodges, Landels, and Macaulay), much of which is suitable for use by students. Where possible, students should study and report on building methods and materials of a particular building or structure; for example, a slide of the interior of the Colosseum (filmstrip 16; slide 24) or of the Pont du Gard will illustrate spectacularly how the principle of the arch was exploited by the Romans. There is a drawing of an arch being constructed on p. 182 of the students' textbook.

The photograph on p. 183 shows part of the panel of buildings from the tomb of the Haterii. Students might enjoy picking out details of the very fine carving, both here and in the part reproduced on p. 177. For example, the knot the workmen are tying at the top of the crane on p. 177 is clearly a reef-knot. Note here that the representation of the arch of Titus is not accurate, but it can be identified from the inscription: ARCVS IN SACRA VIA SVMMA: "The arch at the top of the Sacred Way." The figures in the arches are thought to be gods.

The eye, or skylight-hole, in the center of the Pantheon dome is nearly 30 ft (9 m) across and is the dome's only source of light. The brickwork ring around it acts as the keystone for the vault. The concrete of the dome is in horizontal layers containing different materials, e.g. volcanic rock, which is comparatively light, towards the top. The square coffers (= recesses) were originally enriched with stucco moldings, painted and gilded. A bronze flower occupied the center of each coffer. There is an excellent drawing of the entire Pantheon in MacDonald pp. 98–99, and of a cross-section of the dome in MacDonald p. 101.

Suggestions for Further Work

1 "Imagine yourself as a member of Haterius' building crew and write a first-person account of the construction of the arch of Titus, including the final efforts to get it finished on time. Use the information in the stories and background material of Stages 29 and 30 and any other reference material available to you."

2 Ask junior high or high school students, with the help of reference material like the books mentioned above, to research into particular building techniques (e.g. arch, or dome) or buildings (e.g. Pantheon) and present their findings in the form of a diagram, computer program, or model. There are ample drawings and photographs in MacDonald and Sear. If the academic program does not allow them time to build models, students may do them in vacations and exhibit them during foreign-language field days or at Junior Classical League conventions.

STAGE 31: IN URBE

BRIEF OUTLINE

Reading passages Background material	the city of Rome patronage: patrons and clients
Chief grammatical points	ablative absolute purpose clauses and indirect command with *nē*

NARRATIVE POINTS

Date	*Setting*	*Characters Introduced*	*Story Line*
Switchback (cont): Autumn, A.D. 82	Rome: Subura, Haterius' house on the Esquiline Hill	Euphrosyne (Greek philosopher recommended to Haterius), Haterius' *praecō*, Quintus Haterius Chrysogonus (freedman of Haterius, living in Greece), Eryllus (Haterius' *arbiter ēlegantiae*)	Euphrosyne watches in astonishment the ritual of *salūtātiō* at Haterius' house. Arrogant *praecō* refuses her admittance, but she stoically endures his rudeness.

GRAMMATICAL POINTS

ablative absolute
  e.g. *sōle occidente, saccāriī ā tabernā ēbriī discessērunt, omnī pecūniā cōnsūmptā.*
ablative of description
  e.g. *quae tamen, clāmōribus fabrōrum neglēctīs, vultū serēnō celeriter praeteriit.*
dative noun + participle at beginning of sentence
  e.g. *praecōnī regressō servus, "ecce!" inquit, "domina mea adest."*
increased incidence of purpose clause and indirect command with *nē*
  e.g. *servum iussit festīnāre nē domum Hateriī tardius pervenīrent.*

SENTENCE PATTERN

increased variety in word order in sentences using passive voice
  e.g. *ā crepidāriīs calceī reficiēbantur.*

Title Picture

This shows a boat unloading opposite the Tiber Island (see p. 199 of the students' textbook). The bridge in the background is the Pons Fabricius, which still survives (see filmstrip 20; slide 26).

Model Sentences

A day in the life of waterfront Rome (cf. filmstrip 22; slide 41). Grain arrives on ships, and is unloaded by the dockworkers, who collect their pay and then go off to spend it in a nearby inn.

The ablative absolute is here introduced. Each absolute clause, except the last, is preceded by a finite version of the same event, e.g. *nautae nāvem dēligāvērunt* precedes *nāve dēligātā*. The ablative absolute clauses are temporal rather than associative, and invite translations introduced by "When . . .," "As . . .," "While . . .," and "After . . ."

Concentrate on the subject matter rather than the sentence structure of these sentences. Pick out one or two of the ablative absolute clauses, and put each on the blackboard together with translations suggested by the class. Put up alternative translations and make clear from the first that flexibility in translation is always stylistically preferable to mechanical conversion. Ask students the case of all the words in these clauses. Once they have established it as ablative, postpone further discussion until after they have read the first story and met more examples.

If students have difficulty in translating the present participles, encourage them to use the clues in the picture (e.g. in picture 2 dawn has not yet broken, and in picture 3 the dockhands are still working), and to translate e.g. *illūcēscente* and *labōrantibus* as "was dawning" and "were working." Then ask them to recall the suffixes (*-ns* or *-nt-*) by which they can identify the forms as present participles, meaning "dawning," "working," etc.

The following words are new: *illūcēscēbat, saccāriī, expōnere, distribuit, occidere.*

adventus

This passage at first describes (like the model sentences) the dockside of Rome, then the Subura. The final paragraph introduces patron and client, a theme which will be developed in the next story. The entire scene is viewed through the eyes of a newly arrived Greek girl, to be identified later as the Latin-speaking philosopher Euphrosyne. This Greek girl, having disembarked from a ship amidst the bustle on the bank of the Tiber, makes her way, accompanied by a slave who is heavily laden with her baggage, through the chaotic streets of Rome, where all manner of people are engaged in various activities. Ignoring the catcalls directed at her by some workmen, the girl advances through the city, toward Haterius' house. At this time of the morning, the crowds in the streets are swelled by the clients who are hurrying to their patrons' houses for their morning visit.

Students should use the map on p. 199 of their textbook to locate the Tiber river, the Subura residential area, and the forum. They might also use the background material as either an introduction or a follow-up to the story.

Some Suggested Questions

Why are so many people, rich as well as well as poor, up and around at this time of day? In what way is the status of the senators emphasized?

What activities are taking place by the Tiber? Where have the boats come from? Why are the granaries near the river?

Whose *adventus* is referred to in the title? Where is she going?

Why might the letter carried by the girl be important and what sort of things might you expect it to say? (Cf. Stage 26, where Quintus produces a letter from Barbillus.)

What sort of area does the Subura seem to have been?

Where are the beggars sitting? Why were crossroads (and also bridges) such favored haunts of beggars?

Pick out two phrases which show that the girl is unaffected by the workmen's reaction to her.

Students might also discuss the contrast between the lives of rich and poor (touched on again in the first and last paragraphs; remind students of the beginning of "nox" in Stage 29) and the hazards of street life in the Subura (third and last paragraphs).

Both this story and the next contain examples of all ablative usages recently introduced. The following ablatives with a main verb all occur in "adventus":

multitūdine clāmōribusque hominum . . . obstupefacta est (lines 11–12).
puellam verbīs procācibus appellāvērunt (lines 17–18).
servī multitūdinem fūstibus dēmovēbant (line 25).

If students still have difficulty with these usages, ask leading questions, e.g. "What was she surprised by?," and then, after the story has been completed, discuss the examples again.

salūtātiō

When Euphrosyne arrives at the house of Haterius, she finds it thronged by early-morning callers: clients hoping for a handout or an invitation to dinner. An arrogant herald issues instructions and dinner invitations to some, and then, scattering a few coins among the remaining crowd, orders them to accompany Haterius later to the forum. These clients scrabble in the dirt for the coins flung to them by the contemptuous herald. Euphrosyne, meanwhile, has witnessed this scene with astonishment.

After the crowd has been dispersed, Euphrosyne orders her slave to knock at the door which has by now been shut once again. When the herald returns in response to the knock, the slave announces Euphrosyne's arrival as if she were an expected guest, but is rudely rebuffed by the herald. When the slave attempts to explain that Euphrosyne has been sent by Haterius' freedman Chrysogonus, a freedman of Haterius' who lives in Athens, this only provokes further insolence from the herald, and when the slave mentions the name of Eryllus, Haterius' *arbiter ēlegantiae* at whose summons Euphrosyne has come, the herald shoves the slave into the mud for his pains, and shuts the door rudely in the travelers' faces. Euphrosyne attempts to soothe the slave with a bit of Stoic philosophy, and recommends to him that they return on the following day.

In Stages 29 and 30, Haterius appeared as a client of Salvius; we now see him from another standpoint, performing the role of patron to his own clients.

The story illustrates several features of the patron–client relationship: the *salūtātiō*, or morning visit, which clients regularly made to patrons; the *sportula*, or "handout," once a little basket of food but now usually a handful of coins, distributed carelessly among the crowd; the variety of small tasks required of clients by patrons, including the obligation to stand around and wait attendance; the arrogance of the patron's slaves to the clients (cf. Juvenal, *Satires* V.63–75); the arrogant patron, who disdains any personal appearance at the *salūtātiō* and relays his orders through the *praecō* instead. On the patron-client relationship, especially in connection with the *salūtātiō*, Balsdon, *Life* pp.21–24, has a helpful discussion. When the class discusses the topic, bring out the interdependence of patron and clients: they need him for the *sportula* but he needs them to escort him in public and to run errands, thereby parading his power and influence.

Link the story with the background material and with a selection from primary sources. See notes in background material below, pp. 119–22.

The young girl Euphrosyne was a philosopher, with a Greek name, about whom we know nothing except what is stated on her Roman tombstone:

EVPHROSYNE
PIA
DOCTA NOVEM MVSIS
PHILOSOPHA V(IXIT) A(NNIS) XX

(*C.I.L. 33898/I.L.S. 7783*)

The inscription in large, beautiful letters appears on a marble stele which was found in 1888 in Rome, in the area east of the present Villa Borghese. Because the historical Euphrosyne was buried in Rome, we are left to imagine that the young girl of our story was on her first visit to the city where in fact she was later buried. She is portrayed as an attractive disciple of Stoic teachings, serious enough to proselytize for her beliefs. She is soon rebuffed.

Take the occasion of Euphrosyne's name to demonstrate Greek letters on the blackboard by writing EVPHROSYNE first in Roman, then in Greek, ΕΥΦΡΟΣΥΝΗ. (The name means "Joy.") Draw attention to the equivalences and differences between the Roman and Greek letters. Some of the nine Muses, who are poetically imagined on the tombstone as Euphrosyne's teachers, might also illustrate the relation between Roman and Greek letters, e.g. CLIO / ΚΛΕΙΩ or MELPOMENE / ΜΕΛΠΟΜΕΝΗ.

A student might answer the second part of question 3 in the textbook by a drawing (*corpus . . . ingēns et obēsum*, lines 6–7). You might extend the question by asking, "Which Latin words give us a clue to the herald's character? Does the herald behave in a way that the description of his character would lead us to expect? How is it that he, as a slave, can get away with treating Roman citizens in this way?" If students have difficulty with the second half of question 5, remind them of the name of young Quintus' savior, Caecilius' freedman Lucius Caecilius Felix, and the explanation of freedmen's names in Unit 1, Stage 1, pp. 11, and Stage 6, p. 97. The answer to question 6 illustrates the well-known rhetorical device of a speaker saving till last the word or name which an audience is most anxious to hear. Students will know the device from watching speeches of nomination at political conventions or suspensefully delayed awardings of a first prize.

In Part II of "salūtātiō," students might explore the phrase *arbiter ēlegantiae* (line 16). Once they have pictured someone whose job was to monitor public fashions or fads and advise his employer accordingly, they might go on to compare modern equivalents like Sunday newspaper supplements, *Vogue*, *GQ* and other magazines which feature what's new in physical fitness, music, computers, and other hobbies. Eryllus, who will appear in Stage 32, is modeled on C. Petronius, the *arbiter ēlegantiae* of Nero. Students might be interested in reading, in translation, Tacitus' account of Petronius' colorful life and death (*Annals* XVI.18–19).

Ask students to weigh Euphrosyne's words to her slave (lines 26–27). Her advice is both sensible and thoroughly in accord with Stoic philosophy, but unlikely to persuade many of her hearers, ancient or modern. Ask younger students if they, in the slave's position, would have preserved an *aequus animus*, and if not, whether this means Euphrosyne's advice was bad.

Part II is suitable for reading aloud expressively or acting out. Four readers will be required: narrator, slave, herald, and Euphrosyne. Both Parts I and II are on the audiocassette.

From this and the previous story, ask the students to pick out examples of the passive. Drill passive forms by transforming the form in the text, e.g. "What did *reficiēbantur* ('adventus,' line 16) mean? What would *reficiuntur* mean: *refectī erant*? Give two translations of *refectī sunt*." Make sure that students know the passive, since they are about to meet it again in the different context of deponent verbs.

First Language Note (Ablative Absolute)

You may wish to complete this long note in installments, perhaps paragraphs 1–3 in one lesson, and paragraph 4 in another.

Encourage the students to be flexible while translating. E.g. students should be able to produce "When their leader was killed," "Since their leader had been killed," "After the killing of their leader," etc. for *duce interfectō* (sentence 4 of paragraph 3). Using an example like sentence 5 of paragraph 3, raise the possibility of translating it with an *active* perfect participle ("Having heard the shouts," etc.) Remind the class of any previous discussion of the question, "If *parātus* means 'having *been* prepared,' how did the Romans say 'having prepared the dinner?'" (see below, pp. 163–64). Or help students develop for themselves the Latin sequence: *parāvērunt cēnam, cēna ab eīs parāta est*, and *parātā cēnā*, by asking appropriate guide questions, e.g. "What were two ways of saying in Latin, 'they prepared the dinner?' Another way of saying, 'the dinner (was) prepared?'"

The independence of the ablative absolute from the main structure of the sentence (illustrated implicitly in paragraph 1 of the note) is better demonstrated than explained. Invite students to read out the ablative absolute clauses in paragraph 3. Then invite others to read out the examples in paragraph 3, *omitting* the ablative absolute. Finally, with questions like "Does it still make sense without the ablative absolute?" and "Is it a complete sentence?" establish the point that the ablative absolute is not centrally connected with the rest of the sentence. Reinforce the point if necessary by referring to the word *absolūtus* ("detached") from which the construction takes its name.

Drills

Exercise 1 Type: vocabulary
Grammatical point being practiced: compound verbs with *ab-*, *circum-* and *in-*

Further practice of compound verbs could include:

discēdere (go away)	→ *dīmittere*
percurrere (run through)	→ *perrumpere*
convocāre (call together)	→ *convenīre, compōnere*
trānsmittere (send across)	→ *trānsīre, trānscurrere*

prōpōnere (put forward) → *prōcēdere, prōcurrere, prōferre*

Those students who have now grasped the principle underlying formation of compound verbs should be given encouragement and a warning: although the meaning of an unfamiliar compound verb can often be deduced from knowledge of its component parts, emphasize that such knowledge should be used as a clue rather than an infallible guide, since the meaning of the component parts, particularly the preposition, is likely to vary when used in compounds. Illustrate the latter point with, e.g. *āmittere* and *invenīre*.

Exercise 2 Type: completion
Missing item: verb
Test of accuracy: correct number of verb
Grammatical point being practiced: 3rd person singular and plural, present and imperfect passive

In sentences 2, 3, 5, and 6, there is a deliberate variation of number (singular subject with plural agent, or vice versa) to reinforce the point that the nominative, and not the agent, controls the number of the verb. If students get this wrong, producing e.g. *oppugnābantur* for sentence 5, respond by saying, "Look again: you are thinking of sentences like *barbarī oppidum oppugnābant*, where the sentence was about the barbarians and what they did, and so the verb was active; this time the verb is passive, and the sentence is about the town and what was done to it."

Exercise 3 Type: completion
Missing item: noun *or* verb *or* participle
Test of accuracy: sense and syntax
Grammatical point being practiced: sentence structure

Second Language Note (Purpose Clauses and Indirect Command with nē)

Students have met several examples of these constructions with *nē* in recent stages. Encourage them to experiment with different ways of translating the examples in paragraphs 2 and 3. The examples in paragraph 2 could be compared to the corresponding direct commands *nōlī nāvigāre, nōlīte līberōs interficere*, etc.

The Background Material

You might assign the material on the city of Rome immediately before or after students read "adventus," and postpone the material on patronage until after students read "salūtātiō."

The City of Rome

The area and population of Rome in the first century A.D. are matters of controversy among scholars. The figures in the students' textbook depend on a disputable assumption that the city's population spilled only slightly beyond the area of 7¾ square miles (20 square km) demarcated by the toll-posts. Even if this assumption is mistaken, the point made by the comparison in the textbook is not significantly affected. The Los Angeles and Greater Manchester statistics are for 1976 and 1983 respectively.

The class might consider some of the reasons why expansion could not relieve the massive overcrowding in first-century Rome. If *īnsulae* were allowed to rise very high, they would suddenly collapse or catch fire; Augustus fixed the limit at 70 ft, 21 m (cf. Stage 30, p. 185, of students' textbook). The city was not enlarged outwards with large suburban residential areas (a prominent feature of modern cities) because there were none of the modern forms of rapid transportation.

Relate the places mentioned in the students' textbook not only to the map on p. 199, but also, whenever possible, to photographs. These can be slides (e.g. filmstrip 1–20, slides 19–26, and IV.28–29), photographs like those in Dudley, MacDonald, Nash, Scherer, Sear, and van der Heyden and Scullard or pictures of reconstructions like those in Macaulay, MacDonald, and Sorrell and Birley. Photographs and postcards of the older quarters of present-day Rome (like the photograph on p. 200) can illustrate features of the ancient city which still persist: high buildings, for example, sometimes built around internal courtyards, and narrow streets teeming with life.

The map on p. 199 has deliberately been simplified to show only the main features mentioned in the text. Remind students that the whole area was filled with many buildings of every kind.

At the end of the first century, there were nearly a dozen aqueducts bringing water into the city of Rome. The Aqua Claudia, shown in the photograph on p. 149, was 46 miles (74 km) long, but only about 9 miles (14 km) was raised on arches. It was considered one of the best sources of water and so was taken to the palaces on the Palatine hill. Students may remember the picture in Unit 1, Stage 10, p. 155, which shows the water's final destination, a tap.

This photograph on p. 149 (cf. the larger view in MacDonald, pl. 16) shows part of the large reconstuction model ("plastico") of Rome at the time of Constantine. It was made in 1937–38 and is now in the Museo della Civiltà Romana.

The more students associate each place with its function, the more vividly will they imagine it. Ask them: If you were a first-century Roman, where would you go . . .

. . . to give thanks after recovering from a fever? (Answer: temple of

Aesculapius on Tiber Island)
. . . for a cheap haircut? (Subura)
. . . for a summer's evening stroll away from the crowds? (Campus Martius)
. . . to watch a chariot-race? (Circus Maximus)
. . . to hear an open-air political speech? (Rostra in forum)
Add similar examples. The answers given are not the only possible ones.

Ask the class to list as many ways as they can in which the lives of the rich in first-century Rome differed from those of the poor; they should make use of what they have learned in the stories and background material, supplemented by any additional information they possess or deductions they can make. Areas of difference might include: food (banquets of rich in "nox"—meager meals obtained by poor with *sportula*); housing (mansions and palaces of rich—*insulae* of poor); water (rich connect with main water supply—poor use fountains); summer residence (rich escape to *vīllae*, like Haterius, Stage 30, p. 174—poor stay behind in hot, unhealthy city). This would easily tie in with a reading in translation of parts of Juvenal, *Satires* III.

The topics of city life, which students might research and discuss, are vast, though dependent on the time available. There is helpful information (some of which could be gathered by students themselves, while some would require your guidance) in Carcopino pp. 13–64, Cowell pp. 13–34, Dilke, Frederiksen (in Balsdon (ed.) *Roman Civilisation* pp. 151–68), Leacroft, Meiggs pp. 234–51 (an important description of *īnsulae*), Nash, Paoli pp. 1–53, and Platner and Ashby. Older students could research the theme of city life in translations of the relevant literary evidence:

1 police and fire patrols (Justinian, *Digest* I.xii.1, xv.3; Lewis and Reinhold II.26–28).
2 Augustus' building program (Suetonius, *Augustus* 28.3–30.2; Lewis and Reinhold II.67–69)
3 aqueducts (Frontinus, *The Water Supply of Rome* II.98–129; Lewis and Reinhold II.69–72)
4 dimensions of city (Pliny, *Natural History* III.v.66–67; Lewis and Reinhold II.222)
5 utilities and services (Strabo, *Geography* V.iii.8; Lewis and Reinhold II.223–24)
6 the great fire (Tacitus, *Annals* XV.38–44; Lewis and Reinhold II.224–27)
7 baths (Lucian, *The Bath* 4–8, and Seneca, *Moral Epistles* LVI.1–2; Lewis and Reinhold II.227–28)
8 life in Rome (Juvenal, *Satires* III; Lewis and Reinhold II.239–42). The quotation in the students' textbook, p. 201, is adapted from Juvenal, *Satires* III.243–48.

Patronage

The story "salūtātiō" has reflected the commonest type of Roman patronage; the distribution of *sportula*, on behalf of a wealthy patron, to his dependent clients. The background material provides further information about this and other types of patronage, which operated across the whole spectrum of Roman society. Students may be able to identify some modern patrons like sponsors of the arts or donors to political causes, or modern clients like reporters who build "networks" of "contacts" in high places.

The following is a selection of source material relevant to points mentioned in the text:

Horace, *Satires* I.6.54–64 (introduction to Maecenas; cf. *Letters* I.16.1–16 for the Sabine farm)
Pliny, *Letters* II.9 (candidacy of Sextus Erucius)
Pliny, *Letters* IV.1 (donation of temple to Tifernum)
Pliny, *Letters* IV.13 (contribution to schoolmaster's salary at Comum)
Pliny, *Letters* VI.23 (Cremutius Ruso to speak with Pliny in court)
Martial, *Epigrams* VI.88 (punishment for not addressing patron as "*domine*")
Juvenal, *Satires* V.24–155; Pliny, *Letters* II.6; Martial, *Epigrams* I.20, III.60 (graded dinner-parties)

Duplicate some of this material and distribute it in class for interpretation and discussion.

Encourage students to notice connections between the different topics they study. Here, for instance, link Maecenas' gift of the Sabine farm to earlier discussion of the *vīllae* owned by the rich (see above, p. 121). Compare the patron–client relationship to the Roman view of the relationship between gods and men, described in Stage 23. Finally, compare patronage with another important Roman institution, *amīcitia*. Patronage flows from higher social status to lower; *amīcitia* exists between social equals. A tactful *patrōnus* might blur this distinction by referring to the recipients of his patronage as his *amīcī*.

Suggestions for Discussion

1 Help students attempt an assessment of the uses and abuses of the patronage system. Divide the blackboard into two columns, "pro" and "con," and invite the class to contribute their views, supported as far as possible by examples taken from the stories and background material. Arguments in favor might include: support for the humbler citizen in the law courts, protection against economic disaster in an era when the state did not make welfare payments, and financial help for the needs of the community, as provided by Pliny for Comum. The arguments against

might be: hypocrisy, advancement by personal influence, lack of incentive to get ahead by one's own efforts, the patron's exploitation of his clients. On occasion, the patron could bully a client into criminal or immoral activities by withholding invaluable protection if he or she refused. In its less pleasant aspects, the patron—client system foreshadowed the infamous political machines of American cities, other urban "rackets" and secret "hit" gangs.

2 The analysis above might lead to a comparison between Roman and modern systems of social security. Younger students may have had too little experience to develop it, but some aspects should be accessible to all. For example, "Do people today depend on rich neighbors as a client did on a patron? What are the ways in which the community, state/province, or federal government today helps people in need? Which kinds of needs are the responsibility of our boards/departments of health, education, or social welfare? Do you think that, especially in a large city, there are advantages in knowing by name a few persons to whom one can go for advice and help?"

Words and Phrases Checklist

Focus attention on the paradigm of *īdem* in the LI Section, p. 271. For some suggestions, see below, p. 159.

STAGE 32: EUPHROSYNĒ

BRIEF OUTLINE

Reading passages Background material	Roman society philosophy and other beliefs
Chief grammatical points	deponent verbs gerundive of obligation (with transitive verbs) future participle

NARRATIVE POINTS

Date	*Setting*	*Characters Introduced*	*Story Line*
Switchback (cont.): Autumn, A.D. 82	Rome: Haterius' house on the Esquiline hill	Titus Flavius Sabinus (consul), client-visitors, and Haterius' other dinner guests: Apollonius, Lucius Baebius Crispus (senator), Rabirius Maximus (architect)	Euphrosyne is finally admitted, after Eryllus wonders why she has not arrived from Athens. She is to provide entertainment at banquet, but her lecture on Stoic philosophy does not go down well with drunken Romans.

GRAMMATICAL POINTS

deponent verbs
e.g. *hōc cōnsiliō captō, ad flūmen Tiberim ut nāvem cōnscenderet profecta est.*

gerundive of obligation with transitive verbs
e.g. *illa nōbīs dīligenter audienda est.*

double indirect question with *necne*
e.g. ibi praecō ingressus est, Haterius rogāvit utrum philosopham abēgisset necne.

increased incidence of ablative absolute without a participle
e.g. *mē enim auctōre, philosopha quaedam hūc invītāta est.*

SENTENCE PATTERN

increased incidence of postponement of subordinating conjunction
e.g. *ad flūmen cum advēnisset, Euphrosynēn in nāvem cōnscēnsūram cōnspexit.*

Euphrosynē revocāta

After trying unsuccessfully for seven days to gain entrance to Haterius' house, Euphrosyne makes preparations for her return to Athens. On the same day Eryllus convinces Haterius that his birthday dinner that evening will be a great success because of the novel entertainment: a woman philosopher. Eryllus is concerned, however, because she has not yet appeared. Haterius calls for the herald, and discovers that it is he who has kept the philosopher away. Haterius angrily sends the herald off to intercept Euphrosyne before she should depart from Rome, and the herald, by his tearful entreaties, just manages to persuade Euphrosyne not to embark on the ship she is on the point of boarding when he finds her.

The story of Euphrosyne's recall offers several possibilities for discussion:

1 Why does Euphrosyne at first fail to gain admission? Possible answers: the private feud between Eryllus and the *praecō*; the power wielded by the *praecō*, though only a slave, at the *salūtātiō*; the practice, evidently normal, of gaining an entrée to the patron's house by bribery.
2 Why had Eryllus sent for a philosopher? It happens that she is to provide entertainment at the birthday party. Neither Eryllus nor Haterius shows the slightest interest in philosophy as such; Eryllus' second speech makes it clear he has summoned Euphrosyne because philosophy is fashionable. You may here wish to introduce some of the material below on the philosophies popular during the early Empire.
3 Why does Haterius agree to Eryllus' suggestion of a philosopher? He suspects all philosophers of being old and stern, but when Eryllus promises a philosopher who is young and female, Haterius enthusiastically agrees.

The background material (pp. 220–21) contains examples of questions inquired into by Greek and Roman philosophers. Add others: "What is justice?" "How should a city be governed?" "How can we tell truth from falsehood?" and above all "How ought human beings to behave?" In first-century Rome, the philosopher was not only (or not at all) a contemplative inquirer but a public entertainer, sometimes performing literally on the street corner, where he combined the roles of teacher, preacher, and salesman in a manner not unlike that of the modern Hindu guru proselytizing in the West (cf. Pliny, *Letters* I.10). The attitude of Romans to philosophers veered erratically between enthusiastic interest and violent hostility, resulting periodically in expulsion of all philosophers from Rome. Philosophy was often politically suspect; it supplied ideological backing for opponents of the principate (see pp. 221–22 of the students' textbook). But in A.D. 82, the year in which this stage is set, Epictetus, the famous Stoic, was teaching in Rome and philosophy was temporarily in favor.

Deponent verbs now appear in their finite form. The first four examples are accompanied by line drawings and glossed; all four verbs have already been met in participial form. With the aid of these clues, together with the storyline and your comprehension questions, students are often able to take this new grammar in their stride. In practice, students rarely mistranslate a deponent verb as if it were passive, since many examples are either intransitive or govern an obvious object. When the students themselves begin to notice and comment on the new feature, confirm their observations where appropriate, answer their questions, and let the discussion develop; but the initiative should come from students rather than from you.

All examples of deponent verbs in this story are in the perfect tense and nearly all are in the 3rd person. After the first four examples, they are left unglossed if they have previously been met in their participial form. The 1st person form *adeptus sum* (lines 12–13) has been glossed; check that this, together with the context, enables students to cope successfully with the unglossed *adeptus es* in line 18.

cēna Haterīī

Haterius' banquet is a lavish affair attended by a motley crowd of guests, including friends and clients, a man of consular rank, and sons of freedmen. The furnishings are elaborate, and various tricks are produced to impress and entertain the guests, but the central attraction of the evening is the philosopher Euphrosyne, whom Haterius does not present until after his guests have been well wined and dined. After her dramatic appearance, heralded by trumpet fanfare, Euphrosyne is invited to share some philosophy with the partygoers.

Haterius' dinner-guests are a heterogeneous group. Some are wealthy but lowborn; others are nobly born but poverty stricken. The presence of the consul Sabinus (who in real life was a cousin of the Emperor Domitian) is something of a coup for Haterius, especially in view of the latter's social ambitions, which students should be able to recall from Stage 30. Connect the drawing on p. 210 with the diagram of the placing of dinner guests in Unit 1, Stage 2, p. 31. For further information on this and other details of Roman dinner-parties, see Balsdon, *Life* pp. 32–53 and Paoli pp. 92–99.

Some details of the dinner are taken from Petronius, *Cena Trimalchionis*. Haterius' obsessive desire to impress his guests results in a vulgar display. Ask students, "What impression of himself is Haterius trying to make on his guests? By what methods does he try to do this?" Answers might include the bright-colored and expensive Tyrian-dyed cushions, the gold rings with jewels inset, the silver toothpick, the gimmick of the stuffed boar, the pretentiously labeled wine, and Haterius' boastful and elaborate introduction of Euphrosyne. Ask students whether all this makes a favorable impression on them; if not, why not? They may be able to suggest present-day examples of people trying to keep one-up on their neighbors.

Haterius (lines 32–33) associates Athens with philosophers rather in the way that California is conventionally associated with film stars or Canada with fur trappers; students can suggest other examples. To the first-century Roman, Athens was associated with philosophy mainly for its connection with Stoicism and Epicureanism.

The class will now be very familiar with the use of comprehension questions to explore a passage, and might usefully try to devise some of their own, e.g. each student being required to compose, say, up to three questions on lines 6–20 of the story for fellow students to answer.

Deponent verbs continue to be practiced; examples of the imperfect and pluperfect tenses are now included.

First Language Note (Deponent Verbs)

This note deals with the three tenses of deponent verbs which the students have so far met (imperfect, perfect, and pluperfect) and adds the present tense. This extension is easy for students, since the formation of the present is similar to that of the imperfect, and pluperfect tenses of deponent verbs to appear in Stages 32–34. The forms of the perfect tense in these stages are predominantly 3rd person, with occasional 1st and 2nd person examples, whose meaning is readily established from the context and by the analogy with the 3rd person forms and the perfect passive. The perfect and pluperfect tenses of deponent verbs are fully set out in the Unit 3 LI Section, p. 281.

Help students with the final examples in paragraph 3, which have no supporting context. Encourage them to refer back to paragraph 2 if they are hesitant about the tense. Drill the contrasts between singular and plural (*ingreditur—ingrediuntur, secūtus—secūtī erant*) and between 3rd person singular masculine and feminine in the perfect and pluperfect (*profectus erat—profecta erat*).

Students should study the language note in installments: paragraphs 1–3 in one lesson, paragraphs 4 and 5 in another. Paragraphs 4 and 5 make the point that students have already been meeting deponent verbs in their perfect participial form. The distinction between perfect active and perfect passive participles, familiar since Stages 21 and 22, is restated in the context of deponent and "ordinary" verbs. Students should translate the examples in paragraph 5. Elicit from them the observation that there is nothing about the form of a perfect participle which indicates whether it is active or passive; what matters is whether the verb is deponent or not.

philosophia

With frequent interruptions on the part of the guests, by now well in their cups, Euphrosyne attempts to tell a parable of Stoic philosophy, whose message is essentially that happiness has nothing to do with material or physical well-being, that one who maintains a calm spirit even in bitter adversity is in possession of true happiness. This idea is of course lost on the guests, who are not, for the most part, even listening. Euphrosyne, perceiving their incomprehension, is just about to try again with another parable, when a fight breaks out among the guests, and pandemonium ensues. Far from being distressed by this turn of events, Euphrosyne makes a well-staged exit, issuing as she goes an observation of trenchant irony about the Romans: masters in the material sense, but spiritually enslaved.

Some Suggested Questions

Does Sabinus (line 4) really not know what a poor man is? If he does know, why does he ask?

Why are the guests so startled (*obstupefactī*, line 17) by what Euphrosyne says in lines 14–15? Do you think her words were deliberately aimed at Haterius? (This question has no clear-cut answer. Euphrosyne's naïve manner in telling her fable might suggest that her remark is an innocent blunder, but her parting shot in line 55 hints at a rather sharper character.)

For what qualities does Euphrosyne praise the hero of her story? Do you think it is just a coincidence that he lives in the country, not in the city? (Points for consideration might include the farmer's disregard of riches and status, his constant hard work, lack of opportunities for profiteering, his careful management, and his reverence towards the gods, who affect his life more directly than the townsman's. Relate the latter point to the photographed wall-painting on p. 213 of the textbook, where the painter has introduced wayside shrines into the rural surroundings.

Why does Rabirius try to prevent Sabinus from making advances to Euphrosyne (*nōlī eam tangere!* line 46)?

What does Haterius try to do during the brawl? What were his original reasons for holding the party?

The questions in the students' textbook are open-ended and allow a variety of opinions. Students might work out the answers, without your help, perhaps divided up into half a dozen groups. Let some groups try question 1, and others question 2, before the entire class comes together for discussion under your direction.

Question 1. Students will already have realized that Euphrosyne and her audience are completely at cross purposes. She thinks they want to learn about Stoicism; their comments make it plain their interest lies elsewhere. For the kind of dinner-entertainment they might have been expecting, cf. the Unit 2, Stage 16 model sentences, the dancing-girls of Juvenal, *Satires* XI.162–64, or the coarse buffoons of Pliny, *Letters* IX.17. Euphrosyne also fails to present her theme in a way that interests her audience. She presents her sermon in story form (an approach that students may have experienced in Sabbath or Sunday School), but her manner is rather preachy. In any case, the way of life presented in her story has nothing in common with the lifestyle of her hearers.

Question 2. Harder than Question 1. Are the satisfactions of self-sufficiency, a clear conscience, and achievement through hard work deeper than the satisfaction of owning many material possessions? Are the poor man's satisfactions sufficient compensation for his misfortunes? Euphrosyne's paradox (lines 34–35) is expressed more sharply in Epicurus' aphorism (consistent with Stoicism as well as Epicureanism) that the wise man is happy even when on the rack (Diogenes Laertius, *Lives of Philosophers* X.118).

The story is suitable for reading aloud. Seven readers are required: narrator, Euphrosyne, Sabinus, Apollonius, Baebius, Rabirius, and Haterius, with optional party-noise from the rest of the class. If time allows, have students rehearse their reading and then record the final reading on a cassette for replay a month or two later. Thus they will practice their oral comprehension while simultaneously enjoying the sound of their own voices. Have students compare the expressiveness of their own recording with that of the version on the audiocassette which accompanies this course. Thus they will practice their oral comprehension still again.

If students have difficulty with Euphrosyne's last remark, take them through *en Rōmānī, dominī orbis terrārum* first, then ask which word in the final phrase makes a contrast with *dominī*, and when they have located *servī*, ask "What does she say the Romans are slaves of?" Invite idiomatic translations of *ventris Venerisque servī*.

All three stories in Stage 32 provide opportunities for reviewing the forms and uses of the subjunctive. Ask students to pick subjunctives from the text and explain why the subjunctive has been used in each instance.

Second Language Note (Gerundive of Obligation with Transitive Verbs)

The students have been meeting the gerundive in sentences like *mihi effugiendum est* for some time now, and should have little or no difficulty in bridging the transition to sentences like *nōbīs nāvis reficienda est*. Further discussion of the construction, in particular of the use of *est* and the agreement between noun and gerundive, should wait until students have met more examples (see below, pp. 161–62, under LI Section).

Drills and Suggestions for Further Practice

Exercise 1 Type: vocabulary
Grammatical point being practiced: verbal nouns in *-tus, -sus*

If you wish to add that nouns of this kind all belong to the fourth declension, you should not present the point as an abstraction, but demonstrate it in a practical way, e.g. by referring to the paradigm of *manus* in the Unit 3 LI Section p. 262 and asking students the Latin for "groans," "songs," "about the arrival," "about the return," etc. (Answers: *gemitūs, cantūs, dē adventū and dē reditū.*)

Exercise 2 Type: sentence composition from pool of Latin words
Grammatical points being practiced: nominative, genitive, and accusative, singular and plural: 3rd person singular and plural of imperfect and perfect.

This is the first time the genitive has been included in an exercise of this type. If you wish, allow students to choose words from further categories listed on the blackboard, e.g. *intereā, subitō* or other adverbs, or prepositional phrases like *in carcere, prope templum,* etc.

Exercise 3 Type: completion
Missing item: adjective
Test of accuracy: agreement of number, gender, and case
Grammatical point being practiced: agreement of noun and adjective

Remind students, if necessary, how an adjective agrees with its noun, particularly how agreement does not necessarily mean identity (or "rhyme") of endings. Ask why *līberālem* is the right answer in the example which precedes the exercise.

Exercise 4 Type: transformation
Grammatical point being practiced: imperfect subjunctive in indirect command

Among the specific points practiced in this exercise are the 1st and 3rd persons of the imperfect subjunctive, positive and negative commands, and the use of *sē* to refer back to the original speaker. To balance these demands on the student, generous help has been given with the formation of the imperfect subjunctive in the first four questions; but in questions 5 and 6 the students must carry through more of the transformation for themselves.

Begin, at this time, some consolidation work based on the Review Grammar in the Unit 3 LI Section. See below, pp. 157–65, for commentary.

Third Language Note (Future Participle)

Students should by now be sufficiently familiar with participles to make appropriate comment on the new feature for themselves. Ask why *cōnscēnsūram* and not *cōnscēnsūrus* is used in the third example in paragraph

1. While students are translating, encourage variations on "about to . . . " and "going to . . .," e.g. "on the point of . . ." and (with *esset* in indirect questions) "would . . ." Students should offer their own comments on the differences in form between perfect and future participles, set out in paragraph 3, and translate further examples of future participles, e.g. those from the checklists in Stages 31 and 32: *additūrus* (32); *appellātūrus* (32); *compositūrus* (32); *conductūrus* (32); *conversūrus* (32); *effūsūrus* (32); *neglēctūrus* (31); *oppressūrus* (32); *refectūrus* (31); *scissūrus* (32); *sectūrus* (31); *vectūrus* (31); *vīnctūrus* (31); *volūtūrus* (31).

The Background Material

Roman Society

Students often ask what would be the modern equivalents of sums of money like those mentioned in the text; but the difference between ancient and modern conditions makes comparison impossible. It is useless to compare, say, the cost of a bushel of wheat in the 1st century with its cost in the 20th, or the earnings of a Roman legionary with those of his modern counterpart, because such equations depend on unprovable assumptions about the economic context such as that the average first-century Roman spent on wheat the same proportion of his total personal expenditure as does the average twentieth-century American or Canadian. Useful comparisons can, however, be made *within* the first-century context. A client collecting his sportula on 100 days of the year would receive 625 sesterces (abbreviated "HS.") each year from this source. A laborer's daily wage is often estimated by a rather hazardous inference from *St. Matthew* XX.2 at 4 HS., in which case a laborer working 200 days out of a year would earn 800 HS. in that time. When we look at the upper end of the scale, the figures in the ancient evidence are usually capital sums; for purposes of comparison with the less well-off, they need to be converted into income. If (following Carcopino p. 79) we assume an interest rate of 5%, the 400,000 HS. which constituted the property qualification of an *eques* would earn 20,000 HS. a year—an income evidently regarded as modest but comfortable by Juvenal, in *Satires* IX.139–41 and XIV.332–26. The senatorial capital of 1 million HS. would earn 50,000 HS. a year; Pliny, who described himself, truthfully or otherwise, as "not rich," had capital of about 20 million HS. (income from interest: 1 million HS. a year), and his rival Regulus had three times as much. At the high extreme were exceptional persons like Seneca (capital of 300 million HS.) and the Emperor Claudius' freedman Narcissus (400 million HS.). For further details, see Balsdon, *Life* p. 354 and Carcopino pp. 79–81. From all these figures, a picture emerges of a dramatic disparity between rich and poor in Roman society. The students might discuss these inequalities, and the role of the patron–client system in reducing them; they might compare the role of taxation and government assistance as present-day methods of reducing inequalities.

The exact qualifications for membership of the *ōrdō senātōrius* and the *ōrdō equester* were extremely complicated, and the account in the students' textbook deliberately omits some of the complexities. If students ask about the difference between the *ōrdō senātōrius* and the Senate, it should be enough to say that a member of the senatorial class was not entitled to sit in the Senate unless and until he had reached the office of *quaestor*; an account of the *cursus honōrum* containing more information on this and other aspects of the senatorial career appears in Unit 4, Stage 37.

Two important sections of Roman society, freedmen and women, are not discussed in the textbook at this point, but are dealt with in Stage 34 and Unit 4, Stage 38 respectively.

Encourage students to link the present background material with that on patronage, and to think of ways in which patronage might enable people to move up the pyramid. Pliny's gift to Romatius Firmus (*Letters* I.19), enabling him to become an *eques*, provides one example; the bestowal of the honorary *lātus clāvus* by the emperor provides another. Among equestrians who refused promotion were Maecenas and Atticus in the first century B.C., and the men mentioned in Pliny, *Letters* I.14, III.2. Invite the class to suggest reasons for such refusals. These could include a wish to avoid the risks and toils of a political career at the higher level, or a preference for being a prominent *eques* rather than an undistinguished senator, or a wish to pursue an active commercial career, from which senators were barred by law and social convention.

Explore further the reference in the students' textbook (p. 220) to "casual and irregular employment." There was clearly an immense need for porters in Rome, especially in view of the restrictions on wheeled traffic (Stage 31, p. 201), and students might suggest examples, like dockworkers, luggage-carriers, *aquāriī*, and sedan-chair carriers. They might also recall some of the massive building projects mentioned earlier (Stage 30, p. 185), and this could lead to discussion of the role of the emperor as a provider of employment (cf. Suetonius, *Vespasian* 18).

Astrology, Philosophy, and Other Beliefs

On philosophy generally and Stoicism in particular, use some of the material above, pp. 124–25 and 127–28. Refer to the use of "stoic" in English for someone who endures pain or misfortune bravely and uncomplainingly. Explain the reference to Virtue as being "burned by the sun" (p. 221), since students are likely to associate sunburn with lolling lazily on a beach rather than toiling all day in the heat of a Mediterranean sun. Contrast the Romans' association of *umbra* with *ōtium* and link this with the illustration of Haterius relaxing under a tree (p. 207, bottom).

The Stoic tradition that Epictetus' lameness was caused by brutal treatment represents him as calmly saying to Epaphroditus, "If you go on doing that, you'll break my leg," and a moment later, equally calmly "I told you so." Although the anecdote is hardly convincing as biography (an alternative tradition ascribes Epictetus' lameness to rheumatism), it exemplifies well a characteristic Stoic attitude. Epictetus' master, Epaphroditus, appears as a prominent character in Stages 33 and 34.

Present some of Seneca's Stoic maxims to the class either in translation or in the original Latin, e.g. *magna servitus est magna fortuna* "great wealth is great slavery" (*ad Polybium de Consolatione* VI.5) and *qualis quisque sit, scies, si quemadmodum laudet, quemadmodum laudetur, aspexeris* "you can tell a man's character by noticing how he gives and receives praise" (*Epistulae Morales* LII.12). After you have guided the class to the meaning of the maxims, invite students to say whether they agree with them.

On astrology, see Unit 2 Manual, pp. 79 and 86. Pliny, *Letters* II.20, describes a fraudulent use of astrology and divination to wheedle a legacy from a dupe. Juvenal, *Satires* VI.565–91, colorfully denounces astrologers and their customers. Lewis and Reinhold II.409 has an example of an ancient horoscope. Discuss the reasons for astrology's perennial attraction. What makes people look at newspaper horoscopes? Do the students look at horoscopes? Do they believe in them?

Students might enjoy picking out the various signs of the zodiac which are clearly delineated on the relief shown on p. 221. The central roundel shows a ritual enactment of the slaying of the bull by Mithras. To the left and right stand Cautes and Cautopates: one with torch raised, symbolic of the Bull and the rising Sun, the other with torch pointing down, symbolic of the Scorpion and the setting Sun. The whole symbolized the struggle between the forces of good and evil, light and darkness, death and rebirth in nature.

The same ritual is shown in the drawing on p. 222, which is based on the reconstruction of the Carrawburgh Mithraeum in the Newcastle Museum of Antiquities. In a cavelike building, the initiates recline on benches flanking the aisle.

Suggestions for Further Work

1 "Imagine that you are Euphrosyne and have returned to Chrysogonus in Athens. Describe to him your impressions of Rome." Encourage students to include things that might have impressed Euphrosyne favorably as well as unfavorably, and to refer to Stages 29–31 as well as 32 for material.

2 Read extracts from Petronius' *Cena Trimalchionis* in translation. The

following sections all touch on topics dealt with or referred to in this Stage: 32–33 extravagance at dinner; 34 wine; 35, 39 astrology; 47, 49 stuffed pig; 53 acrobats. See also the werewolf story in 62 and Trimalchio's instructions about his tomb in 71.

3 "Write a continuation of Euphrosyne's lecture, keeping to her original theme that Virtue matters more than Pleasure or Riches, but using a story or argument which would have a better chance of persuading Haterius and his friends than Euphrosyne's 'poor man' story. If you wish, start from the idea of a 'rich man' story, as Euphrosyne intended to when she was interrupted."

Younger students will need considerable help and preliminary discussion with this difficult exercise. The theme "Money isn't honey" could be developed by painting a picture of a rich man, tormented by conscience, hated by those whom he exploits, friendless, or befriended only by spongers and toadies. Alternatively, the theme "You can't take it with you" could be explored. Refer to the custom of displaying a skeleton or similar *memento mori* at banquets (remind students of the skeleton mosaic in Unit 3, Stage 28, p. 133, and consult Petronius, *Cena* 34, and other references in Paoli p. 97), and to the parable of the rich fool in *St. Luke* XII.16–21.

Words and Phrases Checklist

Discuss the way in which *aequus* "level" came to mean both "calm" and "right, fair."

STAGE 33: PANTOMĪMUS

BRIEF OUTLINE

Reading passages / Background material	Christianity / entertainment
Chief grammatical points	future and future perfect active

NARRATIVE POINTS

Date	*Setting*	*Characters Introduced*	*Story Line*
A.D. 83	Rome: Haterius' house on the Esquiline hill, Domitian's palace on the Palatine hill	Tychicus (a Christian convert), Paris (famous pantomime actor), Myropnous (pipe-playing dwarf and Paris' accompanist), Epaphroditus (Domitian's freedman), Empress Domitia Augusta, Olympus (slave of Domitia)	Paris' performance at Haterius and Vitellia's house is interrupted by Tychicus, proclaiming Christ and Judgment Day. Paris gives a private performance for Empress Domitia, but they are interrupted by arrival of Epaphroditus and his soldiers. Paris escapes.

GRAMMATICAL POINTS

future and future perfect active (all persons)

e.g. *lūdī! lūdī! Imperātor ipse victōrī praemium dabit.*

future of *sum* (all persons)

e.g. *nūlla erit fuga.*

priusquam + subjunctive

e.g. *sed priusquam ille plūra ageret, vir quīdam statūrā brevī vultūque sevērō prōgressus magnā vōce silentium poposcit.*

increased incidence of ablative of description (see example immediately above)

conditional clauses (indicative)

e.g. *sī tē apud mē ille invēnerit, poenās certē dabis.*

SENTENCE PATTERN

continued use of complex sentence structure

e.g. *Domitia contrā, quae quamquam perterrita erat in lectō manēbat vultū compositō, Olympō imperāvit ut aliquōs versūs recitāret.*

Title Picture

This picture introduces the *pantomīmus* Paris and shows him with one of his masks. Note its closed mouth, which differentiates it from the types worn in other kinds of drama, e.g. the tragic mask shown as the title picture in Unit 1, Stage 5.

Model Sentences

Three forthcoming entertainments are announced: a performance by Paris in the theater; chariot races in the Circus; gladiatorial combats in the Colosseum.

The future tense is now introduced. The context, and the repeated *crās*, should be sufficient clues. Confirm the meaning of the new endings if students ask about it; otherwise postpone comment until students have read "Tychicus."

The pictures and captions contain many opportunities to discuss details of the three types of entertainment described: the nature of Paris' performance; the dwarf Myropnous who accompanies him on the double pipes; the central platform (*spīna*) around which the chariots in the Circus raced; the turning-posts (*mētae*—a word which students may recall from "lūdī fūnebrēs" in Unit 2, Stage 15); the seven eggs, one of which was removed at the end of each lap; the palm of victory; the feverish interest and involvement of the emperor (Domitian's enthusiasm for chariot-racing was obsessive; later in his reign he established two *factiōnēs* of his own, purple and gold); the contest of *rētiāriī* and *murmillōnēs* in the Colosseum. The performance of the *pantomīmus* appealed on the whole to a more cultivated taste than the combats in the Colosseum; some indication of this is suggested in the drawing of the respective *praecōnēs*. Chariot-racing was by far the most popular of the three entertainments. More details of all three, especially of the *pantomīmī*, appear in the stories and background material.

The following words are new: *pantomīmus, tībiīs, duodecim*, and *aurīgae*.

Tychicus

A performance by Paris in the garden of Haterius' villa (illustrated on p. 228), before Haterius' wife, Vitellia, and her friends, is interrupted by a fiery sermon from the Christian Tychicus, a client of Titus Flavius Clemens. (Whereas Tychicus is fictitious, Clemens is historical (see above, p. 6.).) Even as he is proselytizing, Tychicus is seized by Vitellia's slaves, dragged away, and finally thrown out of the garden, to the derisive shouts of all the audience but a few Christian sympathizers.

Tychicus' outburst is not directed at the content of Paris' performance but at the ecstatic, almost religious adulation lavished upon Paris himself by the audience. The denunciations which pour from Tychicus' lips may be contrasted with the story told by Euphrosyne in Stage 32 in which she propounds a frugal, disciplined quietism; the early Christians not only preached a gospel of peace but also proclaimed in fierce tones the imminent end of the world and the last judgment. Ask the students, "Of Euphrosyne's sermon and Tychicus' prophecy, which would be the more cheering message for persons who were poor and miserable?" Link the answer to this question with the final sentence of the story which hints that Christianity found support especially among the less wealthy and the downtrodden.

Tychicus' speech contains some echoes of the Vulgate, e.g. St. Paul, *I Thessalonians* IV.16–17; *ipse Dominus, in iussu, in voce archangeli, et in tuba Dei descendet de caelo; et mortui, qui in Christo sunt, resurgent primi. deinde nos, qui vivimus, qui relinquimur, simul rapiemur cum illis in nubibus obviam Domino in aëra, et sic semper cum Domino erimus* (from *Nova Vulgata . . . Editio*).

Use comprehension questions to deal with the difficult last sentence of the first paragraph: "Was Haterius there? Where had he gone? Why? What state was he in? Now translate the sentence."

priusquam is used with the subjunctive in line 11. Encourage the class, by attention to the context, to translate "Before he could . . ." rather than "Before he did . . ."

The future tense, introduced in the model sentences, is practiced further in Tychicus' speech, where *rēgnābit* (line 30) is pointedly contrasted with *nunc rēgnat*, and is anticipated by *in perpetuum*. Tychicus' next sentence begins with *mox*. The context, therefore, provides strong clues to futurity. Once students appreciate that Tychicus' protest is leading naturally to threats about future judgment, they will easily recognize the meaning of the new forms of the verb.

Development of ablative usages continues in this stage, with the inclusion of the descriptive phrases *statūra brevī* and *vultū sevērō* (lines 11–12).

in aulā Domitiānī

Paris, now at Domitian's palace, acts the story of Mars and Venus in a private performance for the empress Domitia, while his friend and accompanist, the dwarf Myropnous, plays the pipes. Suddenly Domitia's slave, Olympus, who has been watching the door, announces that Epaphroditus is approaching with a contingent of soldiers. An anxious exchange between Paris and Domitia follows, in which Domitia tries to persuade Paris to flee before they are found together by the malevolent Epaphroditus and punished. Paris, undaunted by this prospect, agrees only to hide, and climbs a pole to the compluvium, while Myropnous conceals himself behind a tapestry. In order to assume a semblance of calm, Domitia instructs Olympus to read to her.

Epaphroditus enters and immediately accuses Domitia of having hidden Paris somewhere in the room. She feigns innocence, so Epaphroditus orders his soldiers to search the whole room—including, when all else fails, the roof. At this Domitia is much alarmed, but the clever Myropnous saves the day: baiting Epaphroditus by twitching the fabric behind which he is hiding, he then pulls down onto Epaphroditus' head the whole assembly, including a heavy pole, which knocks the freedman senseless, whereupon Domitia, recovering her composure, orders the soldiers to take him away. As he is being dragged out, Paris delivers a brief sarcastic eulogy.

Paris was the most famous pantomime actor of his day, and a favorite in the imperial household (Juvenal, *Satires* VI.87 and VII.87–92). Commemorative hendecasyllabics by Martial, *Epigrams* XI.13, gracefully echoing Catullus 3.1, say that in Paris' tomb lie

ars et gratia, lusus et voluptas,
Romani decus et dolor theatri
atque omnes Veneres Cupidinesque . . .

He apparently came from Egypt and probably took the name Paris when he became a pantomime actor as it seems to have been a common stage-name.

Domitia, wife of Domitian, was the daughter of Nero's most successful general, Cn. Domitius Corbulo. Domitian married her in A.D. 70, and when he succeeded to the principate in A.D. 81, gave her the title Augusta. For her affair with Paris, see above, pp. 6–7.

Myropnous, the dwarf musician, belonged in real life to the late second century A.D. He is shown on a Florentine tombstone of that date (see Bieber pp. 236 and 305), playing the *aulos*, or double pipes. The relief clearly shows his large, misshapen head and crippled legs (a drawing based on it appears in Unit 4, Stage 40).

Epaphroditus (mentioned in passing in Stage 32 of the students' textbook; also above, pp. 6–7, 133) was a freedman who became the secretary in charge of petitions (*ā libellīs*), first of Nero and later of Domitian. He was one of the group of powerful ministers who were in charge of important government bureaus.

The language of the story is for the most part straightforward, and students might work through Part I independently working by themselves or in pairs or groups, writing down the answers to the printed comprehension questions. Subsequent class discussion might include a comparison of the students' answers to question 7, which is more wide-ranging and open-ended than the others. Compare Paris' reactions to the approach of Epaphroditus with those of Domitia; some students may feel that Paris cuts a more heroic figure than the nervous Domitia, others that there is something unnatural about his cold-blood.

Let the class comment on the nature of the roles taken by Paris in this and the previous story: sensual, emotional, physical, catering to mildly salacious or morbid tastes. For the love affair between Mars and Venus, see Homer, *Odyssey* VIII.266ff., and for a description of its enactment by a pantomime actor, based on an account by Lucian, *De Saltatione* 63, see pp. 238–39 of the students' textbook.

Other possible questions:

Why does Domitia come so close to tears (line 7)? Which part of the story might provoke this response from her? Or is she responding to the skill of the artist rather than anything in the story?
Why has Domitia asked Olympus to guard the door? Or what evidence is there in lines 8–9 that Domitia is either nervous or guilty about Paris' performance?
Why does Paris describe Epaphroditus as *psittacum Domitiānī* (line 21)?

Students might also note the great power of Epaphroditus. Although an ex-slave, he can frighten even the emperor's wife through his hostility and the activities of his spies.

The final sentence of Part I may cause difficulty; help students with easy comprehension questions of the kind set out above, p. 137, and in the Unit 3 LI Section, p. 296.

In Part II, students often detect Domitia's self-betrayal when she answers Epaphroditus' inquiry about an unnamed pantomimus with a mention of Paris. The question "Why does Domitia turn pale at Epaphroditus' words in line 12?" will test whether they are following the story. They might discuss the significance of the coin placed on the lips as Charon's fare (a picture of Charon and his boat appeared in Unit 3, Stage 22, p. 37) and also the quasi-sepulchral style of Paris' final ridicule of Epaphroditus. The formula *hīc iacet*, followed by three names, title, and cause of death, was common on tombstones. For simplification, *Augustī lībertus* has been placed here after the cognomen, rather than in its more usual position after the nomen.

The story provides plenty of opportunity for reviewing grammatical points. Compare *exstrūcta erat* (I, line 1) with *exstruēbātur* and *exstrūcta est*, and discuss the reason for the feminine ending *exstrūcta*. *cōnspicātī sumus* (I, line 11) and *perscrūtātī estis* (II, line 12) provide practice with the 1st and 2nd persons of deponent verbs; cf. *cōnspicātus sum*, *cōnspicātī erāmus*, and *perscrūtātus es*. Base further drill of deponent verbs on the introductory notes to Part Three of the LI Section (p. 312).

First Language Note (Future Tense)

Encourage students to comment on the paradigms. In particular, elicit the observation that the personal endings (*-ō* or *-m*, *-s*, *-t*, etc.) contain nothing that has not been met already in other tenses; that the endings of the second conjugation are easily recognized by analogy with the first, and those of the fourth by analogy with the third (a point you can easily demonstrate with examples like *portābunt/docēbunt*, *trahēmus/capiēmus/audiēmus*, etc.); that the 1st person singular form of the third and fourth conjugation is something of an "oddball."

Gather further examples on the lines of paragraph 4, numbers 6 and 7, e.g. *rogābimus, manēbunt, pugnābis, capiet, relinquētis, reveniam.* For the moment, do not mix examples of the future before they can profitably identify non-textualized examples of it.

The paradigms in the students' textbook follow the convention that in written English "shall" is used rather than "will" in 1st person forms if the context is one of futurity only and not of volition. Whether and to what extent the students, too, should follow this convention is a matter for your discretion. Do not allow, however, overemphasis of this English grammatical detail to distract attention from the main point of the language note, i.e. the new Latin endings and their significance.

Drills and Suggestions for Further Practice

Exercise 1 Type: vocabulary
Grammatical point being practiced: diminutives

The affectionate or contemptuous overtones of diminutives will be better understood by students when met in the context of a poem or speech than in a word-list. Nevertheless, you can illustrate the point if you are prepared to supply a context. For example, students may remember one of the previous occurrences of *homunculus* as used by Eutychus to Clemens (Unit 2, Stage 18, p. 102, line 23) or by Modestus to Bulbus (Unit 3, Stage 22, p. 30, line 2) or by Paris speaking of Epaphroditus in the present stage ("in aulā Domitiānī" I, line 28); ask them, "Does it refer only to size or does it suggest anything else about the attitude of the speaker?" Similarly, illustrate overtones of endearment or affection from *filiolus*, as used by a mother of her son.

The class might discuss *libellus*, in particular the development in its meaning from "little book" to "document" and so "petition"; hence *ā libellīs* "(secretary) in charge of petitions," the official title of Epaphroditus. You might set out the connection between *libellus* and the English word "libel."

Exercise 2 Type: completion
Missing item: participle
Test of accuracy: sense
Grammatical point being practiced: ablative absolute

Students must fill out the blanks not on the basis of morphology but by studying the situation described in the whole sentence; an incorrect choice will be either nonsensical (sentences 1, 2, 5, and 6) or inappropriate in the context (sentences 3 and 4). The sentences offer several opportunities to vary the translations of the ablative absolute, e.g. "When the signal was given . . .," "On the loss of his ship . . .," "Turning their backs . . .," etc.).

Exercise 3 Type: transformation
Grammatical point being practiced: present and imperfect passive

Some strictly aural work at this point will provide you with a check on the students' ability to comprehend without translating, as well as give them useful practice in listening as opposed to reading. Ask them to follow by ear alone (i.e. without books) while you read a story from an earlier stage or play a tape with a story which students previously recorded, e.g. "philosophia" of Stage 32 (see above, p. 129), pausing or pressing the pause key from time to time and checking by means of comprehension questions that the story is being followed, or by asking students to put up their hand every time a participle, or the name of a person or a place, is mentioned in a particular paragraph. Base similar practice on the "Longer sentences" section of the Unit 3 Review Grammar (pp. 295–96).

Second Language Note (Future Perfect Tense)

The examples in paragraphs 1 and 4, though designed primarily to introduce and practice the future perfect, also give further practice in the simple future and incidentally prepare for subsequent discussion of conditional clauses. If students ask whether the future perfect is used with any introductory word other than *sī*, give them an example with *cum*, e.g. *cum ad urbem advēnerō, amīcum tuum vīsitābō*. Contrast this use of *cum*, with reference to future time, with the more familiar use of *cum* with the subjunctive, where the reference is always to the past.

The Background Material

Discuss the section "Christianity" immediately after the story "Tychicus," discuss the section "Entertainment" at any point in the stage.

Christianity

Students might consider the reasons why the Christians were unpopular and occasionally persecuted. Do not focus on the legal basis of persecutions (a complex subject) but, rather, on the reasons for anti-Christian feeling. Prompt students to make observations like the following:

1 Most religions were able to co-exist happily with the official Roman religion and even identify their own gods with Roman ones (as Sulis, for example, was identified with Minerva), but such easy-going mutual

tolerance was quite unacceptable to the monotheistic Jews and Christians. The Christians' failure to worship the Roman gods made them unpopular, because of the belief that failure to sacrifice to the gods brought divine punishment to the state or society as a whole. St. Augustine, *De Civitate Dei* II.3, quotes a proverb: "No rain because of Christians," which illustrates why some people believed Christians were anti-social. Refusal to worship the Roman gods was not in itself a criminal offense, but it could be used as evidence that an accused person was a Christian, as Pliny's letter to Trajan (*Letters* X.96) shows.

2 Misinterpretation of phrases in the Christian liturgy like "Love one another" and "This is my body . . . take and eat . . ." gave rise to lurid suspicions of sexual orgies, incest, infanticide, and cannibalism.

3 The Roman authorities were generally suspicious and apprehensive of anything that looked like a secret society, fearing political subversion. This anxiety, often focusing on *collēgia*, is evident on several occasions in the Pliny–Trajan correspondence, most strikingly perhaps in *Letters* X.34, where such apprehensions led Trajan to veto the formation of a fire-brigade.

4 The peace was often disturbed by confrontations between Jews and Christians. *Acts* XXI has a lively account of a fracas of this kind. Suetonius, *Claudius* 25, when referring to Jews *impulsore Chresto assidue tumultuantes*, may have garbled another similar incident.

Nero's persecution of the Christians is described by Tacitus, *Annals* XV.44; the quotation from Trajan in the students' textbook is part of the famous exchange between Pliny and Trajan (Pliny, *Letters* X.96 and 97). The class might study these two letters in translation. St. Paul's reference to the *domus Caesaris*, mentioned on p. 237 of the students' textbook, is in *Philippians* IV.22. The Cambridge School Classics Project's *Roman World* material, Unit I, Book 1, *Lugdunum*, includes a description of the second-century persecution at Lyons, and other contemporary material abusing or defending Christians.

Continue the narrative in the textbook with a mention of later developments in Rome's relations with Christianity. By the Edict of Toleration (A.D. 311) and the Edict of Milan (A.D. 313), Christianity became a legal and officially tolerated religion. The first Christian emperor was Constantine (sole emperor A.D. 324–37), who nevertheless continued to support and participate in the official state religion; for example, his new city Constantinople was consecrecated with both Roman and Christian rites. Christianity became the official religion of the empire under Theodosius (A.D. 379–95).

On p. 237 is shown the central roundel of the mosaic pavement from the villa at Hinton St. Mary, Dorsetshire. It has now been relaid on the landing in front of the Roman Britain gallery in the British Museum, London, and it dates from the fourth century A.D. The bust is almost certainly intended to represent Christ, with the "chi-rho." This monogram was used by early Christians to refer to the name and person of Jesus Christ. It is composed of the first two letters of ΧΡΙΣΤΟΣ, the Greek form of "Christ."

Entertainment

Pantomime. For good detailed accounts, see Balsdon *Life* pp. 274ff. and Bieber pp. 165–66, 227 and 235–37. The word *pantomīmus* is used both of the dance and the dancer. He was partly a ballet dancer, partly a mimic. The orchestra accompanying him varied from small to huge; instruments included the double pipes (as played by Myropnous in the stories), lyre, trumpets, and *scabella* (wooden clappers operated with the foot). According to Lucian, *De Saltatione* 61, who wrote in the Antonine period and is our chief source on pantomimi, the dancer was required to know the whole of Homer, Hesiod, and the Greek tragedies. Lucian defends the art vigorously against criticisms of immorality and bad taste: "It exercises the body and sharpens the wits; it delights and instructs the spectator with stories from the past, charming his eye and ears with pipes and cymbals and graceful movement . . . it improves the moral character, too, by filling the audience with indignation at the deeds of the villain and pity for the sufferings of the victim" (*De Saltatione* 72). The degree of detail expected of a pantomimus' gestures, and the way in which strict conventions controlled his performance, are well illustrated by the anecdote of the unfortunate pantomimus who muddled the two sets of gestures for "Cronus devouring his children" and "Thyestes devouring his children" (Lucian, *De Saltatione* 80)!

Chariot-racing. Balsdon, *Life* pp. 314–24, gives a full and entertaining account, with a rich supply of anecdotes from which you can select a few for retelling. For a *dēfixiō* cursing charioteers and horses, see Unit 3, Stage 22, p.37 and above, pp. 36–37. Read and discuss Pliny's criticisms of chariot-racing (*Letters* IX.6), in particular his claims that racing is essentially repetitive and that spectators are less interested in the speed of the horses and the skills of the charioteers than in seeing their own team win. Ovid has a light-hearted description of watching the races with a female companion in *Amores* III.2, translated in the Cambridge School Classics Project *The Roman World* material, Unit II, item 14. An inscription commemorating the great charioteer Diocles (*I.L.S.* 5287, also *C.I.L.* VI. 10048) is translated in Dudley pp. 214–15 (but with wrong reference) and in Lewis and Reinhold II.230–32.

The questions on the chariot-racing relief on p. 240 are examples of the kinds that you can ask about many of the pictures. Remind students that such visual evidence is an important part of our knowledge of the Roman world. Encourage them to pick out details, like the reins tied tightly around the charioteer's body, and connect them with other information they have. Question 2 may cause difficulty. The conical pillars mark the turning-point (*mēta*) at the end of the central platform (*spīna*) and were about 15½ ft (4.75 m) high so that the charioteers could gauge their distance from the turn. The egg-shaped pinnacles on top are not the eggs that marked the number of laps completed, but part of the pillars. The inscription reads *ANNIAE ARESCVSA* but its significance is unknown. The relief dates from the first century A.D. and is now in the British Museum.

Gladiatorial combats. Students will remember much of the material in Unit 2, Stage 8. The gladiatorial salutation to the emperor, *moritūrī tē salūtāmus*, offers a link with the language note on the future participle in Stage 32, p. 218. Carcopino pp. 256ff. has a detailed account of the Colosseum.

Dinner entertainment. Balsdon *Life* pp. 44–49 and Paoli p. 98 are helpful. Use some of the following source material: Pliny, *Letters* IX.17 (cultured and coarse entertainment; Pliny is more tolerant towards the latter than might have been expected); Petronius, *Cena* 53 (acrobats); Pliny, *Letters* V.19 (the versatile entertainer Zosimus); Martial, *Epigrams* XI.52.16–18 (a host promises not to recite even if his guest does); Pliny, *Letters* III.5.11–12 (Pliny's uncle objects to an interruption at a reading); Juvenal, *Satires* XI.162–64 (Spanish dancing-girls); Horace, *Satires* II.8 (an extravagant meal); Pliny, *Letters* VII.24 (Ummidia Quadratilla); Horace, *Satires* I.5.50–70 (a slanging-match between two clowns).

Suggestions for Further Work

1 Explore the narrative of St. Paul's journeys in *Acts of the Apostles* for references to Roman law, government, and religion. In chapter 18, for example, the governor of Achaea, Seneca's brother Gallio, refuses to get involved in a Jewish-Christian dispute; in chapter 19, the silversmiths who sell souvenir models of the great temple of Diana at Ephesus protest vigorously against Paul's preaching; and in chapter 22, Paul lays claim to Roman citizenship, somewhat to the amazement of the Roman officer in charge who has obtained his own citizenship only through bribery; in chapter 24, Paul appears before Antonius Felix, brother of Claudius' freedman Pallas, who is mentioned in Stage 34 of the students' textbook; and in chapter 25, Paul appeals as a Roman citizen to Caesar against a sentence of flogging. Also, in chapter 10, Cornelius, a Roman centurion stationed at Caesarea, sympathized with Judaism and invited Peter to his house (cf. the possible connection with Judaism of the Emperor Domitian's cousin, T. Flavius Clemens, mentioned in Stage 33, p. 228, line 15 (see above, pp. 6 and 136)).

2 Compare Stoic and Christian attitudes to slavery by looking at

Seneca, *Epistulae Morales* 47 and Paul's letter to Philemon.

3 Younger students may be interested in some of the cryptograms used as signs and passwords by the early Christians, like the ROTAS-OPERA-TENET-AREPO-SATOR word-square (details in Augarde 32–33); also in other ancient Latin word puzzles listed by Augarde, Index, under "Latin."

4 "Write a description of a chariot-race, perhaps in the form of a running commentary on the race as it takes place." As an alternative, students may wish to record said description on an audiocassette tape, simulating the style of a radio commentator. They may get ideas for incidents from the Sidonius Apollinaris story described in Balsdon, *Life* p. 317. Follow this exercise with a reading in translation of the account of the chariot race in Sophocles, *Electra* 698–763.

5 College students with an interest in or majoring in communication studies might enjoy reading or hearing part of Quintilian's description of the gestures of an orator (*Institutio Oratoria* XI.3.92–106) and imitating each gesture as it is described.

6 Younger students might enjoy writing a scenario (annotated with steps, postures, and gestures) for a Roman-style pantomime, based on a Classical myth; making masks (with mouth closed) for each character; selecting background music from classical or rock recordings; and performing the pantomime for fellow students.

STAGE 34: LĪBERTUS

BRIEF OUTLINE

Reading passages	the freedman Epaphroditus
Background material	freedmen
Chief grammatical points	present passive infinitive 3rd person singular and plural, future passive

NARRATIVE POINTS

Date	*Setting*	*Characters Introduced*	*Story Line*
A.D. 83	Rome: Haterius' house on the Esquiline hill	Chione (slave-girl of Domitia)	Epaphroditus and Salvius (who has come back from Britain) lay a plan to entrap the lovers Domitia and Paris; by means of false messages, Domitia and Paris are ambushed together in Haterius' house. Myropnous tries to save them by setting a diversionary fire, but Paris dies in a fall from the roof, and Domitia gives herself away when she goes to embrace his body. Salvius is promised consulship by the emperor for his part in the plot, but Myropnous vows revenge. Domitia is sent away.

GRAMMATICAL POINTS

present passive infinitive (including deponent)

e.g. *tum Chionē, ē cubiculō dominae ēgressa, iussit lectīcam parārī et lectīcāriōs arcessī.*

3rd person singular and plural, future passive (including deponent)

e.g. *īnsidiae parābuntur; ambō capientur et pūnientur.*

dum + subjunctive

e.g. *in silentiō noctis diū exspectābat dum redīret ancilla.*

SENTENCE PATTERN

increased complexity in compound sentences

e.g. *tribūnus aliōs iussit aquam ferre ut flammās exstinguerent, aliōs gladiīs dēstrictīs omnēs domūs partēs perscrūtārī ut Paridem invenīrent.*

Title Picture

This shows Epaphroditus in his toga, which he became entitled to when he was freed. On the table behind is his *pilleus*, the felt cap worn by freedmen and freedwomen on ceremonial occasions.

ultiō Epaphrodītī

Epaphroditus seeks revenge for his humiliation in the previous stage. Although he has the support of the jealous emperor (who is suspicious of the relationship between Domitia and Paris), he cannot move openly. But Salvius, returning to Rome after an absence in Britain (see Unit 2 Manual, pp. 5 and 23–4), connives with him and engineers a suitable plan.

In this Stage, as in Stage 33, Epaphroditus appears as a figure of great power and influence. His network of spies and agents (*ministrī*) was mentioned in Stage 33 (p. 230); in the present Stage, he is able to call on the obedient services of the praetorian guard. Such power, wielded by an ex-slave, may surprise students. But although the events of Stage 34 are fictitious, there is considerable evidence for the power exercised by imperial freedmen. For example, in the crisis caused by the activities of Claudius' wife Messalina in A.D. 48, when Claudius was helpless, his freedman Narcissus took the responsibility for ordering Messalina's death (Tacitus, *Annals* XI.37); and his three chief freedmen sponsored the rival candidates for the positions of Claudius' next wife (*Annals* XII.1ff.).

The 3rd person form of the future passive is introduced in this story. Students normally are able to cope successfully, probably without realizing that it is new. The context helps, and the new form is a combination of two elements which they have already met: the future active, met in Stage 33, and the 3rd person passive ending *-ur*, met in Stage 29.

īnsidiae

Domitia receives a sudden summons to the house of her friend—Haterius' wife—Vitellia, who has supposedly fallen ill. Her slave girl Chione organizes transportation to Vitellia's house, and arranges for a doctor, and the party sets off on a dark night in the pouring rain. On arriving at Vitellia's house, they are startled to find it apparently deserted, although fixed up for a banquet. Domitia surmises that Vitellia was taken ill while dining, and begins to make her way to Vitellia's bedroom; she sends Chione back for a lamp, but the slave-girl never returns, and when Domitia, impatient, enters the bedroom, she finds it empty. At this point she begins to suspect a trap, but as she is hurrying through the empty rooms, in an attempt to flee, she is suddenly startled by the voice of Paris, who, having been lured to the house on the pretext of a dinner-party, is still unaware of the danger. Domitia, however, alerts him, and urges escape while possible.

Domitian's suspicions about Paris and Domitia's relationship, followed by Paris' death in A.D. 83 and the emperor's divorce of Domitia, are historical (see above, pp. 6–7; also Dio Cassius, *Roman History* LXVII.3), but the dramatic circumstances in the textbook are fictitious.

Most of the printed questions are straightforward, and students could attempt answering them while working independently, during the first reading of the passage (see above, p. 138, on "in aulā Domitiānī"). Add further questions as appropriate, e.g. "Why did Domitia pause on the threshold of Vitellia's room?" After question 5, invite students to discuss whether Domitia's explanation is probable, or even possible. Use question 9 to establish that Salvius' plan is not primarily a murder plot, but a "frame-up," already foreshadowed in lines 10–13 of "ultiō Epaphrodītī": Paris and Domitia are to be caught together in suspicious circumstances. Paris' earlier enactment of the discovered love affair of Mars and Venus is to be re-enacted, this time unwittingly and in grim earnest.

Ask students, "What mood or atmosphere is built up in lines 24–28?", then "Which words contribute to this mood?" Have students pick out *dēsertam* (line 24), *obscūrum* (line 26) and *in silentiō* (line 27). Suspense and menace are also built up through presentation of the central character Domitia at first in a group, then with only one companion, and finally alone. Such effects are employed with great skill by Tacitus, for example in *Annals* XIV.8 (Agrippina) and *Histories* III.84 (Vitellius), and by film directors like Alfred Hitchcock, e.g. in *Psycho*.

The story contains two examples of the present infinitive passive, and two deponent infinitives. (One example of a deponent infinitive, *ulcīscī*, has already appeared in the previous story, line 1.) In each case, let the context establish the sense; for example, *parārī* (line 6) is anticipated by *parāre* (line 5). Confirm, if necessary, that the *-ī* ending is an infinitive; students may well have noted the deponent infinitive already in the introduction of Part Three of the Unit 3 LI Section (p. 313). Further discussion should normally be postponed until students have read the language note.

The story is suited for review of participles. Ask students to spot participles in the text, and then say which case or number or gender they are, which noun they agree with, whether they are present, perfect active (deponent) or a perfect passive, or whether they are being used with *est* etc. to form a perfect tense.

Encourage idiomatic translation of the sentences involving *dum* (line 28) and *priusquam* (lines 33–34) with the subjunctive. (One example of *priusquam* appeared in Stage 33, "Tychicus," line 11.) Sentences involving *priusquam* and *dum* are included in the "Uses of the Subjunctive" section of the Unit 3 Review Grammar, p. 293, paragraph 7.

exitium

Domitia and Paris, along with Myropnous (who has come with Paris), discover Vitellia's house is surrounded by the praetorian guard. Paris remains optimistic about their chances of escape; through the back door, he suggests, and accordingly he orders Myropnous to barricade the front door. This Myropnous does, and when he hears the soldiers beginning to force entry using axes, he sets fire to the barricade.

Meanwhile, Paris and Domitia have found the back door guarded by two soldiers, whom Paris distracts by running around the garden, in order to allow Domitia to escape unnoticed. The ruse is successful until Paris climbs a tree to get onto the roof, loses his balance on the slippery roof-tiles, and crashes to his death. Domitia, hearing the crash and fearing the worst, abandons any thought of her own safety, and runs back to bid farewell to the body of her lover. Thus she is arrested by the soldiers, and the head of Paris is delivered to Epaphroditus: the freedman has achieved his revenge.

A fast pace is essential for the rapid narrative of this story. Read the story aloud or let students listen to the version on the audiocassette. If they can follow it easily, go over some of the easier sections with comprehension questions alone, without a formal translation. After completing the story, return to selected lines or sections for a more leisurely consideration of character (Myropnous, Domitia, Paris), historical details (e.g. the praetorian guard), or grammar (e.g. ablative absolute).

Insure that students realize that in the drawing on p. 248 Paris is posing behind the statue in order to hide from the praetorian guard (see II line 9). A blackboard plan of the house on the lines of the diagram in Stage 1, p. 15, and showing *iānua, ātrium, triclīnium, culīna, cubicula, hortus, postīcum* and *faucēs* (passage from *iānua* to *ātrium*) may also help them to visualize the sequence of events.

Some Suggested Questions on Part II

What unpleasant discovery did Paris and Domitia make at the back door?
Why did Paris dart out before dashing back into the garden?
Where did he hide?
What noise did Paris hear?
Where did Paris leap from? Where to? Why did he miss his footing?

Paris' agility in lines 18–20, already evident in Stage 33, p. 230, line 30 where he climbs quickly up the pillar, is a reminder that his profession as a pantomimus called for physical strength as well as artistic talent.

Approach the long sentence *intereā Domitia . . . venīret* (lines 23–24) at first with simple comprehension questions of the kind suggested above, p. 137 and in the Unit 3 Review Grammar p. 296, paragraph 4.

ingredientur (I, line 6) is the first example of a deponent verb in the future tense. Let students infer its meaning from the context. There are more examples in the next story.

First Language Note (Present Passive Infinitive)

Invite comments on paragraph 3, and if students do not themselves raise the question of the form of the third conjugation, ask them which passive infinitive is the odd one out.

Paragraph 5 deals with the deponent infinitive; comparison with paragraph 3 can be used to demonstrate the essential nature of the deponent verb. Ask, for example, "In what way is it like the active one?" Discussion like this puts the rather abstract statement that deponent verbs are passive in form but active in meaning into more intelligible terms.

honōrēs

Paris is dead, and Domitia has been sent out of Italy. In return for his services, Salvius is promised the consulship, and his career reaches a new peak. He did in fact hold the office sometime before A.D. 86. Epaphroditus is promised the *ōrnāmenta praetōria* (described in the students' textbook, p. 258). Myropnous, overhearing their conversation and learning of Salvius' responsibility for Paris' death, vows revenge.

After Domitian sent away Domitia, he took his niece Flavia Julia, widow of the consul Sabinus who attended Haterius' dinner-party in Stage 32, p. 209, into the palace as his mistress. But in A.D. 84, he took Domitia back, and thereafter both she and Julia lived together with him. Domitia was probably an accessory in the successful conspiracy in A.D. 96 against Domitian's life.

Epaphroditus was put to death on Domitian's orders in A.D. 95.

Students have already met two examples of a noun and participle in the dative case placed at the front of the sentence (*praecōnī regressō*, Stage 31, p. 193, lines 4–5; *Hateriō hoc rogantī*, Stage 32, p. 214, line 38). Refer them to these prior examples if they have difficulty with *Salviō aulam intrantī* in line 1 here.

Use *comitābitur* (line 10) to demonstrate to students that the context often makes it plain whether a particular verb is passive or deponent. Tell the class "There is a deponent verb *comitārī* and also an ordinary verb *comitāre*, both meaning 'accompany.' But it is clear from the sentence that *comitābitur* here means 'will accompany,' not 'will be accompanied.' Why?"

Discuss the word order *ē latebrīs rēpsit Myropnous* (lines 18–19) and contrast it with English translations.

pereat in the final line anticipates the introduction of the present subjunctive in Unit 4.

The consular symbols in the drawing on p. 251 are based on those shown on a series of coins issued by the consuls in the last years of the Republic. The *fascēs*, a bundle of rods tied with a red thong, was carried before a senior magistrate by a lictor. A consul had twelve lictors. The axe in each bundle was carried only outside Rome. The folding ivory *sella curūlis* was the chair of office on which a senior magistrate sat when conducting official business.

Second Language Note (3rd Person Singular and Plural, Future Passive)

As noted above, p. 147, the introduction of the future passive into the linguistic scheme develops naturally out of previous work and should cause little or no difficulty. Use comparison between the passive forms (paragraph 2) and the deponents (paragraph 4) to re-emphasize the point that the deponent verbs are exactly like the passive of ordinary verbs in form, differing from them only in meaning.

Drills

Exercise 1 Type: completion
Grammatical point being practiced: nouns in *-ātiō*

Use this exercise to exemplify the point that a Latin word normally has several different English translations. Thus, students may translate *coniūrātiō* either as "conspiracy" (by analogy with "conspire" in the adjacent column) or as "plot" (from recollection of its use in Unit 2, Stage 13, pp. 6–7); for *salūtātiō* they may produce the general term "greeting" (by analogy with the familiar *salūtāre*), or the specific term "morning visit," remembered from Stage 31, pp. 191ff. Encourage this flexibility; it will become crucial when students reach original Latin literature.

Exercise 2 Type: completion
Missing item: verb
Test of accuracy: correct number
Grammatical point being practiced: future tense

Exercise 3 Type: translation from English, using restricted pool of Latin words

Grammatical points being practiced: imperfect passive, indirect command, perfect passive participle, relative pronouns, ablative absolute

Exercise 4 Type: transformation
Grammatical point being praticed: perfect and pluperfect passive

This exercise is similar to Stage 33, exercise 3, but is more demanding, as it requires the manipulation of the pluperfect and perfect tenses. A 1st person example is included in sentences 5a and 5b.

The Background Material

There is much helpful information on freedmen and freedwomen in Crook (especially pp. 50–55) and Duff, and the number of relevant references in Latin inscriptions and literature is immense. Use a selection from the following material with students, elicit some points in discussion, present others, and choose particular students to research and report on other points. But do not overwhelm the class with detail.

The following sub-headings roughly follow the order in which the information is presented in the textbook:

Definition of freedman. Remind students of the difference between a freeborn man (*ingenuus*) and a freedman *(lībertus)*. Both are free *(līberī)*, but the *ingenuus* has always been so, whereas the *lībertus* has previously been a slave.

Legal status of freedmen. The legal status granted to ex-slaves was noticeably more generous in ancient Rome than in other slave-owning societies like classical Athens or the American South in the nineteenth century, since the freedman of a Roman citizen became a Roman citizen himself. Although an ex-slave's citizen rights were subject to the limitations described in the students' textbook, the limitations were relatively few and his children were wholly exempt from them.

Motives for manumission. These might be financial (see textbook, p. 255) or humanitarian. A slave might also be manumitted as a reward for long service or for some exceptional action (as was Felix, in Unit 1, Stage 6, p. 90, lines 19–20, for rescuing baby Quintus from the thief).

Obligations to ex-master. The technical term for the work performed by a freedman for his ex-master was *operae*; the number of days on which *operae* were to be performed was normally specified at the time of manumission. Strictly speaking, the *operae* of a freedman had to be of the same kind as he had performed while a slave and were to be performed only for the ex-master; Crook, pp. 52 and 192, notes some entertaining exceptions to this rule. *operae* came to mean not only "work" but "workers" (often "hired workers," hence the meaning "hired thugs" which students met in Unit 2, Stage 18).

A proposal that ex-masters should have the power to re-enslave undutiful freedmen was strongly supported in the Senate but rejected by Nero (Tacitus, *Annals* XIII.26–27).

Prejudice against freedmen. Dionysius of Halicarnassus (*Roman Antiquities* IV.24.4–8, quoted in Lewis and Reinhold II.53) is angry and abusive about freedmen; Persius (*Satires* V.78ff., quoted by Crook p. 50) is sour and sarcastic. Some of the material referred to above, pp. 122–23, in connection with "graded dinner-parties" indicates the readiness of some masters to humiliate their freedmen. Horace, *Satires* I.6, defends himself vigorously against those who sneered at him for being a freedman's son.

Opportunities for freedmen. It has been said that freedmen were "probably the most intelligent class of the community" (Buckland and McNair p. 186). Crook, p. 50, points out that this generalization underestimates the range which the class covered, but he adds: "nevertheless, the freedmen class certainly did include many people of high intelligence, literacy, energy, and ambition." Perhaps the freedmen who came off least well at manumission were those whose "assets" in the labor market had declined with the years—for example, those who had originally been purchased for their biceps or pretty face.

Freedmen's sons who achieved high status. These include Horace, the brutal ex-praetor Larcius Macedo (Pliny, *Letters* III.14), and Pertinax (emperor in A.D. 193).

The relief shown on p. 256 comes from Mariemont, Belgium. A lictor is touching the kneeling slave with a rod (*vindicta*). A slave already freed (on the left) is shaking hands with a fourth person, probably his master. Both slaves are wearing the *pilleus*.

You and your students should work together when interpreting the inscriptions in the students' textbook. The translations are as follows:

1 In memory of Titus Flavius Homerus, a generous ex-master, Titus Flavius Hyacinthus erected (this tomb). *C.I.L.* VI.18109

2 In memory of Julius Vitalis, a well-deserving freedman, his ex-master (erected this tomb)

3 Titus Flavius Eumolpus and Flavia Quinta built (this tomb) for themselves, their freedmen and freedwomen and their descendants. *C.I.L.* VI.18052

4 Titus Flavius Cerialis erected (this tomb) in memory of Flavia Philaenis his freedwoman and wife who served him well. *C.I.L.* VI.18017

Notice the abbreviations:

D.M.	*dīs mānibus*	"to the spirits of the departed"
B.M.	*bene merentī*	a conventional phrase meaning "who was a good man" or "who deserved this kindness"
B.M.F.	*bene merentī fēcit/fēcērunt*	

Imperial freedmen. These followed the normal rule of taking their ex-master's praenomen and nomen on manumission. Thus Epaphroditus, on being manumitted by Nero, would be known in full as Tiberius Claudius, Neronis Augusti libertus, Epaphroditus. A simplified version of this name and title is used in the students' textbook, Stage 33, p. 233.

The more power was concentrated in the hands of the emperor, the greater became the influence of the emperor's personal entourage. Augustus had used his slaves and freedmen as secretaries and clerks; Claudius went further by developing a "civil service," in which the various departments were headed by freedmen. In addition to the secretaries mentioned in the students' textbook, there were also secretaries *ā cognitiōnibus* (responsible for administration of judicial inquiries) and *ā studiīs* (libraries and literary services). The power of such men reached its peak under Claudius and Nero.

Pliny's indignant letters about Pallas are *Letters* VII.29 and VIII.6. The senatorial debate about the grant of *ōrnāmenta praetōria* to Pallas is described by Tacitus, *Annals* XII.53. Crook, p. 63, points out that the great fortunes of men like Pallas and Narcissus were subject to the rule that on a freedman's death a proportion of his property reverted to his ex-master (in this case, the emperor).

Imperial freedmen are often at the center of dramatic episodes in first-century Roman history. For example, the freedman Narcissus was sent to put an end to the mutiny of the army at Boulogne on the eve of the invasion of Britain in A.D. 43. According to Dio, *Roman History* LX.19, the soldiers' rebelliousness dissolved into mirth at the sight of an ex-slave giving orders from the general's tribunal; they greeted him with shouts of *"iō Saturnālia!,"* a reference to the festival at which slaves dressed up in their master's clothes. For the roles played by Claudius' freedmen at and after the death of Messalina, see above, p. 147. Tacitus, *Annals* XIV. 3–8, gives a vivid picture of the part played by the freedman Anicetus in the murder of Agrippina. A less dramatic, but remarkably long career was enjoyed by the imperial freedman (name unknown; his son was called Claudius Etruscus), born in Smyrna about A.D. 3, who served continuously (except for a brief period of exile in his old age) under ten successive emperors, from Tiberius to Domitian, and died in A.D. 92 (Statius, *Silvae* III.3).

Words and Phrases Checklist

In the second part of this checklist, a number of common deponent verbs are gathered together. Ask students to translate the three forms given for a particular verb, e.g. *cōnor, cōnārī, cōnātus sum;* then pick out for translation some examples from the forms given in the list, e.g. *sequī, hortātus sum, profectus sum, adipīscor*; finally, drill variations on them, e.g. *sequēbantur, hortātī erant, profectī estis, adipīscitur.*

The Language Information Section

This section, like the corresponding section for Unit 2, contains three parts called Review Grammar, Reference Grammar, and Complete Vocabulary.

Part One: Review Grammar (pp. 262–297) is intended as a review section to be studied by students only after they have completed (or nearly completed) the Unit. Students should begin work in the Review Grammar soon after they have reached Stage 33, postponing those sections which review Stages 33 and 34 until after they have finished the Stages. Although all the forms and the rules of sentence structure in Unit 3 are described briefly, the Review Grammar gives priority to numerous examples so that students can see the rules illustrated as well as described. Often, manipulation exercises are appended so that students can test their ability to apply the rules.

Part Two: Reference Grammar (pp. 298–311) presents students with access to complete paradigms of the Latin forms which they have learned by the end of Unit 3. (It includes some verb forms which have not yet been learned.) It is designed for older or linguistically more able students who may appreciate a bird's eye view of the grammar to be presented in Unit 3 and are capable of getting a feel for what the Latin in the Unit will be like. Do not confuse this feel for the language, however, with the actual mastery of it; mastery comes only with time and practice of language in context, followed by the consolidation which the Review Grammar—not the Reference Grammar—provides.

The Reference Grammar also contains longer and more formal descriptions of the rules of sentence structures in Unit 3 and a list of the Latin sentence patterns introduced in the Unit. These should be studied by students who are able enough to benefit from the more formal analysis of language after they have successfully completed work on the Stages and Review Grammar.

Part Three: Complete Vocabulary (pp. 312–38) contains all the words in the stories of Unit 3 and in the "Words and Phrases Checklists" in Unit 3 with their meanings. Its format is explained in the notes which preface this part (pp. 312–13). Emphasize paragraph 3, which describes the listing of verbs with up to four principal parts (e.g. pōnō, pōnere, posuī, positus *put, place, put up*), as perfect participles are first introduced in Stage 21 and students are now able to begin learning complete sets of principal parts. Also emphasize paragraph 4, which illustrates some of the different ways in which the conjugations form their perfect tense and perfect passive participle, as many students should now be able to begin differentiating verb forms among the four conjugations (or five, if you treat—as does this textbook—the third conjugation "-iō" as a separate conjugation).

The comments following are concerned with individual sub-sections of the Language Information Section. The sub-sections dealing with nouns, adjectives, and pronouns have now, with the inclusion of the ablative, virtually reached the final form in which they will appear in the Unit 4 LI Section. The sub-sections dealing with verbs, and with various syntactic points, now contain most of the commonest forms and constructions, but have still to be expanded in Unit 4 by the addition of various passive and subjunctive forms, and constructions like indirect statement and conditionals with the subjunctive.

PART ONE: Review Grammar

Nouns (pp. 262–64). The 4th and 5th declensions are now added on p. 262. Although students have already seen examples of the nominative and accusative in the text, the paradigms are now set out for the first time.

If students are worried by the appearance of two more noun types, point out that the 4th declension embraces a relatively small number of words and the 5th declension even fewer, and that the 5th declension completes the set. In the 5th declension, note that *diēs* m. is not typical of the gender of this declension, but *rēs* f. is.

Draw the attention of students to:

1 the presence, in many endings, of a common vowel: "u" in the 4th declension, and "e" in the 5th;
2 similarities between some cases of the 4th and the 2nd declensions (e.g. *manum* and *servum*) and between the 4th and the 3rd declensions (e.g. *manibus* and *cīvibus*).

Although the ablative forms are provided in the paradigms of all the declensions, note that the ablative case by itself, viz. without a preposition, is not introduced until Stage 28, where it is discussed in a language note. This is also the first stage where the use of the ablative after prepositions is formally discussed, although it has occurred in the text from the earliest Stages.

Supplement the exercises in paragraphs 2 and 3 with, for example:

Change from the singular to plural:

dominus amīcō cibum praebuit.
cubiculum servī prope culīnam erat.
captīvus manum ad custōdēs extendit.

Change from plural to singular:

pater <u>*iuvenibus*</u> *effigiem dēmōnstrāvit.*

mercātor <u>*nōmina nautārum*</u> *recitāvit.*

Paragraph 4 seeks to show, by practical demonstration rather than abstract statement, that the stem from which the oblique cases of 3rd declension nouns are formed does not necessarily appear in the nominative singular. When students have produced *duce, ducibus*, etc., have them translate some of the words in context, e.g. *mīlitēs, ā duce laudātī* . . . or *servī, itinere dēfessī* . . ., etc., thus reminding them of the function of the ablative and not leaving the examples as isolated words.

Drill similarly examples in other cases. Ask students to give the accusative singular and plural of assorted 3rd declension nouns (e.g. *flōs, iter, legiō, flūmen*), and thus help them review the identity of nominative and accusative forms of the neuter. In particular, drill the 3rd declension neuters which, in the nominative singular, look like a 2nd declension noun: *corpus* (28); *facinus* (26); *opus* (30); *scelus* (29); *tempus* (31).

For a suggested exercise on 4th declension nouns, see above, p. 157.

Adjectives (pp. 265–66). Lead the exercise in paragraph 4 orally, writing the students' suggestions on the blackboard. Extend it by asking them to express the noun, too, in Latin; or put on the blackboard the noun in Latin and ask them to supply the adjective in agreement with it, using the tables on p. 265. In four of the sentences (1, 3, 4, 7, 9–11, and 13–14), the noun and adjective are of different declensions, thereby reinforcing the point that agreement does not necessarily mean identity of ending.

Sentences 10 and 12 require ablatives. After students have completed the examples, ask them why the required case is ablative; some will remember the note on prepositions in Stage 28, p. 136 and perhaps recall which particular preposition would be used here, and some who have studied Latin from other textbooks will know the label, "ablative of agent." Extend the exercise with further oral work, using nouns and adjectives on pp. 262–63 and 265, including 4th and 5th declension nouns. If students ask about word order, confirm that noun + adjective is commoner than adjective + noun, but do not let this point distract their attention from the main topic, i.e. the correct endings.

Comparison of adjectives (pp. 267–68). Continue the sentences in paragraph 5 with more examples, perhaps mixed, to reinforce awareness of both ways of translating the superlative.

Pronouns (pp. 269–74). Paragraphs 2 and 5: *sē* and *ipse*. The contrast in their usage is not a problem when reading Latin for comprehension. Illustrate the difference by putting pairs of sentences on the blackboard, e.g.:

1a *Salvius ipse praemium Belimicō dedit.*

1b *prīncipēs sē Salviō trādidērunt.*

2a *captīvus perterritus sē necāvit.*
2b *custōdēs ipsī captīvōs necāvērunt.*
3a *Quīntus "pestis, furcifer, asine," sibi inquit.*
3b *Belimicus Agricolae ipsī multa ac falsa nūntiāvit.*

Paragraph 7: if students are asked to comment on *īdem*, they will probably say that *īdem* consists of the various forms of *is*, with *-dem* on the end. Confirm this, and encourage further comment. When they spot the exceptions to the rule (*eundem, eōrundem*, etc.), invite them to suggest reasons why these forms should have been used rather than the non-existent *eumdem, eōrumdem*, etc. Thus, prepare the way for some aspects of compound verbs which students will meet later, e.g. the combination of *cum* + *dō* to produce *condō*, *cum* + *dūcō* to produce *condūcō*, etc.

Paragraph 8: in this exercise, ask the class to translate the noun as well as the demonstrative in sentences 1–5.

Paragraph 9: the relative pronouns, *cuius* and *cui*, are now added to the paradigm. The sentences practice identifying the relative clause, the relative pronoun, and its antecedent. You may do this orally before students translate the sentences. The pattern contained in sentences 5 and 6, where the relative pronoun refers to an accusative noun in a main clause which does not have an expressed subject, may cause some difficulty. Examples of this construction in Unit 3 include:

fībulam, quam puella alia tibi dederat, Vilbiae trādidī. (Stage 22, p. 27, lines 13–14)
Vilbiam meam, quam valdē amō, auferre audēs? (Stage 22, p. 33, lines 27–28)
omnēs mīlitēs, quī Dumnorigem custōdīverant, poenās dare iussit. (Stage 24, p. 58, line 4)
amīcōs igitur, quibus maximē cōnfīdēbat, ad sē vocāvit. (Stage 28, p. 128, line 16)
ventrem, quī . . . dolēbat, prēnsāvit. (Stage 28, p. 132, lines 23–24)

Paragraph 10: the connecting relative. Students do not meet this until Stage 26. They often find it awkward at first. With younger students, *do not* review this use at the same time as other uses of the relative.

Regular Verbs (pp. 275–80). Some students may be discouraged by the quantity of verb morphology on these pages. Reassure them by making some of the following points:

1 Some parts of the verb are met much oftener than others; most of the forms which occur most frequently are already familiar to students (present, imperfect, perfect, and pluperfect indicative active; imperfect and pluperfect subjunctive active).
2 The personal endings of the verb's active forms differ very little from tense to tense. Show this by putting a present subjunctive like *audiāmus* on the blackboard, and demonstrate that although it is a part of the verb they have never seen before, they know, without being told,

whether it refers to "I," "you (sg. or pl.)," "s/he, it," "we," or "they."

3 The context of the sentence often makes the significance of the verb-ending obvious. The present subjunctive can again be used as an illustration. Put *in hōc theātrō adsumus ut fābulam spectēmus* on the blackboard, and demonstrate that anyone who can cope with the first four words will also get the rest of the sentence right, including the unfamiliar form *spectēmus*. Here weaker students who are unaware that *spectēmus* is spelled differently from *spectāmus* have less trouble than students with good memories!

In a reading course, as opposed to a composition course, there is no great virtue in requiring students to learn paradigms by heart; what matters is that they should be able to recognize the forms and translate them correctly in their reading, or (if confused) be able to find their way around the paradigms in a reference-work like the LI Section. But some students, still anxious about the large number of verb forms, may ask to be allowed to learn them. Explain to them that recognition matters more than memorization; stress the importance of being able to *translate* a form, not just recite it as part of a paradigm. Point out that not all tenses are of equal importance, so that there is much more point in learning, say, the imperfect than the future perfect. But it is merely doctrinaire to forbid students to learn paradigms. Their belief that memorization of paradigms will help them with their reading can sometimes be a self-fulfilling prophecy.

Indicative Active (pp. 275–76). In paragraph 1, the conjugation of *capiō*, paradigms of which have appeared from the Unit 1 LI Section onwards, causes few problems. If it does, illustrate the "double category" of this verb by comparing it with the imperfect tense of *audiō* and with the present tense of *trahō*. Other verbs like it, besides its compounds, are *cupiō*, *faciō*, and *rapiō*.

Paragraph 2: Do not explore the problem posed by the similarity between the 2nd conjugation's present tense and the 3rd and 4th conjugation's future tense until students have securely grasped the general principles behind the future tense's formation. For most students, postpone the problem until Unit 4.

Paragraph 3: Usually, conduct this exercise orally. Monitor the students' ability to find the correct translation for each item in the future-tense paradigms in paragraph 2. Make sure they know the meaning of each stem, and recognize the personal endings. Help them isolate the letters which mark the tense as future (-b-, -bi-, and -bu- in the first and second conjugations; -a-, -ē-, and -e- in the third and fourth conjugations).

Paragraph 4: In this and similar transformation exercises, students should translate, transform, and retranslate *each* word before moving on to the next; they should not work through the whole list translating, then again transforming etc., since the main purpose of the exercise is to help students associate change of form with change of meaning.

Indicative Passive (pp. 277–78). In paragraph 2, as a reminder that the 3rd person singular can also be translated by "she" or "it," invite students to improve on "he is being praised" for *laudātur*, and practice similar variations with the other examples. Be guided by the experience and confidence of the class in doing paragraphs 5 and 6. If students are very competent, or have reached a late stage of Unit 3, cover the paragraphs quickly as oral work. But if the students hesitate, give them ample time; let them discuss the examples among themselves in pairs or groups, and postpone if necessary the pluperfect example in paragraph 6 ("they had been carried"), which is the most difficult. Translate, then discuss the examples in paragraph 7. Drill further non-masculine forms of the participle, including some 3rd person singular examples where no subject is expressed and "she" or "it" has to be supplied (e.g. *laudāta est, dēlētum est,* etc.), and end with a discussion of one or two examples of other persons (e.g. *iussa sum, ductae estis,* etc.) where English lacks a differentiating pronoun.

If, in the later stages of a Unit, students are having problems with a particular morphological item, e.g. one of the passive tenses, have them go back and re-do an exercise from the LI Section which has been worked several days before. Insecure students can find this a very effective type of remedial work, but employ it sparingly because of the danger of boredom.

Subjunctive Active (p. 279). In paragraph 1, illustrate the importance of *context* in determining the correct translation of a given subjunctive, i.e. with *ut* or *cum*. You will find examples of sentences incorporating the subjunctive in the sub-section called "Uses of the Subjunctive" in the students' textbook, pp. 290–93.

Paragraph 2: This exercise, though ostensibly about the morphology of the subjunctive, provides helpful practice in a range of constructions met between Stages 24 and 27. Do not let students attempt it until late in the Unit, by which time you may ask, "Why is it subjunctive?"

Other Forms (pp. 279–80). Students should compare the paradigm of the present participle in paragraph 3 with that of *ingēns* on p. 265; compare the inflections of participles and gerundives in paragraphs 4–6 with those of *bonus* on p. 265.

Because there is no natural English equivalent to the Latin gerundive, the latter is here translated not in isolation, but in the context of complete sentences. If students ask questions like "What does *portandus* mean by itself?", say "having to be carried." Although such an answer has its drawbacks, especially when applied to impersonal uses like *currendum est,* it goes some way towards explaining the presence of *est* in *amphora portanda est*, and the agreement between *amphora* and *portanda*. Quote and explain some gerundives which have found their way into English, e.g. addenda, agenda, corrigenda, and the names Amanda and Miranda. Drill gerundives further in sentences where the agent is not expressed, e.g. *urbs dēlenda est.* Students have met one example of this sentence pattern (*Haterius . . . laudandus est)* in Stage 32, p. 214, line 23.

Deponent Verbs (pp. 281–82). This section is more advanced and more demanding than the language note on deponent verbs in Stage 32, 211–12; 1st and 2nd person forms have been included in the perfect and pluperfect tenses, and the practice in paragraphs 3 and 4 presupposes considerable familiarity with deponents. For easier practice of deponent verbs in this LI Section, see below, p. 167, on the Introduction to the "Complete Vocabulary" part.

When students attempt paragraph 5, ask them to find specific correspondences between the passive forms of *portō* and *trahō* and the forms of the two deponent verbs in paragraph 1 (e.g. *portātur—cōnātur; tractī erant—locūtī erant*) and encourage comment both on the similarity of form and on the extent of difference in meaning, e.g. "*-bantur* always indicates 'they' and is always imperfect; but if the verb is deponent it means 'they' were doing something, and if the verb is ordinary it means 'they' were having something done to them." Comment of this kind, however, will be more useful if it comes from students rather than from the teacher. Deponent verbs, though usually easy to cope with in reading, are often difficult to discuss. Comment from the teacher will be confusing if the students have not already grasped the point for themselves, and superfluous if they have.

The students' earlier experience of participles can be used to reinforce the comparison between "ordinary" and deponent verbs. Thus, put up the following examples on the blackboard:

parābātur he was being prepared	*cōnābātur* he was trying	
parātus erat he had been prepared	*cōnātus erat* he had tried	etc.

After students have discussed and compared these examples and their meanings, they should look again at the distinction drawn in Stages 21 and 22:

parātus having been prepared	*cōnātus* having tried	etc.

Students may be able to see for themselves how the difference between the participles fits into a general pattern of difference between "ordinary" and deponent verbs.

Anxious students may ask "How can I tell whether an ending like *-bantur* is passive or deponent?" On the whole, the later they raise this question, the more fully you can answer it, since an answer at a later stage can make use of the students' increased experience of, and familiarity with, deponents. Demonstrate that the sentence as a whole normally gives clues to the nature of the verb (ask students to compare *puella ē templō ēgrediēbātur* and *servus ad rēgem dūcēbātur*), that the "Complete Vocabulary" part of the LI Section will always supply an answer (illustrate with the threefold pattern of deponent-verb principal parts, e.g. *ēgredior, ēgredī, ēgressus sum*), and that students already know from experience whether some verbs are deponent or not (e.g. they can handle *ingressus est* correctly through familiarity with the active participle *ingressus*).

Irregular Verbs (pp. 282–84). If the students ask, confirm that there is no passive of *esse, posse, velle, nōlle* or (except for some isolated forms) *īre*.

These verbs provide a convenient opportunity for students to practice handling the various technical terms ("3rd person," "plural," "pluperfect," etc.). Ask students to describe assorted examples (*nōlam, fert, ībant, nōn vult, vellēmus*, etc.) in the way described in the Unit 2 LI Section, p. 183, paragraph 4. At the same time, require a translation; have students add the labels "indicative" and "subjunctive" if they have a good grasp of them.

On the rather difficult exercise in paragraph 3, see the comments above, p 160, on the similar exercise in paragraph 4 of "Verbs: *indicative active*."

Paragraph 5: drill further orally along these lines.

Uses of the Cases (p. 285). This section is intended primarily for students to refer to during their reading. It contains all the major case-usages encountered so far.

Uses of the Participle (pp. 286–89). In paragraph 4, 2nd part: younger students sometimes confuse the object of a transitive participle with the noun which the participle "describes." If they have already translated the participle correctly but cannot label it, ask "Which noun does the participle agree with?," then do some further work on the rules of agreement as set out in the next paragraph.

Paragraph 5: when students have translated these examples, ask them to classify the participle in terms of present, perfect active, or perfect passive. Extend this exercise orally by asking students to identify the case, number, and (where straightforward) gender of participles on this page and in the textbook stories.

Paragraph 7: vary the perfect participles here with other contextualized examples, e.g.:

nūntius ad rēgem ductus
nūntius ā castrīs profectus.

If you are reviewing this material early in the Unit, a student may ask,

"If *parātus* only means 'having been prepared,' how did the Romans say things like 'having prepared the dinner, the cook went to sleep'?" Such a question will allow you to prepare the way for the ablative absolute in Stage 31, by saying, "The Romans had various ways of putting sentences of that kind. One way was to say "with the dinner having been prepared, the cook went to sleep.' You will meet examples of this kind in Stage 31." At the moment, do not analyze further.

Paragraph 10: ask students whether each noun-and-participle pair is singular or plural.

Paragraph 11: encourage variety in translating ablative absolutes. When students have become more confident in handling these phrases, explore the meaning of the term "absolute" further (for suggestions for preliminary discussion, see above, pp. 114 and 118). Students could note the result of removing the noun-and-participle phrases from the sentences in paragraph 10.

Uses of the Subjunctive (pp. 290–93). Each paragraph states the Stage in which that particular use of the subjunctive is introduced. Be careful not to try to review a usage until students have met sufficient examples of it. Paragraph 3: encourage variety of translation of the purpose clause ("to," "in order to," or "so that").

Paragraph 6: encourage students to comment on the two illustrative sentences. The more they say about the idea of result in the one and the idea of purpose in the other, the more they will be assessing the meaning of the sentence as a whole.

Paragraph 7: younger students sometimes confuse indirect commands with purpose clauses. Do not be overly concerned; the meanings are adjacent and experience will produce more accurate discrimination. If students hesitate over the *ut* in, for example, *mīlitibus imperāvērunt ut plaustra reficerent*, ask the question, "'They ordered the soldiers . . . ;' how should the English sentence go on?"

Paragraph 8: if students are invited to comment on the examples of *priusquam* and *dum* used with the subjunctive, they may be able to discern, and express in their own words, the idea of "purpose" which underlies this construction. Bear in mind, however, that the students have not yet met *priusquam* (or *dum* in the sense of "until") with the indicative, and so have nothing with which to contrast the subjunctive use.

Longer Sentences (pp. 295–97). This section provides practice in the more complex sentence patterns developed in Stages 21–28. It presents three types and you may wish to be aware of them. If a type causes difficulty, make up more examples. The types are:

1 "branching" of one participial phrase or subordinate clause out of another. Examples are 1c, 4c, 7, and 10;
2 "nesting" of one participial phrase or subordinate clause inside

another. Examples are 2c, 5, 8, and 11;

3 "stringing" of two participial phrases or two subordinate clauses, each grammatically related to and dependent on the main clause but not to each other. Examples are 3c, 6c, 9, and 12.

Students have met "branching" and "nesting" from Stage 18 onwards, and "stringing" from Stage 20 onwards, in the form of subordinate clauses. In Unit 3, all three types have included participial phrases as well as subordinate clauses. But do not present this classification to younger students here, although they may consider it later. If students have trouble with paragraph 3, take them back to shorter versions of the sentence which is causing them trouble, or encourage them to read through the longer sentence twice before trying to translate it.

Paragraphs 4 and 5: the sentences in these paragraphs are all examples of "nesting." The examples vary the basic pattern in a number of ways: the subordinate clause sometimes precedes, sometimes interrupts, and sometimes follows the main clause; the subject of the main clause is sometimes the same as that of the subordinate clause, and sometimes different; and in some examples an extra subordinate clause is added. Encourage students to read each sentence in paragraph 5 twice before they try to translate it. If they have difficulties, use comprehension questions as in paragraph 4, or build up to each sentence through shorter sentences, as in paragraphs 1 and 2.

Use comprehension questions, of the kind printed in paragraph 4, when students are attempting unusually complex sentences in the textbook stories. See above, pp. 97 and 141 for additional examples.

Word Order (p. 294). If necessary, give students more practice in the deviations from "normal" word order (nominative + accusative + verb). Two of the commonest are: verb + nominative + accusative (practiced here) and accusative + nominative + verb (practiced in the Unit 2 LI Section, p. 185, paragraph 4).

Paragraph 5: while students are studying this note, invite comments. You may, if you wish, have students study this along with the Stage 28 language note (pp. 136–37 of the students' textbook) on prepositions. The note will enable students to express their comments in terms of "adjective + preposition + noun +" or "preposition + adjective + noun."

PART TWO: Reference Grammar

For complete paradigms of nouns, adjectives, and pronouns students are referred to the Review Grammar. The models of ordinary and irregular verbs charted in Sections V–VI (pp. 300–02) contain some forms which the students will either not have met or have met rarely, unless they have studied some Latin from textbooks which have an order of grammatical presentation different from that in this course. Older students, if they wish and can, may memorize some of the anticipatory forms when they first see them here.

The description of syntax in Sections VII–X (pp. 303–10) is provided largely for the benefit of older or extremely able students who can think about a language as well as comprehend it.

In Section VII, the summary descriptions of subordinate clauses are divided into *adverb clauses* and *noun clauses*, i.e. those (adverbial) which describe when, where, why, or how the main event in the sentence takes place, and those (nominal) which replace a noun, usually the direct object, in a sentence. Listed among the adverbial subordinate clauses are:

(1)	*cum*-clauses in the past	=“when” or “while”
(2A)	*dum*-clauses with indicative	=“while”
(2B)	*dum*-clauses with subjunctive	=“until”
(3)	purpose clauses (introduced by *ut, nē, quī,* or *ubi*)	=answer “why?” or “where?”
(4)	result clauses (introduced by *ut*)	=answer “how?”

Listed among the nominal subordinate clauses are:

(5)	indirect questions (introduced by interrogative pronoun, adjective, or adverb or with *num* or *utrum . . .an*)	=direct object after verb of asking, etc.
(6)	indirect commands (introduced by *ut* or *ne*)	= direct object after verb of ordering, persuading, warning, etc.

Section VIII focuses on participles, especially those forms new to Unit 3, the perfect participles, both passive and active (= deponent). The contrast between the *meanings* (the forms are similar) of the perfect passive and active participles is explained in sub-sections 1 and 2. In sub-section 3, perfect participles whose meanings are completed by prepositional phrases are described as *participial phrases.* Note that another form of participial phrase, the ablative absolute, is described in Section IX, sub-section 3 (Unit 3, p. 309).

In Section IX, the descriptions of the uses of the ablative case—the most complex of the cases in Latin—are organized as follows:

(1) Ablative with a Preposition
  (A) Ablative with *ā/ab, cum* (=with), *dē, ē/ex, in, prō*, and *sine*
  (B) Ablative of Agent: noun or pronoun in ablative with *ā/ab*
(2) Ablative without a Preposition: ablative of means or instrument
(3) Ablative Absolute.

Section X describes the gerundive, its forms and context, and, here, its nuance of obligation; gerundives not-of-obligation have been postponed until Unit 4.

Section XI lists, with examples, some of the most important sentence patterns which students have met in Unit 3. Students who know these patterns will have one more set (along with inflections and contextual fabric) of "clues" toward sentence meaning. Encourage younger students to identify these major patterns as they are reviewing the stories of Unit 3, especially the "nesting" and "stringing" patterns illustrated in Section XI.9. (p. 311). Older or more able students will be able to study or memorize the patterns before reading the stories and thus recognize examples when they first come to them.

PART THREE: Complete Vocabulary

Spend a little time helping the class to study the notes (pp. 312–13) which introduce this part; otherwise, they may misunderstand and/or misuse the vocabulary which follows (pp. 314–38). After students have studied Stages 21–22, ask invidual s to look up a verb and, with the help of the lexical meaning, translate each of the principal parts. Is the verb ordinary or deponent? How do you know? Intransitive or transitive? How do you know? Also, while students are translating stories in the Stages themselves, appoint a "secretary" for the class or for each group, whose duty it will be to look up problematic words and help the class decide on the correct translation of a particular form.

Other Aids

Make students aware very early in the course of the study aids included at the back of their textbooks, the "Guide to Characters and Places" (pp. 339–42), "Index of Cultural Topics" (pp. 343–44), "Index of Grammatical Topics" (pp. 345–46), and "Time Chart" (pp. 347–49). All of these will become increasingly useful when students try to consolidate their knowledge of Unit 3 at review or examination time.

Diagnostic Tests

For a discussion of the purpose of the diagnostic tests, and suggestions for their use, see the Unit 1 Teacher's Manual, p.110. The words and phrases in boldface are either new to students or have occurred infrequently in the reading material up to the Stage indicated.

Test 7

This test should be given after the class has finished Stage 22. Give the story to students in three separate parts, preferably in three consecutive periods.

Part I: Introduction

This should be translated orally and informally with the class, so that the students become familiar with the situation and context of the story. This will probably not take more than fifteen minutes at the end of a lesson.

amōrēs Modestī

Modestus, ubi Aquās Sūlis vīsitābat, multās puellās **adamāvit**, sed celeriter **dēseruit**. Scapha, filia mercātōris, prīma eum dēlectāvit. Modestus eī rosās dedit quās ex hortō Memoris **abstulerat**.

"volō tē hoc dōnum accipere," inquit, "quod puellam pulchriōrem quam tē numquam vīdī. sine tē vīvere nōn possum." 5

"ō Modeste," respondit Scapha **ērubēscēns**, "ego quoque tē **cōnspicāta**, statim adamāvī. volō dōnum parvum tibi dare, quod vir magnae **benignitātis** es."

ubi haec verba dīxit, gemmam pretiōsam Modestō dedit.

Part II: Written Translation

After a brief oral recapitulation of Part I, the students should be asked to translate Part II. Allow a whole period for this written translation.

postrīdiē Ampelīsca, **ōrnātrīx** perīta, ad fontem sacrum prōcēdēbat. 10 Modestus, eam **secūtus**, post columnam sē cēlāvit. Ampelīsca, deam precāta, postquam nōnnūllōs **sēstertiōs** in aquam iniēcit, ā fonte sacrō abībat. Modestus eī obstitit.

"ego tē nōn nōvī," inquit, "sed volō tē hoc dōnum accipere, quod puellam pulchriōrem quam tē numquam vīdī. sine tē vīvere nōn 15 possum."

haec verba locūtus, gemmam, quam ā Scaphā accēperat, eī dedit. Ampelīsca, maximē attonita, **prīmō** dōnum accipere nōlēbat, sed, ā Modestō **identidem** rogāta, cōnsēnsit.

tum Modestus "necesse est nōbīs," inquit, "iterum convenīre. multa alia dōna tibi dare volō."

"ō Modeste!" exclāmāvit Ampelīsca, "quam līberālis es! ego quoque tibi aliquid dare volō." 20

et ānulum aureum, quem in **digitō** habēbat, eī trādidit.

Part III: Comprehension Test

The passage and the comprehension questions should be given to students in the next Latin lesson. A points-scheme has been suggested but you may wish to award points differently.

post paucōs diēs, Modestus ē thermīs **ēgressus**, aliam puellam prope templum stantem cōnspexit. ubi eī appropinquāvit, 25

"hercle," inquit, "nōnne tū es dea Minerva ipsa?"

"minime," respondit puella, "ego sum Scintilla."

"et quid in hōc oppidō agis, Scintilla?" rogāvit Modestus.

"**ostreās** in forō vēndō," respondit Scintilla.

"quam fēlicēs sunt illae ostreae," inquit Modestus, "quod manūs 30 tuae eās **tangunt**."

tum ānulum aureum, quem ab Ampelīscā accēperat, Scintillae dedit.

"volō tē hoc dōnum accipere," inquit, "quod puellam pulchriōrem quam tē numquam vīdī. sine tē nōn vīvere possum." 35

Scintilla ānulum acceptum intentē spectāvit. subitō Modestum vehementer verberāre coepit.

"parce! parce!" clāmāvit Modestus. "cūr tū, cui ānulum dedī, mē pulsās?'

Scintilla īrāta respondit, "tē pulsō, quod ānulum agnōscō. 40 Ampelīsca, soror mea, mīlitī Rōmānō, quī amōrem **aeternum** prōmīsit, hunc ānulum dedit. tū es mīles iste. Ampelīsca, ā tē dēcepta, trīstissima est. nunc igitur tē pūniō."

Modestus, ā Scintillā ita verberātus, quam celerrimē effūgit.

		Points
1	Where had Modestus been? Where did he see the girl?	2
2	"nōnne tū es dea Minerva ipsa?" (line 27). Why do you think that Modestus said this to the girl?	2
3	What did the girl tell Modestus about herself?	2
4	Why did Modestus say the oysters were fortunate?	2
5	What present did Modestus give the girl? How had he gotten it?	2

6 Why was Modestus surprised by the girl's reaction? 2
7 Why did the girl recognize the present? 2
8 Why was Ampelisca "trīstissima" (line 44)? 2
9 What is the last thing we hear about Modestus in this story? 2
10 Having read all three parts of the story what have you learned about Modestus' character? 2

20

You may like to note how students are coping with the following features in particular:
neuter plurals: *haec verba* (line 9); *multa alia dōna* (21).
participial phrases: (i) perfect passive: *Ampelīsca . . . ā Modestō identidem rogāta* (17–18); *Ampelīsca, ā tē dēcepta* (42–43); (ii) perfect active: *Ampelīsca, deam precāta* (11–12); *haec verba locūtus* (18).
volō: with accusative and present infinitive *volō tē . . . accipere* (4 and 14), as contrasted with examples with present infinitive alone *volō . . . dare* (7); *ego . . . volō* (21–22).
relative clauses containing oblique cases of the relative pronoun: *quās . . . abstulerat* (3); *quam . . . accēperat* (16); *quem . . . habēbat* (23); *quem . . . accēperat* (32); *cui ānulum dedī* (38).
complex sentences: *Ampelīsca . . . abībat* (11–13); *haec . . . dedit* (17); *Ampelīsca . . . cōnsēnsit* (17–18).
position of dative: the test contains many examples of the dative. (particularly *eī*) in a variety of positions within the sentence; check that students can recognize their forms and functions.

Test 8

This test should be given after the class has finished Stage 26. Follow the same procedure as for Test 7.

Part I: Introduction: for Oral Translation

Agricola Calēdoniōs vincit
Agricola, cum Britanniam quīnque annōs administrāvisset, **contrā** Calēdoniōs bellum gerere **cōnstituit**. nāvēs igitur ēmīsit ut portūs barbarōrum explōrārent. ipse **simul** in Calēdoniam cum magnīs **cōpiīs** prōcessit.
Calēdoniī, ubi nāvēs Rōmānōrum vīdērunt, valdē commōtī, sē ad bellum parāvērunt. 5
Agricola, cum barbarīs appropinquāret, cōpiās suās in trēs partēs **dīvīsit**. barbarī, hoc cōnspicātī, in **nōnam** legiōnem, quae erat pars **invalidissima, noctū** impetum facere cōnstituērunt. castra ingressī,

cum custōdēs interfēcissent, mīlitēs dormientēs oppugnāvērunt. 10
Agricola, postquam ab **explōrātōribus** cognōvit quid accidisset, ad
castra cum novīs cōpiīs statim contendit. pugna erat **ātrōx**. tandem
barbarī, magnā cum difficultāte superātī, in silvās et **palūdēs**
effūgērunt.

Part II: Written translation

Before this is undertaken it will be helpful to review the military vocabulary of Part I and to make sure everyone is clear about the story so far.

post illam pugnam Rōmānī in ultimās partēs Calēdoniae 15
contendēbant. Calēdoniī, cum uxōrēs **līberōs**que in loca tūta
dūxissent, magnās **cōpiās** collēgērunt. ad montem Graupium
prōgressī, sē ad pugnam parāvērunt. tum Calgācus, prīnceps
Calēdoniōrum, quī erat vir summae virtūtis, haec verba dīxit:
"ō Calēdoniī, hodiē nōs prō **lībertāte patriae** pugnāmus; nam istī 20
Rōmānī omnēs aliōs Britannōs iam superāvērunt. Rōmānī, quī
numquam contentī sunt, omnēs hominēs vincere cupiunt; ad omnēs
partēs **orbīs terrārum** legiōnēs dūcunt; ab omnibus **gentibus**
pecūniam **opēs**que rapiunt; fēminās līberōsque in **servitūtem**
trahunt. necesse est **aut** Rōmānōs **expellere aut** prō lībertāte 25
pugnantēs perīre."

Part III: Comprehension Test

Calēdoniī, cum verba Calgācī audīvissent, vehementer plausērunt et
magnō cum clāmōre pugnam poposcērunt.
Agricola, quamquam Rōmānī quoque pugnāre valdē cupiēbant,
pauca dīcere **cōnstituit**: 30
"vōs mīlitēs Rōmānī, multōs labōrēs passī, tandem in ultimās
partēs Calēdoniae pervēnistis. vōs saepe, cum per silvās, per flūmina,
per montēs mēcum iter facerētis, **fīnem** labōrum vidēre nōn
poterātis. saepe **dubitābātis** num dī Rōmānīs favērent. hodiē tamen
tōta Britannia est nostra. vincite et barbarōs in mare **pellite**." 35
haec locūtus Agricola mīlitēs impetum facere iussit. Rōmānī
fortiter pugnābant, sed hostēs ferōciter resistēbant. multī **utrimque**
periērunt. Agricola ipse ex equō dēscendit ut **ante vexilla** cum
mīlitibus stāret. Rōmānī, cum hoc vīdissent, hostēs fortissimē
oppugnāvērunt et fugere coēgērunt. tum equitēs, ab Agricolā iussī, 40
multōs barbarōs fugientēs interfēcērunt. paucī ex illā pugnā
superfuērunt; **aliī** domōs suās incendērunt; **aliī** uxōrēs **līberōs**que
necāvērunt, quod nōlēbant eōs esse servōs Rōmānōrum. postrīdiē

Rōmānī nūllōs barbarōs invenīre poterant **nisi** mortuōs.

1	How did the Caledonii react to Calgacus' speech?	2
2	What were the feelings of the Roman troops before Agricola spoke to them (lines 29–30)?	1
3	Why had the Romans' march north been so difficult?	2
4	According to Agricola, what doubt had his men had about the gods (line 34)?	1
5	What did Agricola urge his men to do in the last sentence of his speech?	2
6	Which side attacked first? Give one reason for your answer.	2
7	What did Agricola do in the battle to encourage his men (lines 38–39)?	2
8	What was the result of his encouragement?	2
9	What job did Agricola give to the horsemen at the end of the battle?	1
10	What did the Caledonian survivors do after the battle (lines 42–43)?	2
11	"necāvērunt" (line 43): why did they do this?	1
12	Which word is given special emphasis in the last sentence? Why is this?	2
		20

Students may find the military content and the rhetorical style of the speeches in this passage more demanding than the straightforward narrative and dialogue of previous tests. Teachers may like to assess whether the students' grasp of morphology, syntax, and basic vocabulary is firm enough to help them overcome any problems presented by less familiar subject matter. The following features have been recently introduced in the course:

adjective + preposition + noun word order: *magnā cum difficultāte* (13); *magnō cum clāmōre (28)*.
cum with imperfect subjunctive: *cum . . . appropinquāret* (7).
cum with pluperfect subjunctive: *cum . . . interfēcissent* (10); *cum . . . dūxissent* (16–17).
indirect questions: *Agricola . . . accidisset* (11); *saepe . . . favērent* (34).
purpose clause: *nāvēs . . . explōrārent* (2–3); *Agricola . . . stāret* (38–39).

You may also like to check on students' ability to handle the numerous participial phrases in the passage and analyze whether they can distinguish correctly between the different cases, tenses, and voices of the participles.

Test 9

This test should be given after the class has finished Stage 28. Follow the same procedure as for Test 7.

Part I: Introduction: for Oral Translation

Modestus aegrōtat

ōlim Modestus et Strȳthiō cēnābant. cibus tamen quem coquus parāverat pessimus erat. subitō Modestus, coquum vehementer **dētestātus** cibum humī dēiēcit.

"iste coquus," inquit, "est **venēficus**. cibum pessimum nōbīs semper parat." 5

"cibum meliōrem comparāre nōn possumus," inquit Strȳthiō. "nam nūllam pecūniam habēmus, melius est perīre quam miserē vīvere."

Modestus, homō summae calliditātis, cum haec verba audīvisset, cōnsilium cēpit. Strȳthiōnem iussit amīcōs quaerere et haec nūntiāre, 10

"Modestus, amīcus noster cārissimus graviter **aegrōtat**. cum eum vīsitārem tam sollicitus erat ut dē testāmentō cōgitāret. ille tamen, quamquam gravī morbō **afflīctus**, maximē **sitit** et **ēsurit**. nōs igitur oportet eī cibum vīnumque ferre."

Part II: Written Translation

Strȳthiō, ā Modestō missus, amīcōs quaesīvit ut verba Modestī eīs 15 nūntiāret. cum Aulum et Pūblicum et Nigrīnam invēnisset tōtam rem nārrāvit.

Aulus, hīs verbīs dēceptus, sibi dīxit,

"volō Modestum mihi aliquid **lēgāre**. mihi necesse est Modestō dōnum splendidum dare." 20

itaque Aulus, amphoram vīnī optimī adeptus, ad cubiculum Modestī laetus contendit. Nigrīna et Pūblicus tamen trīstissimī erant. Nigrīna Modestō magnum **piscem** coquere cōnstituit. Pūblicus ad forum cucurrit ut **pānem** et **ōva** comparāret.

amīcī, ubi cubiculō, in quō Modestus iacēbat, appropinquābant, 25 gemitūs lacrimāsque audīvērunt, Strȳthiō, ē cubiculō ēgressus,

"morbus Modestī **ingravēscit**," inquit. "vōbīs melius est mihi dōna dare et discēdere."

cum amīcī discessissent sollicitī, Modestus et Strȳthiō rīdentēs magnificē cēnāvērunt. post cēnam Modestus tam **ēbrius** erat ut 30 multās hōrās dormīret.

postrīdiē amīcī ad cubiculum rediērunt, ut cognōscerent quid accidisset. Strȳthiō, **reditūs** amīcōrum ignārus, per castra

ambulābat. amīcī, in cubiculum ingressī, circumspectāvērunt.
Modestum immōtum in lectō iacentem vīdērunt. 35

Part III: Comprehension Test

"ēheu! mortuus est Modestus," inquit Nigrīna. lacrimīs sē dedit.

Aulus, nihil locūtus, testāmentum Modestī quaerēbat.

"amīcum fortissimum āmīsimus," inquit Pūblicus. "nōbīs decōrum est eum magnō cum honōre **sepelīre**."

Pūblicus statim ēgressus **libitīnāriō** imperāvit ut ad cubiculum 40 festīnāret. **brevī** tempore advēnērunt libitīnārius et quattuor servī, **arcam** ferentēs. tam gravis erat Modestus ut difficile esset servīs eum in arcam pōnere.

tandem servī Modestum in arcā positum magnā cum difficultāte in umerōs sustulērunt. libitīnārius ē cubiculō prīmus prōcēdēbat, post 45 eum amīcī; servī, ultimī ēgressī, arcam ferēbant.

Strӯthiō, ad cubiculum tandem regressus in libitīnārium violenter incurrit, quī attonitus in servōs incidit. servī arcam tenēre nōn poterant. magnō cum **fragōre** humī dēcidit arca. magnus clāmor erat. omnēs Strӯthiōnem vituperābant. 50

subitō vōcem **raucam** audīvērunt: "nōlīte clāmāre."

amīcī, cum tacitī **respexissent**, Modestum ex arcā surgentem vīdērunt.

"umbra est Modestī," inquit Nigrīna perterrita. "nōbīs fugiendum est." 55

fūgērunt aliī omnēs. Strӯthiō tamen adeō attonitus erat ut fugere nōn posset. Modestum sollicitus rogāvit num mortuus esset.

"minimē," respondit Modestus. "morbum, nōn mortem **simulāvī**. nunc tamen mihi nōn necesse est morbum simulāre: quod nimium vīnī cōnsūmpsī, **rē vērā** aegrōtō." 60

1	"mortuus est Modestus" (line 36). What do you think were the feelings of the three friends at this news? Give reasons for your answer.	3
2	How did the "libitīnārius" come to appear on the scene?	1
3	Whom did he bring with him?	1
4	What was their job? Why did they find it difficult on this occasion?	2
5	"magnō cum fragōre humī dēcidit arca" (line 49). First translate this sentence, and then explain in your own words what sequence of events had led to this happening.	2+3
6	To whom did the "vōx rauca" (line 51) belong?	1
7	What was he doing?	1
8	Which Latin word tells you that he was obeyed?	1

9	What did Nigrina think she was seeing?	1
10	What did she and her friends do then?	1
11	Why did Strythio not do the same thing?	1
12	In line 57 who asked the question?	1
13	From the last sentence do you conclude that the speaker is now (a) dead (b) pretending to be dead (c) pretending to be well (d) ill (e) pretending to be ill?	1
		20

You may like to note how the students are coping with the following features in particular:

vocabulary: most of the vocabulary in this passage should be familiar and several "obvious" words have not been glossed, although they have not occurred in the checklists so far. See whether the students can connect *miserē* (7) with the familiar *miser, calliditās* (9) with *callidus; regressus* (47) with *ēgressus, ingressus; incurrit* (48) with *currō.*
extended participial phrases: *amphoram vīnī optimī adeptus* (21); *reditūs amīcōrum ignārus* (33).
participial phrases containing ablatives: *gravī morbō afflīctus* (13); *hīs verbīs dēceptus* (18).
result clauses: *cum . . . cōgitāret* (11–12); *post cēnam . . . dormīret* (30–31); *tam gravis . . . pōnere* (42–43); *Strȳthiō . . . nōn posset* (56–57).
indirect question: *postrīdiē . . . accidisset* (32–33).
connecting relative: *quī . . . incidit* (48).
"nesting": *amīcī . . . audīvērunt* (25–26).
"branching": *postrīdiē . . . accidisset* (32–33).

Test 10

This test should be given after the class has finished Stage 31. The following procedure is suggested.

Part I: Written Translation

You may like to set the scene for this story by referring to the picture on p. 149 and the map on p. 199 of Unit 3.

senex

in Viā Sacrā prope amphitheātrum Flāvium stābat senex **pauperrimus**. vultus eius pallidus erat, tunica sordida, pedēs **nūdī**. parvam **cistam** manū tenēbat in quā pauca **sulphurāta** posita erant.

"sulphurāta! sulphurāta!" exclāmāvit vōce **raucā**.
ingēns Rōmānōrum multitūdō eum praeterībat: senātōrēs, multīs 5
comitantibus clientibus, ad **cūriam** contendēbant ut **ōrātiōnem**
Imperātōris audīrent; **ōrātōrēs** ad **iūdicia**, sacerdōtēs ad templa
ībant; fēminae dīvitēs ad vīllās familiārium **lectīcīs** vehēbantur,
mercātōrēs per viam prōcēdentēs ab amīcīs salūtābantur; servī,
ingentēs **sarcinās** portantēs, ā dominīs incitābantur. omnēs, negōtiō 10
occupātī, clāmōrēs senis neglegēbant.
tandem sōle **occidente** senex ad rīpam flūminis abīre cōnstituit ut
locum quaereret ubi dormīret. cum Subūram trānsīret, subitō iuvenis
ēbrius, ē tabernā cum duōbus servīs ēgressus, senī obstitit.
"sceleste!" exclāmāvit iuvenis. "tē nōn decet iuvenem nōbilem 15
impedīre."
tum servīs imperāvit ut senem verberārent. senex, ā servīs
verberātus, humī dēcidit exanimātus.

Part II: Comprehension Test

This passage and the comprehension questions should be given to students in the next Latin lesson. A points-scheme has been suggested but you may wish to award points differently.

senex tandem **aegrē** surrēxit. cum **sulphurāta** humī dispersa
colligeret **crumēnam**, quae ā iuvene **omissa erat**, cōnspexit. 20
crumēna dēnāriīs plēna erat. senex magnō **gaudiō** affectus est.
tabernam ingressus caupōnem iussit cēnam splendidam parāre.
senex, cēnā cōnsūmptā, ad flūmen prōgressus prope pontem
Fabricium **cōnsēdit**. dēnāriōs ē crumēnā extractōs **identidem**
laetissimus numerābat. dēnique, cum crumēnām summā cūrā 25
cēlāvisset nē fūrēs eam invenīrent, obdormīvit.
quamquam dēfessus erat, nōn **sēcūrus** dormiēbat. nam **in somnīs**
sē vidēbat in iūdiciō stantem; ab illō iuvene **ēbriō fūrtī** accūsābātur;
tum **convictus** et ad mortem damnātus, ad carcerem trahēbātur;
subitō ē somnō excitātus est, vehementer tremēns. adeō perterritus 30
erat ut pecūniam, quam nūper comparāverat, **abicere** cōnstitueret.
itaque ad rīpam flūminis prōgressus, crumēnā in aquam abiectā,
"multō melius est," inquit, "pauper esse et sēcūrus dormīre quam
dīves esse et poenās timēre."
diē **illūcēscente**, ad Viam Sacram regressus, "sulphurāta! 35
sulphurāta!" exclāmāvit.
multī cīvēs eum praeterībant; aliī clāmōrēs eius neglegēbant; aliī
eum vituperāvērunt; nūllī sulphurāta ēmērunt. ille autem vītam
miserrimam sēcūrus ferēbat.

1	What did the old man find? How did it come to be there? Why was he particularly pleased?	3
2	What did the find enable him to do?	1
3	"cēnā cōnsūmptā" (line 23): what did the old man do next?	2
4	"identidem . . . numerābat" (lines 24–25): give two reasons why you think the old man did this.	2
5	What did he do immediately before he fell asleep? Why?	2
6	Describe what happened in his dream.	5
7	Write down two Latin words that describe the effect of the dream on the old man. What did he do as a result of the dream?	3
8	What reason did he have for this action?	2
9	Where did he go at daybreak?	1
10	Which was the only group of passers-by to take any notice of him?	1
11	Which word in the last sentence sums up the attitude of the old man?	1
12	Do you think the old man made the right decision? Give your reasons.	2
		25

You may like to note how students are coping with the following features in particular:

ablative with adjective: *negōtiō occupātī* (lines 10–11); *crumēna dēnāriīs plēna erat* (21).
ablative with verbs: *manū tenēbat* (3); *exclāmāvit vōce raucā* (4); *lectīcīs vehēbantur* (8); *summā cūrā cēlāvisset* (25–26).
ablative absolute: *multīs comitantibus clientibus (5–6); sōle occidente* (12); *cēnā cōnsūmptā* (23); *crumēnā in aquam abiectā* (32).
3rd person singular and plural imperfect passive: *fēminae . . . vehēbantur* (8); *mercātōrēs . . . salūtābantur* (9); *servī . . . incitābantur* (9–10); *ab illō . . . trahēbātur* (28–29).
3rd person singular perfect passive: *subitō . . . excitātus est* (30).
3rd person singular and plural pluperfect passive: *posita erant* (3); *omissa erat* (20).
nē with subjunctive: *nē . . . invenīrent* (26).
ubi with subjunctive: *ubi dormīret* (13).
decet: tē nōn decet . . . impedīre (15–16).
omission of first of two verbs: *ōrātōrēs . . . ībant* (7–8).
"branching": *tandem . . . dormīret* (12–13); *dēnique . . . obdormīvit* (25–26).
"nesting": *adeō . . . cōnstitueret* (30–31).

Test 11

This test should be given after the class has finished Stage 34. Give the story to students in three separate parts, preferably in three consecutive periods.

Part I: Introduction: for Oral Translation

Agathyrsus et Cordus

erat prope amphitheātrum Flāvium īnsula altissima, quam
aedificāverat lībertus dīves, Agathyrsus nōmine. in hāc īnsulā erant
conclāvia spatiōsa et splendida ubi Agathyrsus ipse habitābat:
parietēs marmore ōrnātī erant; ubīque stābant statuae pretiōsae
quae ex Graeciā importātae erant. 5

in aliīs īnsulae partibus habitābant hominēs multō pauperiōrēs
quam Agathyrsus. pauperrimus omnium erat poēta, Cordus nōmine,
quī in **cēnāculō** sordidō sub **tegulīs** sitō habitābat. tam pauper erat
ut nihil habēret nisi lectum parvum paucōsque librōs. vīta eius erat
difficillima: **quotiēns pluerat**, aqua per multās **rīmās** cēnāculum 10
penetrābat. eum versūs scrībentem **vīcīnī rixīs** vexābant. eō absente,
mūrēs librōs avidē **rōdēbant.**

Part II: Written Translation

ōlim Cordus, in **cēnāculō** recumbēns, versūs scrībere cōnābātur.
subitō magnus clāmor in īnsulā **ortus est**. ille, quī **rixās vīcīnōrum**
audīre solēbat, clāmōrem neglexit quod intentē scrībēbat. mox tamen 15
maiōre clāmōre audītō, ad **fenestram** iit; prōspiciēns spectāculum
terribile vīdit: tōta īnsula flammīs cōnsūmēbātur. vīcīnī, ex īnsulīs
proximīs ēgressī, in viam conveniēbant. quī, simulac Cordum
cōnspicātī sunt,

"fuge, Corde! fuge!" exclāmāvērunt. "moritūrus es. nisi statim 20
dēscendēs, flammae tē dēvorābunt."

quibus clāmōribus audītīs, Cordus quam celerrimē dēscendit. tōta
īnsula **fūmō** iam complēbātur. tam dēnsus erat fūmus ut nihil vidērī
posset. Cordus, quamquam vix **spīrāre** poterat, in viam effūgit, ubi
ingēns turba convēnerat. mediā in turbā, Agathyrsus, vultū sevērō, 25
imperābat servīs ut flammās exstinguerent. aliī, iussīs neglectīs,
pavōre permōtī per viās fugiēbant; aliī immōtī stābant. incertī quid
facerent; aliī ad proximās īnsulās currēbant ut aquam peterent; sed
priusquam aqua comparārī posset, tōta īnsula flammīs cōnsūmpta
est. 30

Part III: Comprehension Test

amīcī Agathyrsī, cum audīvissent quid accidisset, ad eum contendērunt ut adiuvārent. omnēs spē favōris dōna magnifica eī dedērunt. paucīs diēbus, Agathyrsus tot statuās, mēnsās, lectōs accēpit ut plūra habēret quam anteā. mox in eō locō ubi īnsula sita erat domum novam sūmptuōsamque aedificārī iussit. dōna, quae ab amīcīs data erant, per conclāvia **disposuit**. 35

Cordus tamen, librīs lectōque incēnsīs, nihil habēbat neque ūlla dōna adeptus est. cum quondam per urbem **inops** errāret, servō Agathyrsī occurrit.

"nōnne dē Agathyrsī fraude audīvistī?" inquit servus. "ipse īnsulam **cōnsultō** incendit ut domum magnificam eōdem in locō sibi aedificāret. tot dōna accēpit ut tōtam domum sūmptuōsē ōrnāre posset. ēheu! fortūna scelestīs favet." 40

quibus rēbus audītīs Cordus magnā īrā incēnsus. "nōnne iste pūniēndus est?" inquit. "ego ipse fraudem eius omnibus patefaciam. sī tōtam rem versibus meīs nārrāverō, nēmō ab eō **posthāc** dēcipiētur." 45

itaque versūs dē fraude scrīptōs in omnibus urbis partibus recitāvit. mox omnibus Agathyrsus erat odiō. fraude iam patefactā, amīcī Agathyrsī tam īrātī erant ut ipsī domum novam **noctū** incenderent. 50

1	"quid accidisset" (line 31): what does this refer to?	1
2	"dōna magnifica" (line 32): what were they?	2
3	Which Latin words describe the friends' reason for helping Agathyrsus? Translate them.	2
4	What happened to the site on which the apartment building had stood?	2
5	What possessions did Cordus lose in the fire (line 37)?	1
6	Why could he not replace them?	2
7	What deception was Agathyrsus guilty of?	2
8	How did Cordus come to hear of it?	1
9	"fortūna scelestīs favet" (line 43): why was this a suitable thing to say at this point?	2
10	How did Cordus decide to punish Agathyrsus? What did he say his motive was?	3
11	"versūs dē fraude scrīptōs" (line 48): how did people get to know about them?	2
12	What did the friends of Agathyrsus feel about him? What action did they take?	2
13	Why do you think Agathyrsus was not content with life in an "īnsula"?	3
		25

You may like to note how students are coping with the following features in particular:

verbs: imperfect tense of deponents: *cōnābātur* (line 13); perfect tense of deponents: *ortus est* (14); *cōnspicātī sunt* (19); imperfect passive: *cōnsūmēbātur* (17); *complēbātur* (23);perfect passive: *cōnsūmpta est*(29–30); pluperfect passive: *ōrnātī erant*(4); *importātae erant* (5); *data erant* (36); present infinitive passive: *vidērī* (23); *comparārī* (29); *aedificārī* (35); future and future perfect active: *dēvorābunt* (21); *patefaciam* (46); *nārrāverō* (46); future passive: *dēcipiētur* (47).
ablative absolute: *eō absente* (11); *maiōre clāmōre audītō* (16); *quibus clāmōribus audītīs* (22); *iussīs neglectīs* (26); *librīs lectōque incēnsīs* (37).
connecting relative: *quī . . . exclāmāvērunt* (18–20); *quibus clāmōribus audītis* (22).
conditional: *sī . . . dēcipiētur* (46–47).
priusquam with subjunctive: *priusquam . . . posset* (29).
accusative + nominative + verb: *eum . . . vexābant* (11–12).

Appendix A: Cumulated List of Checklist Words

This list is an alphabetized listing of all words which appear in the checklists of Unit 1 (Stages 1–12), Unit 2 (Stages 13–20), and Unit 3 (Stages 21–34). Nouns and adjectives are listed as nominative singulars; verbs as infinitives.

The number in parentheses refers to the stage-number of the checklist in which the Latin word appears.

a

ā (="by") (21)
ā (="from") (17)
abesse (6)
abīre (10)
ac (28)
accidere (25)
accipere (10)
accūsāre (26)
ācriter (33)
ad (3)
addere (32)
adeō (27)
adesse (5)
adhūc (30)
adipīscī (22 & 34)
adīre (20)
aditus (27)
adiuvāre (21)
administrāre (23)
adstāre (24)
advenīre (13)
adventus (27)
adversus (32)
aedificāre (16)
aedificium (13)
aeger (13)
aequō animō (32)
aequus (32)
afficere (30)
agere (4)
agitāre (8)
agmen (15)
agnōscere (9)
agricola (5)
aliī . . . aliī (29)
aliquandō (29)
aliquid (18)
aliquis (25)
alius (15)
alter (13)
altus (31)
amāre (19)
ambō (30)
ambulāre (5)
amīcus (2)
āmittere (12)
amor (22)
amplectī (29 & 34)
ancilla (2)
angustus (31)
animus (17)
annus (21)
ante (31)
anteā (27)
antīquus (14)
ānulus (4)
aperīre (25)
appārēre (27)
appellāre (32)
appropinquāre (17)
apud (14)
aqua (15)
āra (17)
arcessere (20)
ardēre (27)
argenteus (14)
arrogantia (28)
ars (20)
ascendere (21)
at (33)
atque (28)
ātrium (1)
attonitus (14)
auctor (34)
auctōritās (24)
audācia (29)
audāx (24)
audēre (18)
audīre (5)
auferre (26)
aula (14)
aureus (22)
auris (20)
autem (25)
auxilium (16)
avārus (6)
avidē (22)
avis (32)

b

barbarus (21)
bellum (26)
bellum gerere (26)
bene (17)
beneficium (28)
benignus (17)
bibere (3)
bonus (16)
brevis (33)

c

caedere (19)
caelum (22)
callidus (10)
canis (1)
cantāre (13)
capere (10)
captīvus (25)
caput (18)
carcer (24)
carmen (29)
cārus (19)
castīgāre (19)
castra (25)
cāsus (32)
catēna (31)
cautē (19)
cēdere (23)
cēlāre (21)
celebrāre (9)
celeriter (9)
cēna (2)
cēnāre (7)
centum (28 & 33)
centuriō (7)
cēra (4)
certāmen (27)
certāre (33)
cēterī (13)
cibus (2)
cinis (12)
circum (21)
circumspectāre (3)
circumvenīre (29)
cīvis (9)
clāmāre (3)
clāmor (5)
clārus (23)
claudere (15)
cliēns (31)
coepisse (18)
cōgere (25)
cōgitāre (19)
cognōscere (18)
cohors (26)
colligere (26)
collocāre (20)
colloquium (24)
comes (27)
comitārī (34)
commemorāre (23)
commodus (15)
commōtus (26)
comparāre (19)
complēre (12)
compōnere (32)
comprehendere (24)
cōnārī (32 & 34)
condūcere (32)
cōnficere (19)
cōnfīdere (21)
conicere (33)
coniūrātiō (13)
conscendere (24)
cōnsentīre (16)
cōnsilium (16)
cōnsistere (18)
cōnspicārī (23 & 34)
cōnspicere (7)
constituere (28)
cōnsulātus (34)
cōnsulere (30)
cōnsūmere (8)
contendere (5)
contentus (10)
contrā (33)
convenīre (11)
convertere (32)
coquere (4)
coquus (1)
corōna (29)
corpus (28)
cotīdiē (14)
crās (33)
creāre (30)
crēdere (11)
crūdēlis (20)
cubiculum (6)
cum (= "when") (24)
cum (= "with") (7)
cupere (9)
cūr? (4)
cūra (23)
cūrāre (19)
currere (5)
cursus (29)
custōdīre (12)
custōs (13)

d

damnāre (34)
dare (9)
dē (= "about") (11)
dē (= "down from") (19)
dea (18)
dēbēre (15)
decem (20, 28, & 33)
decēre (27)
dēcidere (13)
decimus (33)
dēcipere (22)
decōrus (14)
dēfendere (19)
dēfessus (29)
dēicere (21)
deinde (19)
dēlectāre (16)
dēlēre (14)
dēmittere (30)
dēmōnstrāre (18)
dēnique (20)
dēnsus (12)
dēpōnere (25)
dērīdēre (16)
dēscendere (24)
dēserere (24)
dēsilīre (17)
dēsinere (25)
dēspērāre (17)
deus (14)
dī immortālēs (25)

dīcere (13)
dictāre (14)
diēs (9)
diēs nātālis (9)
difficilis (14)
dignitās (25)
dīligenter (14)
dīligentia (25)
dīligere (28)
dīmittere (16)
dīrus (22)
discēdere (18)
dissentīre (22)
diū (17)
dīves (30)
dīvitiae (30)
docēre (26)
doctus (20)
dolēre (28)
dolor (29)
domina (14)
dominus (2)
domus (20)
dōnum (14)
dormīre (2)
dubium (30)
ducentī (28 & 33)
dūcere (8)
dulcis (19)
dum (34)
duo (12, 20, 28, & 33)
dūrus (21)
dux (31)

e
ē (4)
ecce! (3)
efficere (21)
effigiēs (15)
effugere (16)
effundere (32)
ego (4)
ēgredī (24 & 34)
ēheu! (4)
ēicere (33)
ēligere (22)
emere (6)
ēmittere (9)
enim (23)
epistula (12)
eques (24)
equitāre (20)
equus (15)
errāre (23)
esse (1)
et (3)
et . . . et (33)
etiam (15)
euge! (5)
eum (8)
exanimātus (17)
excipere (33)
excitāre (13)
exclāmāre (10)
exercēre (9)
exīre (3)
exitium (22)
explicāre (25)
exspectāre (3)
exstinguere (34)
exstruere (30)
extrā (25)
extrahere (21)

f
faber (16)
fābula (5)
fābulam agere (5)
facere (7)
facile (8)
facilis (17)
facinus (26)
falsus (26)
familiāris (14)
favēre (11)
favor (31)
fax (27)
fēmina (5)
ferōciter (6)
ferōx (8)
ferre (9)
ferrum (29)
fessus (13)
festīnāre (6)
fēstus (30)
fidēlis (14)
fidēs (26)
fīlia (19)
fīlius (1)
flamma (12)
flōs (16)
fluere (19)
flūmen (24)
fōns (21)
fortasse (18)
forte (19)
fortis (6)
fortiter (12)
fortūna (18)
forum (3)
fossa (15)
frangere (15 & 18)
frāter (10)
fraus (31)
frūmentum (16)
frūstrā (12)
fuga (33)
fugere (12)
fulgēre (17)
fundere (22)
fundus (12)
fūr (6)
furēns (25)

g
gaudēre (27)
gaudium (34)
geminī (13)
gemitus (28)
gemma (17)
gēns (11)
gerere (23)

gladius (8)
grātiās agere (19)
gravis (21)
graviter (17)
gustāre (2)

h

habēre (4)
habitāre (8)
haerēre (17)
haesitāre (25)
haruspex (21)
hasta (17)
haud (34)
haudquāquam (31)
haurīre (13)
hercle! (10)
hērēs (28)
heri (7)
hic (8)
hīc (33)
hiems (20)
hodiē (5)
homō (9)
honor (23)
honōrāre (15)
hōra (21)
horreum (13)
hortārī (34)
hortus (1)
hospes (9)
hostis (22)
hūc (17)
humī (24)

i

iacere (3)
iacēre (12)
iactāre (22)
iam (12)
iānua (3)
ibi (18)
īdem (31)
identidem (32)
igitur (12)
ignārus (27)
ignāvus (8)
ignōscere (32)
ille (9)
illūc (19)
immemor (25)
imminēre (34)
immortālis (25)
immōtus (23)
impedīre (15)
imperāre (27)
imperātor (16)
imperium (10)
impetus (17)
impōnere (34)
in (1)
in animō volvere (31)
incēdere (29)
incendere (27)
incidere (12)
incipere (22)
incitāre (8)
indicium (34)
induere (23)
īnfāns (6)
īnfēlīx (21)
īnferre (20)
īnfestus (24)
ingenium (23)
ingēns (7)
ingredī (22 & 34)
inicere (22)
inimīcus (10)
iniūria (30)
inquit (4)
īnsānus (26)
īnsidiae (27)
īnspicere (9)
īnstruere (26)
īnsula (17)
intellegere (7)
intentē (6)
inter (16)
intereā (24)
interficere (13)
intrāre (2)
invenīre (10)
invītāre (11)
invītus (18)
iocus (27)
ipse (14)
īra (28)
īrātus (3)
īre (10)
irrumpere (20)
iste (14)
ita (16)
ita vērō (13)
itaque (17)
iter (19)
iterum (9)
iubēre (21)
iūdex (4)
iussum (27)
iuvenis (5)

l

labor (32)
labōrāre (1)
lacrima (22)
lacrimāre (7)
laedere (25)
laetus (2)
latēre (25)
latrō (17)
lātus (20)
laudāre (2)
lavāre (14)
lectīca (34)
lectus (15)
lēgātus (26)
legere (11)
legiō (25)
lēniter (33)
lentē (15)
leō (3)
libenter (18)

liber (10)
līberālis (11)
līberāre (20)
līberī (29)
lībertās (32)
lībertus (6)
lingua (28)
lītus (15)
locus (19)
longus (18)
loquī (23 & 34)
lūdus (30)
lūna (20)
lūx (29)

m

magister (30)
magnopere (24)
magnus (3)
mālle (29)
malus (28)
mandāre (28)
mandātum (23)
māne (19)
manēre (9)
manus (= "band") (27)
manus (= "hand") (18)
mare (17)
marītus (14)
māter (1)
maximē (24)
maximus (17)
medicus (20)
medius (9)
melior (16)
mendāx (4)
mēnsa (2)
mercātor (2)
metus (28)
meus (5)
mīles (18)
mīlia (28)
mīlle (28)
minimē! (11)
minimus (22)
mīrābilis (12)
miser (15)
mittere (12)
modo (34)
modus (23)
molestus (22)
monēre (22)
mōns (12)
morbus (21)
morī (34)
mors (20)
mortuus (7)
mōs (31)
movēre (33)
mox (9)
multī (5)
multitūdō (17)
multō (28)
multus (5)
mūrus (11)

n

nam (18)
nārrāre (7)
nāscī (34)
nātus (30)
nauta (15)
nāvigāre (16)
nāvis (3)
nē . . . quidem (32)
necāre (7)
necesse (14)
neglegēns (19)
neglegere (31)
negōtium (17)
negōtium agere (4)
nēmō (18)
neque . . . neque (24)
nescīre (25)
nihil (7)
nihilōminus (32)
nimis (30)
nimium (23)
nisi (33)
nōbilis (14)
nocēre (27)
nōlle (13)
nōmen (25)
nōn (3)
nōnāgintā (28 & 33)
nōnne? (16)
nōnnūllī (21)
nōnus (33)
nōs (10)
noster (11)
nōtus (9)
novem (20, 28, & 33)
nōvisse (19)
novus (13)
nox (18)
nūbēs (12)
nūllus (13)
num (26)
num? (14)
numerāre (13)
numerus (23)
numquam (17)
nunc (11)
nūntiāre (10)
nūntius (8)
nūper (21)
nusquam (24)

o

obscūrus (29)
obstāre (18)
obstupefacere (33)
obviam īre (34)
occīdere (28)
occupāre (26)
occupātus (21)
occurrere (27)
octāvus (33)
octō (20, 28, & 33)
octōgintā (28 & 33)

oculus (20)
ōdī (29)
odiō esse (33)
offerre (9)
ōlim (6)
omnīnō (30)
omnis (7)
opēs (28)
oportet (26)
oppidum (21)
opprimere (32)
oppugnāre (24)
optimē (12)
optimus (5)
opus (30)
ōrāre (31)
ōrdō (13)
ōrnāre (23)
ōs (= "face") (25)
ōsculum (27)
ostendere (9)
ōtiōsus (32)

p

paene (12)
pallēscere (30)
pallidus (28)
parāre (17)
parātus (16)
parcere (22)
parēns (20)
pārēre (23)
pars (18)
parvus (6)
patefacere (24)
pater (1)
patī (24 & 34)
patrōnus (31)
paucī (17)
paulīsper (9)
pauper (32)
pavor (30)
pāx (10)
pecūnia (4)
pendēre (34)
per (6)
perficere (29)
perfidia (26)
perfidus (24)
perīculōsus (18)
perīculum (19)
perīre (16)
perītus (21)
permōtus (32)
persuādēre (20)
perterritus (4)
pervenīre (17)
pēs (8)
pessimus (20)
pestis (7)
petere (= "attack") (5)
petere (= "beg for") (18)
placēre (11)
plaudere (5)
plaustrum (15)
plēnus (21)
plūrimī (19)
plūrimus (19)
plūs (21)
pōculum (7)
poena (25)
poenās dare (25)
poēta (4)
pompa (19)
pōnere (16)
pōns (24)
populus (29)
porta (8)
portāre (3)
portus (10)
poscere (19)
posse (13)
post (9)
posteā (18)
postquam (6)
postrēmō (18)
postrīdie (16)
postulāre (8)
potēns (23)
potestās (33)
praebēre (26)
praeceps (27)
praecō (31)
praeesse (15)
praeficere (28)
praemium (27)
praesidium (18)
praestāre (30)
praetereā (30)
praeterīre (31)
prāvus (23)
precārī (22 & 34)
precēs (20)
pretiōsus (14)
pretium (21)
prīmus (11 & 33)
prīnceps (15)
prīncipia (26)
prior (15)
prius (29)
priusquam (34)
prō (18)
prōcēdere (7)
procul (34)
prōcumbere (18)
proficīscī (32 & 34)
prōgredī (31 & 34)
prōmittere (11)
prope (7)
prōvincia (26)
proximus (27)
prūdentia (22)
pūblicus (31)
puella (5)
puer (8)
pugna (11)
pugnāre (8)
pulcher (7)
pulsāre (6)
pūnīre (15)

q
quadrāgintā (20, 28, & 33)
quaerere (4)
quālis (27)
quam (= "how") (14)
quam (= "than") (10)
quamquam (14)
quantus (22)
quārē? (30)
quārtus (33)
quasi (34)
quattuor (20, 28, & 33)
-que (14)
quī (15)
quia (32)
quicquam (28)
quīdam (32)
quiēs (29)
quīnquāgintā (20, 28, & 33)
quīnque (20, 28, & 33)
quīntus (33)
quis? (4)
quō? (18)
quō modō? (22)
quod (6)
quondam (7)
quoque (2)
quot (26)

r
rapere (11)
ratiōnēs (31)
rē vērā (32)
recipere (17)
recumbere (8)
recūsāre (18)
reddere (4)
redīre (15)
redūcere (29)
referre (26)
reficere (31)
rēgīna (33)
rēgnum (26)
regredī (23 & 34)
relinquere (20)
remedium (20)
rēs (6)
rēs adversae (32)
resistere (18)
respondēre (3)
retinēre (13)
revenīre (9)
revertī (34)
rēx (14)
rīdēre (3)
rīpa (24)
rogāre (7)
ruere (13)
rūrsus (25)

s
sacer (18)
sacerdōs (15)
saepe (8)
saevīre (18)
saevus (26)
saltāre (16)
salūs (29)
salūtāre (2)
salvē! (3)
sānē (26)
sanguis (8)
sapiēns (21)
satis (4)
saxum (15)
scelestus (25)
scelus (29)
scindere (32)
scīre (23)
scrībere (6)
sē (13)
secāre (31)
secundus (11 & 33)
sed (4)
sedēre (1)
sēdēs (30)
sella (14)
semper (10)
senātor (11)
senex (5)
sententia (10)
sentīre (12)
septem (20, 28, & 33)
septimus (33)
septuāgintā (28 & 33)
sepulcrum (30)
sequī (32 & 34)
serēnus (31)
sermō (20)
servāre (10)
servīre (29)
servus (1)
sevērus (33)
sex (20, 28, & 33)
sexāgintā (28 & 33)
sextus (33)
sī (26)
sīc (28)
sīcut (20)
signum (4)
silentium (27)
silva (8)
simulac (16)
sine (17)
sōl (30)
solēre (17)
sollicitus (11)
sōlus (10)
solvere (28)
sonitus (9)
sordidus (17)
soror (30)
sors (29)
spectāculum (8)
spectāre (5)
spērāre (31)
spernere (29)
spēs (28)

stāre (5)
statim (8)
statiō (25)
stola (19)
strēnuē (32)
strepitus (30)
stultus (11)
suāvis (25)
suāviter (13)
sub (27)
subitō (6)
subvenīre (32)
summus (16)
sūmptuōsus (32)
superāre (6)
superbus (31)
superesse (16)
surgere (3)
suscipere (21)
suspicārī (28 & 34)
suus (9)

t
taberna (3)
tacēre (10)
tacitē (7)
tacitus (27)
taedēre (27)
tālis (23)
tam (20)
tamen (7)
tamquam (23)
tandem (12)
tantum (24)
tantus (27)
tardus (22)
tēctum (33)
tempestās (30)
templum (12)
temptāre (20)
tempus (31)
tenebrae (34)
tenēre (15)
tergum (17)
terra (12)
terrēre (7)
tertius (11 & 33)
testāmentum (28)
testis (25)
timēre (12)
timor (30)
tollere (16)
tot (19)
tōtus (8)
trādere (9)
trahere (13)
trānsīre (24)
trēs (12, 20, 28, & 33)
tribūnus (26)
trīgintā (20, 28, & 33)
trīstis (24)
tū (4)
tuba (8)
tum (6)
turba (5)
tūtus (22)
tuus (6)

u
ubi (= "when") (14)
ubi (= "where") (5)
ubīque (31)
ultimus (26)
ultiō (34)
umbra (7)
umerus (19)
umquam (23)
unda (15)
unde (21)
undique (29)
ūnus (12, 20, 28, & 33)
urbs (5)
ut (= "as") (28)
ut (= "that") (26)
ūtilis (11)
utrum (33)
uxor (10)

v
valdē (7)
valē! (11)
vehementer (10)
vehere (31)
vel (34)
velle (13)
vēnātiō (8)
vēndere (4)
venēnum (23)
venia (23)
venīre (5)
ventus (28)
verberāre (11)
verbum (22)
vertere (16)
vērum (24)
vērus (32)
vester (29)
vestīmenta (34)
vexāre (19)
via (1)
victor (15)
vidēre (3)
vīgintī (20, 28, & 33)
vīlla (3)
vincere (15)
vincīre (31)
vīnum (3)
vir (11)
virtūs (22)
vīta (17)
vītāre (22)
vituperāre (6)
vīvere (19)
vīvus (29)
vix (19)
vocāre (4)
volvere (31)
vōs (10)
vōx (19)
vulnerāre (13)
vulnus (20)
vultus (31)

Appendix B: Cumulated List of Word-Search Words

As students approach the final Stages of Unit 3, review with them some of the basic vocabulary in the first three Unitrs, i.e. the words in the Checklists, by asking for the Latin parent word of the following English words, which they have studied in the Word-Search sections.

The following list contains all the Word-Search vocabulary from Units 1–3.

a
aberrant
acrimony
advent
adversary
advocate
affection
affiliate
agent
agitation
alien
allocate
altitude
ameliorate
amicable
ancillary
annually
aperture
apparition
appellation
approximate
ardent
audacious
audience
aural
auxiliary
avarice
aviation

b
barbaric
belligerent
beneficial
brevity

c
canine
captivate
casualty
centrifugal
civilization
cogitation
colloquy
commerce
commotion
compassion
complete
concatenate
concede
concerted
concomitant
confidence
conjure
consecutive
consensus
conservation
conspicuous
contented
contravene
convene
conversely
coronation
cubicle
curator
custodian

d
debt
decapitate
deciduous
delectable
delegate
delete
demonstrable
density
depose
depravity
deride
diligence
dire
disgust
dissolve
doctor
doleful
domesticate
domination
dormitory
dulcet

e
edifice
effect
effulgence

effusive
elocution
emit
endure
enumerate
equine
exercise
exhort
extemporaneous
extinct

f
fabulous
facilitate
feminine
ferocity
fidelity
flume
fortuitous
fracture
fraternal
fraudulent
frustrate
fugitive

h
homicide
horticulturalist
hospital
hostile

i
imbibe
imminent
impassive
impecunious
impede
imperial
imperious
impetuous
imprecation
impunity
incarcerate
inception
incident
incinerate
incite
incorporeal
incredible
indecorous
indignity
indubitably
infant
infidel
inhabit
inscribe
insidious
insuperable
intelligible
interrogation
invent
irate
irremediable
itinerant

j
judicial

l
laboratory
latent
latitude
laudable
lavatory
liberal
library
loquacious
ludicrous

m
magisterial
magnitude
malice
manually
marine
marital
maternity
militant
molest
monitor
morbid
mural

n
nascent
naval
nocturnal
nullify

o
obscurity
omnipotent
operate
opulent
ostensible

p
patronize
paucity
pendulous
perfidy
pessimist
pestilence
petition
placate
populous
portable
potentate
principal
procedure
procrastinate
progressive
provincial
pulse

r
recipient
regal
regress
reiterate
relinquish
repugnant

retard
revive
ridicule

s
sacrilege
salutary
sanguinary
sapient
satisfy
sedentary
sentence
service
servile
solicitude
sororal
spectacular
spectator
state
stultify
stupefaction
suave
suffuse
summit
surge

t
tacit
tedious
tempestuous
terrify
testify
total
transition
turbulent

u
ubiquitous
ultimate
undulate
utilitarian

v
vendor
venial
ventilate
veritable
vex
vitality
vulnerable

Appendix C: Summary of Changes from the North American Second Edition

General

The principles on which the North American Second Edition was designed remain the same for this Edition (see "Objectives of the Course," in the Unit 1 Teacher's Manual, pp. 5–6). The North American Third Edition is compatible with the North American Second Edition. In the Third Edition, however, the students' textbook has been written in American English throughout, with punctuation, spelling, and analogies in the American style. Many new photographs, mainly color ones, have been added. The chart showing the makeup of a Roman legion (p. 81) has been enlarged and clarified. Minor corrections have been made to several drawings (notably the altar of Sulis Minerva at Bath on p. 39, the *aquila* on p. 69, Modestus on p. 111).

Changes from the North American Second Edition of Units IIIA and IIIB include the following:

1 Units IIIA and IIIB, with the accompanying Language Information pamphlets, have been combined into one Unit, now called Unit 3, with an Arabic numeral to avoid confusion between the name of the textbook and "Latin III," the traditional name for third-year high-school Latin. In most high schools, Unit 3 will be used throughout the second year (=Latin II); in colleges and universities, during the second, intensive semester of Latin.

2 The students' material in Units IIIA and IIIB has been bound, with the two former Language Information pamphlets, into a single hardbound volume. There have been added a new Reference Grammar, which will provide students with an introductory overview of forms and rules ; an Index of Cultural Topics (formerly in the Units IIIA/IIIB Teacher's Manual, pp. 152–53); a new Index of Grammatical Topics; and a new Time Chart.

3 The contents of the two former Language Information pamphlets have been collated into a single Language Information Section. Part One of the Language Information Section has had its name changed from "About the language" to "Review Grammar"; the former Part Two, or the "Words and phrases" part, has been renamed the "Complete Vocabulary" and transferred to Part Three, thus making room for the completely new "Reference Grammar," which now becomes Part Two.

The "Guides to Characters and Places" from the two former Language Information pamphlets have been collated into a single Guide but still appear, as previously, immediately after the complete vocabulary.

4 Latin Names and Proper Adjectives are now glossed in sections separate from the other Latin words in the running vocabularies.

5 A new drill, called Word Search, follows the Words and Phrases Checklist in every Stage. This drill uses Latin words in the preceding checklist as clues so that students may match the given definitions with their correct English words.

6 The Teacher's Manual has been streamlined to make it more accessible. New charts outlining Narrative Points, Grammatical Points, and Sentence Patterns have been introduced into the beginning of each of the Stage Commentaries. The Bibliography has been updated. As there is now a Word Search drill in every Stage of the students' textbook, the lists of derivatives formerly in Appendix A of the Units IIIA/IIIB Teacher's Manual have been omitted.

Bibliography

Books marked with an asterisk (*) are suitable for use by junior or high school students: other books, by college or university students (or high school students under the teacher's guidance). Included are some recommended books which, though out of print (O.P.), may sometimes be found in libraries or second-hand bookstores.

Unless stated otherwise, publishers cited are British. But if a book printed in Great Britain is or was available from a North American distributor, the name of the latter—should it differ from that of the British publisher—is listed. If in print, British books without North American distributors may be ordered from Heffers Bookshop, 20 Trinity Street, Cambridge CB2 3NG, England. To establish a personal account (and obtain instructions for ordering), request an application blank from Heffers, c/o Customers' Account Department, P.O. Box 33, Cambridge CB2 1TX, England.

For up-to-date listing of audio-visual materials, consult the annual listings in *Classical World*: the most recent is J.C. Traupman, "Audio-Visual Materials in the Classics: 1988 Supplementary Survey," *Classical World* Vol 81, 1988, pp. 275–304.

For a current list of supplementary materials and examinations available specifically for users of the *Cambridge Latin Course*, write to William D. Gleason, Director, Resource Center, North American Cambridge Classics Project (NACCP), Box 932, Amherst, MA 01004-0932, U.S.A.

Books for Stages 21–28: *Aquae Sūlis* and *Dēva* (Bath and Chester, England)

General

Bagshawe, R.W. *Roman Roads* (Shire Archaeology Series; Shire Publications (pbd) 1985)

Balsdon, J.P.V.D. **Life and Leisure in Ancient Rome* (Bodley Head 1969)

Birley, A.R. *Life in Roman Britain* (North Pomfret, VT: David and Charles, rev. edn 1976)

Branigan, K. *Roman Britain: Life in an Imperial Province* (Life in Britain Series: Reader's Digest 1980)

Cambridge School Classics Project **The Romans discover Britain* and *Teacher's Handbook* (Cambridge U.P. 1981)

**The Roman World Units I and II* (Cambridge U.P. 1978–79)

Carcopino, J. **Daily Life in Ancient Rome* (New Haven, CT: Yale U.P. 1940)

Casson, L. *Ships and Seamanship in the Ancient World* (Princeton, NJ: Princeton U.P. 1971)
Travel in the Ancient World (Allen and Unwin 1974)
Chevallier, R. *Roman Roads* (Berkeley, CA: U. California P. 1975)
Collingwood, R.G. and Richmond, I.A. *The Archaeology of Roman Britain* (Methuen, rev. edn 1969)
Cornell, T. and Matthews, J. *Atlas of the Roman World* (Phaidon 1982)
Cunliffe, B. **Rome and her Empire* (New York: McGraw-Hill 1978 O.P.)
The Regni (Peoples of Roman Britain Series; Duckworth 1973 O.P.)
Dudley, D.R. *Urbs Roma* (Phaidon 1967 O.P.)
Ferguson, J. *The Religions of the Roman Empire* (Aspects of Greek and Roman Life Series; Ithaca, NY: Cornell U.P. (pbd) 1985)
Frazer, Sir J.G. **The New Golden Bough*; ed. T.H. Gaster (Chatham, NY: S.G. Phillips 1959)
Hattatt, R. *Ancient and Roman-British Brooches* (Dorset Publishing Company 1982)
Jones, P.V. (ed.) *Selections from Tacitus, Histories I–III: The Year of the Four Emperors* (Cambridge Latin Texts Series; Cambridge U.P. 1974) and *Handbook* (Cambridge U.P. 1975)
McEvedy, C. *The Penguin Atlas of Ancient History* (Penguin new edn. 1986)
Margary, I.D. *Roman Roads in Britain* (Baker, 3rd edn. 1973)
Ogilvie, R.M. *The Romans and their Gods* (Ancient Culture and Society Series; New York: Norton (pbd) 1970)
Ordnance Survey *Map of Roman Britain* (H.M.S.O., 5th edn due 1989; available from Heffers Bookshop (address above, p. 194))
Paoli, U.E. **Rome, its People, Life and Customs* (White Plains, NY: Longman Inc., rprt of 1963 edn (pbd) O.P.)
Soulsby, D.E. *Selections from Tacitus: Agricola* and *Handbook* (Cambridge Latin Texts Series; Cambridge U.P. 1982)
Tacitus, *Agricola;* ed. R.M. Ogilvie and I.A. Richmond (Oxford U.P. 1967)
Tacitus *The Agricola and the Germania;* tr. H. Mattingly and rev. S.A. Handford (Penguin 1982)
Van der Heyden, A.A.M. and Scullard, H.H. **Atlas of the Classical World* (Nelson 1959 O.P.)
Wacher, J. *The Towns of Roman Britain* (Berkeley, CA: U. California P. 1975)

Aquae Sūlis

Cunliffe, B. **Aquae Sulis* (History Patch Series (pbd); Ginn 1971)
The City of Bath (New Haven, CT: Yale U.P. 1987)
Roman Bath (Oxford U.P. 1969 O.P.)
Roman Bath Discovered (New York: Methuen, rev. edn 1984 O.P.)
The Roman Baths and Museum: Official Guidebook (Bath Archaeological

Trust, rev. edn 1985)
The Temple of Sulis Minerva at Bath, Vol 2: The Finds from the Sacred Spring (Oxford: Oxford University Committee for Archaeology 1988)
Cunliffe, B. and Davenport, P. *The Temple of Sulis Minerva at Bath, Vol 1: The Site* (Oxford: Oxford University Committee for Archaeology 1985)
Hassall, M. "From our correspondent in Roman Britain: The fountain of Sulis," *Omnibus* I (1981), p. 16
"News from Roman Britain," *Omnibus* VI (November 1983), pp. 31–32
"Religion in Roman Britain with example of a project kit on the cult of Minerva," *Hesperiam* No. 2 (1979), pp. 18–33
Stewart, B. *The Roman Baths and Museum* (Unichrome of Bath 1983)
**Waters of the Gap—The Mythology of Aquae Sulis* (Bath City Council 1981 O.P.)

Further information on the latest excavations is available from Bath City Council, Department of Leisure and Tourist Services, Bath, Avon BA1 1LZ, ENGLAND.

Dēva

Carrington, P. "The Plan of the Legionary Fortress at Chester: a Reconsideration," *The Journal of the Chester Archaeological Society* LXVIII (1986), pp. 23–52. Available from the Grosvenor Museum Education Service (see below for address).
Collingwood, R.G. and Wright, R.P. "The Roman Inscriptions in the Grosvenor Museum, Chester"; reprinted from *R.I.B.*, pp. 146–90, with addenda by G. Lloyd-Morgan and D.J. Robinson (Grosvenor Museum Publications 1978)
Grosvenor Museum Education Service *The Deva Investigation Book* (Grosvenor Museum Publications, rev. edn 1982 O.P.)
Petch, D.R. **Deva Victrix* (History Patch Series (pbd); Ginn 1971)
Strickland, T.J. "First Century Deva; Some Evidence Reconsidered in the Light of Recent Archaeological Discoveries," *Journal of the Chester Archaeological Society* LXIII (1980), pp 5–13. Available as an offprint from the Grosvenor Museum Education Service (see below for address).
Roman Chester (Grosvenor Museum Publications 1984)
Strickland, T.J. and Davey, P.J. *New Evidence for Roman Chester* (Grosvenor Museum Publications 1978 O.P.)
Webster, G. **A Short Guide to the Roman Inscriptions and Sculptured Stones in the Grosvenor Museum, Chester* (Grosvenor Museum Publications, rev. edn 1970 O.P.)

Further information, including quiz sheets and project books for school children and a publication list, is available from the Grosvenor Museum

Education Service, 27 Grosvenor Street, Chester, Cheshire CH1 2DD ENGLAND.
See also *J.A.C.T. Bulletin* 63 (Autumn 1983) pp. 26–27 for article on the Museum.

The Roman Army

Students, with guidance from their teacher, could use all the materials in this section.

Abranson, E. *Roman Legionaries at the time of Julius Caesar* (Macdonald 1979)
Anderson, A.S. *Roman Military Tombstones* (Shire Archaeology Series (pbd); Shire Publications 1984)
Birley, R. *Vindolanda: a Roman Frontier Post on Hadrian's Wall* (Thames and Hudson, rev. edn 1979)
Vindolanda in Colour (Frank Graham 1974)
Breeze, D.J. *Roman Forts in Britain* (Shire Archaeology Series (pbd); Shire Publications 1983)
Breeze, D.J. and Dobson, B. *Hadrian's Wall* (Allen Lane 1976; Penguin 1978)
Connolly, P. *The Roman Army* (Armies of the Past Series; Morristown, NJ: Silver Burdett 1975)
Dobson, B. and Breeze, D.J. *The Army of Hadrian's Wall* (Frank Graham 1972 O.P.)
Embleton, R. and Daniels, C. *Hadrian's Wall Reconstructed* (Frank Graham, 3rd edn 1981)
Hodge, P. *The Roman Army* (Aspects of Roman Life Series: Longman 1977)
Jones, D. and Jones, P. *Hadrian's Wall* (Jackdaw Series 41: Cape 1968 O.P.)
Martin, C. "The Gods of the Imperial Roman Army," *History Today* Vol. 19, April 1969
Powell, G. "The Roman Legions and their Officers," *History Today* Vol. 17, November 1967.
Richmond, I.A. "Trajan's Army on Trajan's Column," *Papers of the British School at Rome* Vol 13, 1935, pp. 1–40
Robinson, H.R. *The Armour of Imperial Rome* (Arms and Armour Press 1975 O.P.
The Armour of the Roman Legions (Frank Graham 1980 O.P.)
What the Soldiers Wore on Hadrian's Wall (Frank Graham 1976 O.P.)
Rossi, L. *Trajan's Column and the Dacian Wars* (Thames and Hudson 1971)
Simkins, M. and Embleton, R. *The Roman Army from Caesar to Trajan* (Osprey, rev. edn 1984)
Warry, J. *Warfare in the Classical World* (New York: St. Martin 1981)

Watson, G.R. *The Roman Soldier* (Aspects of Greek and Roman Life Series; Ithaca, NY: Cornell U.P. 1969)
Webster, G. *The Roman Army* (Grosvenor Museum Publications, rev. edn 1973)
**The Roman Imperial Army* (Totowa, NJ: Barnes and Noble, 3rd edn 1985)
Wilkes, J. *The Roman Army* (Cambridge U.P. 1972)
Wilson, R. *Roman Forts: an Illustrated Introduction to the Garrison Posts of Roman Britain* (Bergström and Boyle 1980)

Source Material and Reference

Ferguson, J. *Greek and Roman Religion: a Source Book* (Park Ridge, NJ: Noyes Press 1980 O.P.)
Ferguson, J. and Chisholm, K. *Rome – the Augustan Age: a Source Book* (Oxford U.P. 1981)
Gordon, A.E. *Illustrated Introduction to Roman Epigraphy* (Berkeley, CA.: U. California P. 1983)
Lewis, N. and Reinhold, M. *Roman Civilization: a Sourcebook. I The Republic; II The Empire* (Harper Torchbooks (pbd); Harper and Row 1966)
London Association of Classical Teachers. LACTOR No. 4: *Some Inscriptions from Roman Britain* (L.A.C.T 1969)
LACTOR No. 8: *Inscriptions of the Roman Empire* (L.A.C.T. 1971)
Both these L.A.C.T. *O*riginal *R*ecords include translations and are obtainable from the NACCP Resource Center (see above, p. 194, for address).
R.I.B. – Collingwood, R.G. and Wright, R.P. *The Roman inscriptions of Britain Vol. I: Inscriptions on Stone* (Oxford U.P. 1965)

Books for Stages 29–34: Rome

Augarde, T. **The Oxford Guide to Word Games* (Oxford U.P. 1986)
Balsdon, J.P.V.D. **Life and Leisure in Ancient Rome* (Bodley Head 1969)
Roman Civilisation (Penguin 1969 O.P.)
**Roman Women* (New York City, NY:Barnes and Noble (pbd) 1983)
Barrow, R.H. *The Romans* (Pelican 1975)
Bieber, M. **The History of the Greek and Roman Theater* (Princeton, NJ: Princeton U.P.., rev. edn 1980)
Buckland, W.W. and McNair, A.D. *Roman Law and Common Law* (Cambridge U.P., 2nd edn revised 1965)
Cairns, T. **The Romans and their Empire* (Introduction to World History Series; Cambridge UP. 1970)
Cambridge Ancient History Vol. XI (Cambridge U.P. 1936)
Cambridge School Classics Project **The Roman World Units I and II*

(Cambridge U.P. 1978–79) and *Teacher's Handbook* (Cambridge U.P. 1980)

Carcopino, J. **Daily Life in Ancient Rome* (New Haven, CT:Yale U.P. 1940)

Cornell, T. and Matthews, J. *Atlas of the Roman World* (Phaidon 1982)

Cowell, F.R. **Everyday Life in Ancient Rome* (Batsford 1961 O.P.; Carousel Books (pbd) 1975 O.P.)

Crook, J.A. *Law and Life of Rome* (Ithaca, NY: Cornell U.P. (pbd) 1984)

Cunliffe, B. **Rome and her Empire* (New York City, NY: McGraw-Hill 1978 O.P.)

Dilke, O.A.W. *The Ancient Romans, how they lived and worked* (David and Charles 1975 O.P.)

Dudley, D.R. *Urbs Roma* (Phaidon 1967 O.P.)

Duff, A.M. *Freedmen in the Early Roman Empire* (Heffer 1958 O.P.)

Friedlander, L. *Roman Life and Manners under the Early Empire Vol. II,* ed. M. Finley (Salem, N.H: Ayer, rprt of 1913 edn)

Furneaux, R. *The Roman Siege of Jerusalem* (Hart-Davis 1973 O.P.)

Grant, M. **The World of Rome* (Cardinal, rev. edn 1974 O.P.)

Green, M. **Roman Technology and Crafts* (Aspects of Roman Life Series; Longman 1979)

Hadas, M. **Imperial Rome* (Great Ages of Man Series; Alexandria, VA: Time-Life Books 1965 O.P.)

Hamey, L.A. and Hamey, J.A. **Roman Engineers* (Cambridge U.P. 1981)

Hammond, N.G.L. and Scullard, H.H. (eds) *Oxford Classical Dictionary* (Oxford U.P., 2nd edn 1970)

Hodges, H.W.M. *Technology in the Ancient World* (New York City, NY: Alfred Knopf (Random House) 1970)

Jones, P.V. (ed) *Selections from Tacitus, Histories I–III: The Year of the Four Emperors* (Cambridge Latin Texts Series; Cambridge U.P. 1974) and *Handbook* (Cambridge U.P. 1975)

Josephus *The Jewish War,* tr. G.A. Williamson and M. Smallwood (Penguin 1981)

Landels, J.G. *Engineering in the Ancient World* (Berkeley, CA: U. California P. (pbd) 1978)

Leacroft, H. and Leacroft, R.**The Buildings of Ancient Rome* (Brockhampton 1969 O.P.)

Lewis, H. and Reinhold, M. *Roman Civilization: a Sourcebook. II The Empire* (Harper Torchbooks (pbd); New York City, NY: Harper and Row 1966)

Liversidge, J.*Everyday Life in the Roman Empire* (Batsford 1976 O.P.)

Loane, H.J. *Industry and Commerce of the City of Rome 50BC–AD200* (New York City, NY: AMS Press, rprt of 1938 edn)

Macaulay, D. **City: a Story of Roman Planning and Construction* (Boston: Houghton Mifflin (pbd) 1983)

McCrum, M. and Woodhead, A.G. *Select Documents of the Flavian Emperors* (Cambridge U.P. 1961 O.P.)

MacDonald, W.L. *The Architecture of the Roman Empire* (New Haven, CT: Yale U.P., rev. edn (pbd) 1982)

McKay, A. **Vitruvius: Architect and Engineer* (Inside the Ancient World Series: Macmillan 1978)

McWhirr, A. **Roman Crafts and Industries* (Shire Archaeology Series; Shire Publications 1982)

Meiggs, R. *Roman Ostia* (Oxford U.P., 2nd edn 1974 O.P.)

Nash, E. (ed.) *Pictorial Dictionary of Ancient Rome,* 2 vols (Hacker, rprt 1968 edn)

Nova Vulgata Bibliorum Sacrorum Editio (Vatican City: Libreria Editrice Vaticana 1979)

Paoli, U.E. **Rome, its People, Life and Customs* (White Plains, NY: Longman Inc., rprt of 1963 edn (pbd) O.P.)

Pearlman, M. *The Zealots of Masada* (New York City, NY: Scribner (pbd) 1967)

Platner, S.B. and Ashby, T. **Topographical Dictionary of Ancient Rome* (Oxford U.P. 1929 O.P.)

Sandbach, F.H. *The Stoics* (Chatto and Windus 1975 O.P.)

Scherer, M.R. *Marvels of Ancient Rome* (Phaidon 1955 O.P.)

Sear, F. *Roman Architecture* (Ithaca, NY: Cornell U.P. (pbd) 1982)

Sorrell, A. and Birley, A. **Imperial Rome* (Lutterworth 1970 O.P.)

Stambaugh, J.E. *The Ancient Roman City* (Baltimore, MD: The Johns Hopkins U.P. 1988)

Tacitus *Empire and Emperors: Selections from Tacitus' Annals* tr. Graham Tingay, (Cambridge U.P. 1983)

Tingay, G.I.F. and Badcock, J. **These Were the Romans* (Chester Springs, PA: Dufour (pbd) 1986)

Van der Heyden, A.A.M. and Scullard, H.H. **Atlas of the Classical World* (Nelson 1959 O.P.)

Vickers, M. **The Roman World* (New York City, NY: State Mutual Books 1981 O.P.)

Wheeler, Sir M. *Roman Art and Architecture* (World of Art Series; Thames and Hudson (pbd) 1985)

Wyman, P. **Ostia* (History Patch Series (pbd): Ginn 1971)

Yadin, Y. **Masada* (New York City, NY: Random House 1966 O.P.)